Advance Praise for *Lean Culture Change*

"Lean organizational transformation requires empowerment of and respect for those who do the work. In order to accomplish this, there must be a core leadership structure, strategic vision and system to support them. Leuschel and Lewis lead you on a journey in Lean Culture Change to the roots of building this structure and support. They provide thoughtful and systematic concepts with validated resources and real-life applications to guide and aid you on your journey. Find your True North!"
  — **JENNIFER CONDEL**, Senior Quality Improvement Specialist, The Pittsburgh Regional Health Initiative

"To change a management system and culture so that it integrates core Lean principles, you need to know the details of a Lean system's components and you need guidance on how to proceed. I encourage readers to understand the purposes of each of the components of Daily Management that Steve describes and how the components fit together to create a practical and sustainable foundation for continuous improvement. Every healthcare organization should pay attention to this message."
  — **KEVIN LITTLE**, Ph.D. Informing Ecological Design, LLC, Improvement Advisor, Institute for Healthcare Improvement

"In Lean Culture Change, Leuschel provides a compelling nuts-and-bolts approach to a variety of lean tools with an eye toward the "people" side of Lean—an area that many organizations overlook to their detriment. Here, the importance of mutual trust and respect are emphasized while providing the reader with some easy-to-use recommendations to help their organization continuously improve."
  — **MICHAEL J. URICK**, Ph.D., MBA, MS; Graduate Director of Master of Science in Management: Operational Excellence at Saint Vincent College

"Lean Culture Change is a must read for anyone who wants to better understand how Lean methodologies integrate with the Baldrige Criteria. Used together, they are powerful tools for any organization that wants to systematically improve outcomes."
  — **ROBERT BITNER**, Executive Director, Keystone Alliance for Performance Excellence

"Should you choose to follow the path that Steve has outlined here you will significantly increase the likelihood that you will achieve your goal of a Lean—an efficient, mutually trusting and respectful, problem solving, change embracing, learning organization. I wish to thank my colleague, Steve, for taking the time to pull together the learnings, which we and others have accumulated over the years of organizations learning new pathways to adapting the Toyota Production System rooted in culture."
  — **DR. RICHARD KUNKLE**, Learner of Operational Excellence

"Lean Culture Change presents a detailed account of a simple, yet powerful management framework that enables the effective use of the Toyota Production System/lean tools. The use of this system has been powerful in both healthcare and manufacturing. It's successful implementation requires discipline, attention to detail, and daily practice. Soon, this discipline of daily management results in dramatic culture change evident by years of unleashed pent-up productive activity from those working within the framework."
  — **MICHAEL CULIG**, MD, Chief, Cardiac Surgery, Forbes Hospital

"This lean management system works regardless of personality and leadership and management styles—in fact, it enables us to transform our leadership and management styles. Lean Culture Change has been our guide for this phase of our transformation learning and leading a new leadership and management system."
  — **DOMINIC PACCAPANICCIA**, Chief Operating Officer, Indiana Regional Medical Center

"Most books on lean management provide insight into individual components of a system. However, they fail to give the reader sufficient information to be able to translate the concepts into specific actions or to be able to realize the benefits of a single integrated system. Lean Culture Change is an invaluable resource for those who are serious about truly undergoing a lean transformation by balancing human development and operational improvements."
  — **DAVID MARSHALL**, Director of Healthcare Performance Improvement

LEAN CULTURE CHANGE

Using a Daily Management System

STEVEN LEUSCHEL

ALIGN KAIZEN PUBLISHING

Indiana, PA

Published by
Align Kaizen Publishing
Indiana, PA

Publisher's Cataloging-in-Publication Data
Leuschel, Steven R.

Lean culture change : using a daily management system / Steven R. Leuschel. – Indiana, PA : Align Kaizen Pub., 2015.

p. ; cm.

ISBN13: 978-0-692-48106-6

1. Organizational effectiveness. 2. Organizational change--Management. 3. Corporate culture. I. Title.

HD58.9.L48 2015
658.31—dc23   2015948597

Printed in the United States of America
19 18 17 16 15 · 5 4 3 2 1

Contents

Foreword

by Mike Hoseus

Co-writing the book *Toyota Culture* has given me the opportunity to travel to many parts of the world and come into contact with many organizations working on improving through Lean management. I have observed many misunderstandings of what it takes to be a Lean organization. Most organizations view Lean as a program to eliminate waste and cut costs. Operations are "Leaned out," and the assumption is that if well-trained experts properly implement the tools, the efficiency gains will be self-sustaining. Unfortunately, these companies are missing the very essence of the Toyota Way.

The Toyota Production System aims to intentionally expose problems and engage all members in solving them. These two points are usually missed in the common Lean implementation, where leadership delegates Lean to a set of "champions" and then asks them to report results. Leadership goes about business as usual and the champions are out cutting costs through implementing some of the Lean tools. The problem is that most times these tools are used to reduce people. This results in both losing a valuable resource in those that leave and losing the trust of those that stay. Meanwhile, the improvements that were made do not usually last, because they did not include the people doing the work and were not systematic improvements.

Toyota's approach is much more broad and holistic. It starts with a philosophy that the strength of a company is based on continuous improvement and respect for people. Measurement of success is multidimensional, and that is what reflects the success of the enterprise, not specific projects. The leadership hierarchy is not there to delegate improvement to specialists; rather, leaders at every level play an integral role in daily improvement, and leaders are teachers who develop team members. There are a broad set of methods available for improvement, but the unit of improvement is primarily at the level of the work group, led by a group leader. The group leader is supported by hourly team leaders who facilitate kaizen at the team member level. Improvement is not focused only on large Lean projects, but numerically more on small improvements led by team members, which yields a strong ownership of the process and results. Over time, continuous improvement by identifying and solving problems strengthens the company, which can be regarded as a learning organization.

This book, *Lean Culture Change*, is a helpful resource for you to now "countermeasure" the problems many organizations have in implementing Lean management. In my teachings on *Toyota Culture*, many times the feedback has been, "This all sounds good, but what do I do now?" Lewis and Leuschel make the case that Lean is about more than the tools, and that addressing the culture is key. Not only that, *Lean Culture Change* gives us a time-tested and proven road map to follow in order to address the culture—the "daily management system" (DMS). The DMS is a system that incorporates many key Lean processes and components into a daily routine or practice. It gives everyone in the organization a framework from which to practice their Lean roles and responsibilities. These behaviors soon become habits, and when we have enough people practicing these habits, a Lean culture has emerged.

Lean Culture Change articulates Lean as a complete management system, and this is the key to understanding the difference between implementing Lean tools and leading a Lean transformation in your organization. When I teach about Lean as a complete management system, I utilize the 4Ps to help people understand and in turn teach their people. The 4Ps are Purpose, Process, People and Problem Solving. The power of this book is that the daily management system that Leuschel describes in *Lean Culture Change* incorporates all 4 of these and breaks them down into actionable steps.

The first P is **Purpose.** This is about an organization having a clear "true north" communicated to the organization, and a clear plan to get there. The organization needs to know the vision of where the company is going and what they are trying to accomplish, and then have a plan on how to get there. Toyota uses the *Hoshin kanri* process to align the organization around these "true north metrics" and the plan to improve them. *Lean Culture Change* and its components of balanced scoreboard, annual and master planning, and the monthly meeting cycle gives helpful examples and practical information to help your organization.

Having a way to measure your progress toward true north is manifested through the "balanced scoreboard." Unfortunately, I've seen several balanced scoreboards out of balance. When "Safety First" is an articulated value visualized on the scoreboard, it describes your true north. When articulated and visualized, it is even more important for the actions of your leadership team to reflect this in daily routines. The same is the case for "Quality" before "Productivity" and "Cost." The daily management system provides the framework to practice and demonstrate these true north values on a daily basis and indeed lead to a Lean culture change.

The next P is **Process.** Process is the foundation of the Lean management system. When improving multi-disciplinary processes, a standard must exist. Without a process to improve the standard, i.e., a daily management system, improvement occurs sporadically and slowly at best. In addition, where there is no standard, there is no problem to solve—therefore, a fully integrated Lean daily management system does not work without the foundation of standardization.

I was taught by my Japanese trainers, whenever the process or a person brought up an issue, to first ask, "What is the standard?" Many times, there was not one, so we had to establish one. But if there was a standard, we could then start problem solving. Leuschel discusses very effectively the fact that your daily management system drives the problem solving for the team, department, plant, and organization. Introducing problem solving on a daily basis begins to drive team members to create standards based on problems. *Lean Culture Change* explains the purpose of the Lean tools and how they fit into the rest of the DMS.

The third P is **People.** "People" describes the intention of the daily management system to engage every member of the organization in problem solving and improvement of their job and the product or service for your customer. *Lean Culture Change* gives you the framework from which to make this happen. Of course, you first need to agree not only that you want this to happen, but that this is a standard for your organization. In other words, you must make it clear to your people that it is not only their job to do their job, but that it is also their responsibility to improve their job. There is a big difference between the two and, in my experience, most employees, in any organization, want the opportunity to improve their job; we just don't always give them that opportunity.

Even when we give them the opportunity, this doesn't mean that they are necessarily able to act on it. It is the responsibility of the leader in Lean to develop their people to act on opportunities. This is another "standard" question as you implement *Lean Culture Change*: What is the role of the leader in your organization, whether this is a supervisor, manager, or executive? In Lean, it is the role of the leader to develop their people, and primarily this means to teach and coach problem solving.

In *Lean Culture Change*, Leuschel makes a critical and important distinction about different types of improvement that the daily management system drives. A Lean culture change component of the daily management system is the "improvement system," in which Leuschel lays out the process to engage your people in implementing their ideas. A key point that is made here is that it is *self-implemented* ideas. This is critical to an effective Lean idea system. A box on the wall for employees to put their suggestions into is not an effective way to develop employees to implement their own ideas. Employees have many ideas, and the daily management system provides a process for them to voice and implement them. It also provides the framework (the daily huddle) for the leaders to help coach and develop their people in this process. Leaders can support their people's ideas by helping their people overcome barriers to implementing their ideas, and teach them how to follow up and confirm the effectiveness of their ideas. This component of the DMS is critical, and also allows organizations to deal with problems when employees do not know what is causing them. In this case, further analysis is necessary before a countermeasure/improvement is put in place, which aligns with the last P, Problem Solving.

The fourth P, **Problem Solving**, is the point of the daily management system. "Purpose" gets the organization going in the same direction and helps us solve the right problems. The Lean "Process" and tools help us identify and solve problems, and now we want to engage each and every person in doing this each day. *Lean Culture Change* gives very helpful visuals and examples of simple problem solving, using sheets and boards to help you develop your people in this Lean competency. This is the double bonus of the daily management system if you utilize this book to its full intent. I've seen many organizations only get half of the picture when it comes to their daily management system. They hang up boards and have many Key Performance Indicators identified, but they are only using the "management" half of the system. In other words, they are managing results, and utilizing "traditional management" top-down, command and control techniques, and turning daily meetings into daily beatings. This is taking a Lean tool and NOT using it to drive Lean culture change. The other half of the daily management system is "development." In Lean, we manage results and develop our people. This describes what Rodger Lewis refers to as the "human and operations balance." The daily management system makes development a daily and continual process, if you utilize all of the components, in the way Leuschel lays it out.

The last component described in the book is an important one to sustain gains made by this phase of the daily management system, the audit process. As Leuschel explains in *Lean Culture Change*, the "daily management system" is just that, a system, and one that needs P-D-C-A, or Plan-Do-Check-Act. The audit process detailed will give you a framework to check and adjust. It's important that you have thoughtful reflection, after you start your plan, as to what is working and what is not, in order to adjust what you are doing. These are sound and proven principles, and need to be adapted for your organization.

An effective Lean transformation taps into the potential of your entire organization. Strong leaders are important, but more important is their ability to build the systems that engage the entire organization. People want to be part of a larger vision and purpose and they want to be involved. Everyone wants to contribute their skills and abilities and be productive. We just have to lead and structure the organization in such a way that gives them the chance to do so. Nothing is more important to their success or your organization, and *Lean Culture Change* gives you a way to actually do it.

—Mike Hoseus
Co-author, *Toyota Culture*
Executive Director of Center for Quality People and Organizations

Preface

by Steven Leuschel

Lean, rooted in the Toyota Production System, has resulted in healthcare improvements, including a 53% decrease in inventory, 36% increase in productivity, 41% decrease in floor space, and 65% decrease in lead time, among other operational cost saving improvements (IHI, 2005). Other results include a 95% reduction of patient deaths related to central-line-associated bloodstream infections, reduced patient wait time for orthopedic surgery from 14 weeks to 31 hours, and reduced patient length of stay by 29% (Graban, 2009).

These results have all helped answer the question, "Why Lean?" and helped initiate Lean improvements at many healthcare organizations, but results only begin to tell the story of "How?" Before answering "How?" though, leaders must understand the current state of Lean healthcare and the historical context and influences thus far. Understanding the history gives insight to there having been a better way for Lean and organizational transformation to occur for many years, that has by and large gone unnoticed, compared to the professionalization of events, tools, and current pathways—all of which have roots in the Toyota Production System (TPS).

In 1990, *The Machine That Changed the World* was published, which identified Toyota's Production System as "Lean," and described in great detail what a Lean organization looks, feels, and acts like. Many manufacturing organizations embarked on "Lean journeys" trying to copy the tools and practices Toyota used as countermeasures to problems. In 1992, Toyota started the Toyota Supplier Support Center, supporting Toyota's suppliers and developing internal leaders to solve large-scale operational problems using primarily project-based teams and activities called "Kaizen events" (Dyer & Nobeoka, 2000). This wide-scale exposure to Kaizen events led many organizations to believe that "becoming Lean" was accomplished by "doing events," thus many organizations started down an event-based, tools-based pathway. Note: a longer history of Toyota in North America and a plausible explanation for the professionalization of an event-based pathway is explained further in Appendix A, *A Brief History of Lean in Healthcare*.

As early adopters of Lean in healthcare began using Kaizen events, or **Rapid Process Improvement Workshops/Weeks (RPIWs)**, in 2002. *Going Lean in Healthcare* (2005) cites results of 175 RPIWs, including positive savings in inventory, productivity, floor space, lead time, and set up time (IHI). These results not only provided clear evidence that Lean in healthcare was possible, they also provided a repeatable framework to improve healthcare processes via a Kaizen event–based approach—thus, the momentum of an event-based approach to

Lean continued into many healthcare organizations throughout the United States and the world.

Using Kaizen events and RPIWs as the primary mode of improvement, many healthcare organizations embarked on Lean journeys slashing costs, changing processes, and achieving many financial and clinical results. Kaizen events were exciting, promoted cross-functional teamwork, resulted in improvement, and could be repeated fairly easily following the same process. Therefore they were repeated over and over almost to a fault, all in the name of "becoming Lean."

Some organizations that have hired Lean consultants and used an event-based pathway quote their consultants as saying, "All you have to do is events and that's how you learn Lean." In 2015, Dr. John Toussaint notes: "At one time, we were saving an average of $45,000 for every rapid-improvement event we did, week in and week out. Even then, however, we were setting ourselves up for failure" (para. 17). Yet a thorough root cause analysis has not been performed asking questions like—"Why has healthcare gone down an event-based pathway?" or "What could we have done differently to avoid such a time-consuming mistake by leading with events?"

The purpose of Lean and the Toyota Production System are not to become "Lean," they are to become world-class, perpetuating the underlying value of mutual trust and respect. During the Georgetown ramp-up, leaders began learning both human and operational artifacts of the Toyota Production System to produce organizational change. Over the last several decades some of those leaders exited Toyota and began transforming other organizations— a very small number compared to the number of individuals who experienced Kaizen events as the primary "Lean tool."

A mature Lean organization, like Toyota, uses Kaizen events to develop people and solve problems—not to transform an entire organization. Many Lean professionals learning from Toyota began using the Kaizen events as the primary mode of Lean transformation, because it achieved results and got the attention of leadership. The professionalization of the tools-based, Kaizen event-based approach became the standard for "Lean," as was evident with Lean certifications, belts, consultancies, institutes, and professional literature—all very focused on events, tools, and projects. Early adoptions of Lean in healthcare also support the professionalization of an event-based pathway. Figure A.2 in Appendix A on page 180, attempts to visualize the migration of Lean professionals—skilled at Kaizen events—from Lean organizations—to non-Lean organizations that wanted to become Lean. Generally, these individuals used an event-based approach to begin adapting TPS.

However, not all organizations have started on an event-based approach. In the 1980s, Toyota was being deeply studied and documented, Rodger Lewis, a former General Manager at Toyota, Georgetown, was learning and adapting a sequenced approach to organizational transformation using the Toyota Production System. Lewis left Toyota and went on to use TPS to change organizations and change cultures—not just processes. In the Introduction, Lewis describes his journey and introduces the **Transformation Curve**, a multi-phase, adaptable pathway to organizational transformation rooted in TPS, cultural change, and mutual trust and respect.

The purposes of *Lean Culture Change* are to:

1. Introduce a new definition of Lean—mutual trust and respect.
2. Provide evidence that the continuous improvement industry must P-D-S-A the problem of healthcare initiating Lean with an event-based approach.
3. Introduce Phase 1 Level A of the Transformation Curve so that Senior Leaders and team leaders can adapt the model and begin to create Lean cultural change.

In this book, the main content chapters include, among other things, background information on the artifact, visual examples, a case study, examples, and step-by-step guides on how to get started. Many chapters contain a section entitled "Baldrige Connections." This section serves to highlight how a daily management system begins to answer the questions posed by The Baldrige Excellence Framework and Criteria (2015). Each case study was selected to highlight an artifact within an overall management system and give insight into the learning of that particular organization. Not all organizations in the case studies have used the Transformation Curve. No organization has a "pure" adaptation of the curve.

My hope is that this book does not cast a shadow on past and current Lean journeys, but provides the introduction to a time-tested approach to organizational transformation learned by Rodger Lewis before the word "Lean" had anything to do with improvement and/or Toyota. Lean in healthcare is shifting from events to daily management—but without understanding Lewis' long-term strategic plan for organizational transformation rooted in the Toyota Georgetown ramp-up, healthcare is destined to make other long-term mistakes that could be avoided. I hope that this book enables healthcare leaders to begin Lean culture change rooted in mutual trust and respect.

Introduction
by Rodger Lewis

Coming from Volkswagon to Toyota, I thought I understood how to make cars, lead people, and improve performance, but I did not. When I first started in Georgetown, I did not realize that Toyota's approach to developing people and solving problems was very different than other car manufacturers. I also did not realize that my personal and professional culture would be transformed and align with the Toyota culture, a culture that was far superior to any other culture that I had previously experienced.

I first learned the Toyota Production System (TPS) and the focus on culture during the Georgetown ramp-up in the 1980s. My Senseis, Sekeyi and Hirose, were at my side day in and day out for years as I learned TPS, so that I could lead other Americans through the Georgetown ramp-up, long-term transformation and beyond. This very personal experience helped me quickly learn Toyota's values, which are put into action on a daily basis. By creating a culture of continuous improvement and personal development, the lives of our employees, our community, and our customers improve. During my time at Georgetown I learned TPS from a high level strategically and on a daily living level. Later, I took on challenges to adapt and introduce TPS in other organizations.

I began learning and adapting a systematic approach to introducing and sequencing the tools and building a culture of mutual trust and respect. This detailed and sequenced approach defines the pathway to world-class performance—what many call "Lean." The values of Toyota and the final product (Lean) are not new, and have been written about and studied over the past several decades. Unfortunately, many organizations have taken an event-based pathway to implementation and attempt to bypass culture. Very few people have been exposed to a long-term, organization-wide transformation model rooted in TPS that has been repeated.

Since my time at Georgetown, General Motors, and beyond, it has been my life mission to align other organizations, transforming culture from the top down and bottom up, using a systematic long-term plan. The plan, which I call the Transformation Curve, is a multi-phased, multi-year systematic approach to becoming world-class. It has been adapted from my experience introducing TPS to the people and process and has been applied globally. The Transformation Curve has been refined over the past several decades— Phase 1 Level A is shown in Figure I.1, which is the focus of *Lean Culture Change*.

After being a part of the Georgetown ramp-up, I was recruited by General Motors to start operations in its Opel division in Germany, then Argentina, China, Poland, the United Kingdom, Thailand, and other countries. I was able to take a similar

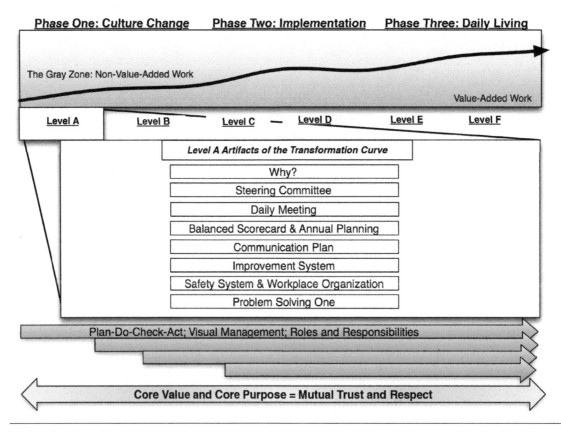

Figure I.1. Introduction to the Transformation Curve's Phase 1 Level A adapted by Rodger Lewis.

approach to what I learned at Toyota, hiring for culture and aligning individual behavior to the desired behavior—growing mutual trust and respect from day one. We designed operations and developed people to become world-class using the original Transformation Curve (i.e. the curve) as our guide and plan. General Motors experienced much success from its adapted version of TPS; however, I actively chose my next journey to implement TPS into an existing organization to adapt the curve even further.

Though a brownfield organization needed similar coaching, like new people hired for a new operation, an existing organization has an existing culture with existing norms, attitudes, and values that are difficult to change. Changing culture to align the entire organization, starting with the pilot hall, was essential in aligning daily behavior before redesigning processes and creating large-scale operational improvement. Our first goal was to win the hearts of the employees by engaging them in improvement cycles, then capture their minds to redesign the work. We changed culture incrementally by putting mutual trust and respect into action through coaching suggestions, focusing on leadership, and becoming a problem-solving organization.

The essence of TPS is *mutual trust and respect*. Many Lean practitioners have preached and practiced that the essence of TPS/Lean is to eliminate waste or create value. These are byproducts if the culture of mutual trust and respect thrives. When creating mutual trust and respect there must be a human and operational balance, which can be achieved using the 3Ps (*People, Passion, Patience*) and 3Gs (*Go and See, Get the Facts, Grasp the Situation*). These must be in balance, and most failures I have seen with transformation have been because the organization is focused on the 3Gs and has neglected the 3Ps.

As I took the approach learned from Toyota back to my home community at Saint Vincent College, I began to see the emergence of Lean within the healthcare industry. In fact, as the initial results of Lean in healthcare were being published, showcasing the results of many Kaizen events, Leuschel and others at Saint Vincent were learning the culturally-based systematic approach to becoming world-class (i.e., the Transformation Curve). Like the manufacturing industry, many healthcare organizations focused on Kaizen events as the main mode for improvement and neglected the culture and daily management system, which drives culture. This is most likely because their primary exposure to Lean was through events, and not a sequenced systematic repeatable approach to transforming organizations to become world-class.

Now, there are TPS models out there that describe the Toyota Production System "House." These are great models for understanding the house of TPS and great models for understanding what world-class looks like. These models, however, do not necessarily tell you *how to build the house*. Becoming world-class involves more than just doing Lean or seeing all the tools work in one model area—there must be a long-term strategic action plan that must be learned and adapted. The Transformation Curve gives you insight on how to adapt, align, and build that strategic plan to become world-class using Lean. *Lean Culture Change* defines the first steps in that strategic plan.

—Rodger B. Lewis

Chapter 1
Culture, Leadership, and Daily Management

This chapter will introduce your team to:

- *The working definition of Lean—mutual trust and respect.*

- *The foundations of Lean Culture Change and the Transformation Curve.*

- *Artifacts of a daily management system.*

- *Proposed sequencing for Lean transformation, Phase 1 Level A.*

Create a Culture of Mutual Trust and Respect

Organizations that have tried to implement tools without understanding the underlying values and culture of the organization have not been successful, have taken far too long to transform, or have even hurt the organization and the individuals in it. Change initiatives over the last 20 years including Total Quality Management and reengineering initiates, like the traditional implementations of Lean, have had a 75% failure rate or have actually harmed organizations to the point of their very survival being threatened. The number one reason for failure is the inability to change the organization's culture. (Cameron & Quinn 2011).

The hypothesized development of an event-based pathway to introducing Lean (described in the *Preface* and further explored in *Appendix A*) is rooted in the concept that artifacts of Toyota's transformation and success were copied while neglecting or downplaying the role of culture. Rodger Lewis, who learned TPS at Toyota Georgetown in the 1980s, has adapted a pathway focused on cultural change first, known as the Transformation Curve, introduced by Lewis in the *Introduction.*

The current and previous definition of Lean, "creating more value for customers with fewer resources" (LEI, 2015) does not fully describe the underlying values and the culture of organizations that have truly adopted the TPS and Toyota's philosophies. The true essence, proposed new definition, and definition used throughout *Lean Culture Change* of **Lean** is mutual trust and respect. This is the core principle of becoming world-class using the Transformation Curve as a guide as seen in Figure 1.1.

Healthcare leaders must understand the underlying value of mutual trust and respect when attempting Lean transformation. When healthcare and other organizations see Lean as an artifact or mindset, they tend to use it as a way to cut costs, eliminate waste, or create value. These are all important and can be activities to promote mutual trust and respect, but if Lean is used outside of a value system based on mutual trust and respect, it can be very dangerous to organizational culture, the individuals impacted by the improvement, and the organization's community.

Lean = Mutual Trust and Respect

Figure 1.1. The definition of Lean used throughout *Lean Culture Change* and the Transformation Curve. Note: adaptations of the Curve have been called multiple names since the Georgetown ramp-up, all with mutual trust and respect as the underlying value/meaning.

Foundations of Lean Culture Change

The foundations of Phase 1 Level A of the Transformation Curve and a daily management system are Plan-Do-Check-Act (P-D-C-A), visual management, and clearly established roles and responsibilities. The foundations, as shown in Figure 1.2, are used to drive culture change. These foundations are embedded into each artifact of the daily management system and the Transformation Curve. The **Cultural Change Pyramid** is explored further in Appendix B, *Lean Culture Change Theory*.

A leader practicing the **3Ps** (People, Passion, and Patience) and the **3Gs** (Go See, Get the Facts, Grasp the Situation), using the foundations found within each artifact of the daily management system, begins to balance the operational improvements with human development.

On the human development side, leaders begin to develop people's problem-solving skills, creating a coaching/learning relationship between team leader and team member. On the operational improvement side, as coaches/learners are focused on solving the right problems, the organization's performance improves. Seeing and solving problems is the core of the daily management system, with P-D-C-A, visual management, and roles and responsibilities being foundational. An overview of the foundations:

☐ **Visual Management.** Cultural objects that support the clear alignment of activities and roles/responsibilities with processes.

☐ **Plan-Do-Check-Act (P-D-C-A).** Cultural activities, which are standardized improvement cycles.

☐ **Roles and Responsibilities.** Defining individuals and teams along with expectations of the daily management system.

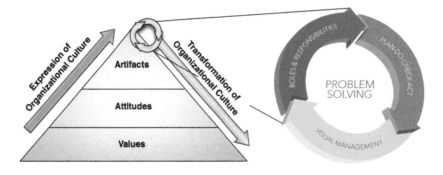

Figure 1.2. Foundations of continuous improvement and their relation to the culture change pyramid. Note. The pyramid, adapted from Schein (1985), Shook (2010), and Gagliardi (1986) is further explored in Appendix B: Lean Culture Change Theory.

Visual Management

There are many forms of visual management in a daily management system, including a few prominent artifacts: a problem-solving board, balanced scoreboard, and improvement system board. Additional visual objects that support these artifacts are a 6-year scorecard, problem-solving sheets, improvement system forms, master plans, and workplace organization standards. Figure 1.3 is an introduction to the connections between these visual artifacts.

Balanced scoreboard. The balanced scoreboard is used to visualize annual targets, top problems, and countermeasures. Daily, monthly, and annual P-D-C-A cycles are activities with the balanced scoreboard at the center. Annual targets are cascaded and visualized on the scoreboard, and the scoreboard is the centerpiece of monthly performance reviews.

Problem-Solving Board. The problem-solving board is an object used to manage problem-solving sheets and lead problem solving. This board, coupled with activities of problem identification and communication, helps track the progress of problems, and gives leaders a standard way to lead problem solving. Daily, weekly, and monthly P-D-C-A cycles surround the problem-solving process.

Improvement System Board. The improvement system board is a visual management artifact to manage daily improvements that are owned and implemented by team members. Daily and monthly P-D-C-A cycles are integrated into the improvement system process using the visual board.

Various Other Visual Objects. Other visual management objects, such as the safety cross, detailed plans, and metrics, are leading indicators, and are integrated with the above-mentioned objects and activities.

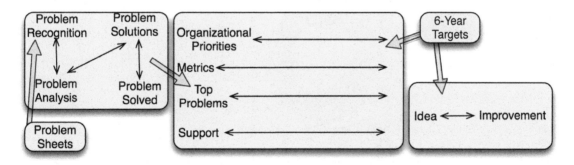

Figure 1.3. Visual artifacts of a daily management system include the problem-solving board (left), balanced scoreboard (center), and improvement system board (right). These objects, aligned with activities and verbal expressions, will align individual and team behavior focused on long-term (6-year) targets. Organizational activities, including structured P-D-C-A cycles and well-defined roles and responsibilities, are necessary to begin Lean culture change.

Plan-Do-Check-Act

Plan-Do-Check-Act, in this phase, are activities that include standardizing some planning and check cycles using the visual management artifacts. Though P-D-C-A cycles are found in various ways within each artifact of the daily management system, the primary P-D-C-A cycles that are standardized during the initial phase of the daily management system are annual, monthly, weekly, and daily cycles. Figure 1.4 shows interlocking P-D-C-A cycles.

Annual. Annual cycles include setting objectives, creating master plans, establishing targets and metrics, setting the improvement theme, and creating the daily management system implementation plan. With an emphasis on planning, this annual cycle informs other more frequent P-D-C-A cycles.

Monthly. Monthly cycles include checking performance to the annual targets, checking the status of annual plans, and generating top problems based on daily problem-solving cycles. As a primary P-D-C-A cycle, the *monthly balanced scoreboard review*, discussed in Chapter 4, is a monthly meeting to plan the top countermeasures and check the status of performance to annual objectives.

Weekly. Weekly check cycles include checking the status/progress of monthly top problems/countermeasures, weekly checks on safety and workplace organization via safety audits, and other weekly checks.

Daily. Daily check cycles include the daily huddle, daily problem solving, daily going to see improvements, and daily checks of leading indicators. The daily huddle is a daily check informed by daily problem solving and improvements that also informs weekly and monthly check cycles.

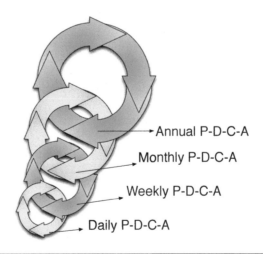

Annual P-D-C-A

Monthly P-D-C-A

Weekly P-D-C-A

Daily P-D-C-A

Figure 1.4. Interlocking Plan-Do-Check-Act (P-D-C-A) cycles. Daily, weekly, monthly, and annual P-D-C-A cycles are cultural artifacts that link daily activities with longer-term goals.

Roles and Responsibilities

Roles and responsibilities are embedded into each artifact of the daily management system and are explored more specifically chapter-by-chapter. Overarching roles and responsibilities for starting Lean culture change include a few central teams. Without top-down implementation (i.e., enforcing P-D-C-A activities), and bottom-up support (i.e., frontline problem-solving and improvements), transformation will take a very long time. Specific teams that must be identified while beginning Lean culture change are as follows: the *Senior Team* (the most executive team in the organization), the *Steering Committee* (a core group of leaders to drive and monitor the progress of the system), a *Pilot Hall/Team* (a frontline team to develop the new artifacts and culture), and the *Continuous Improvement (CI) Team* (a group of internal coaches to train and coach the daily management system).

The Senior Team. Leadership is responsible for much more than setting the direction, making resources available, and supporting the implementation of staff improvements. The Senior Team, or the highest-level team in the organization, is the primary team responsible for Lean culture change and overall organizational transformation. Their initial responsibilities are to be transformed, to learn, and to develop other leaders in the organization. It is essential that the Senior Team learn and align leadership styles while coaching and enforcing other leaders to align behaviors with the standards of the daily management system. This is done through practice and by being a positive role model for other leaders.

As noted, many organizations have taken the approach of implementing a kaizen event-based transformation in the form of formal events or large-scale cross-functional problem-solving activities. These are all necessary, but the daily management system and culture must be in place in order to support, sustain, and improve upon these activities. It is Senior Leadership's responsibility to change the culture by changing the management system and behaviors that align with the management system.

Figure 1.5 demonstrates how individuals on a team, focused on different priorities, come together and transform into an interlocking team to solve a problem or alleviate a crisis. As that crisis dissipates, the team generally reverts back to individual behavior until the next crisis comes along. These high-level crises may instigate team activities on a very infrequent basis, and generally formal root cause analysis does not occur. A daily management system with problem solving at the core, using the culture change artifacts and foundations, creates a daily crisis that aligns individual members into a team. The Senior Team sets the tone for the organization's culture, and must lead as a team to create and communicate the standards surrounding the culture change artifacts.

Steering Committee. Leading culture change is not a Lean program or a system that merely is supported by the Senior Team, but rather a new way of doing things, led by the Senior Team. As the master plan for Lean transformation is created, communicated, and tested in the pilot hall, a steering committee may be necessary to take a deeper dive into the current state of Lean culture change and take the next steps. The steering committee monitors the status of alignment, and introduces new tools and standards to further the daily management system and create further alignment.

The **Steering Committee** is a subset of the Senior Team, plus additional members case-by-case, that sets and monitors the direction of the new daily management system. The team may include members such as the Chief Executive Officer, Chief Operating Officer, Vice President of Human Resources, Chief Financial Officer, Chief Quality Officer, Chief Medical Officer, President of the Medical Staff, and Continuous Improvement Team Leader. Generally, operations, finance, and human resources are mandatory and others are added case-by-case.

Other primary roles and responsibilities include:

- *Learn, adapt, set, and update the standards of the management system.*

- *Set the direction and pace of implementation.*

- *Ensure the success of the pilot hall.*

- *Monitor the deployment of the Transformation Curve.*

- *Create and check the status of the management system master plan.*

- *Establish the communication plan and strategy.*

- *Ensure the Senior Team is pointed in the same direction and prepared to lead as one team, not as a group of individuals.*

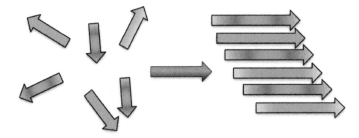

Figure 1.5. The Senior Team must move from a reactive state to an integrated, proactive state. As problems are solved, repeatable processes are put in place and integrated throughout the organization. Figure based on Baldrige Excellence Steps Toward Mature Process (NIST 2015).

The Pilot Hall. An initial step in changing culture and aligning continuous improvement efforts throughout any organization is leadership learning and beginning to grasp, adapt, and create the standards of this system. As the model in Figure 1.6 shows, an external coach is recommended who understands the elements of a daily management system and has implemented the daily management system, starting with leadership. If this general model is followed, the tools that the Senior Team will grasp, adapt, and begin to standardize include the daily huddle, balanced scorecard/scoreboard, Problem Solving One, and monthly meeting. Creating the system is based on skill, not time.

The next step is to align a pilot hall with the Senior Team. The purpose of the pilot hall is to create the standard of what the system will look like and what the organization will look like when the system is fully deployed. The pilot hall is a place for other leaders in the organizations to go, see, and learn, and a place to standardize the tools. All the system artifacts include those in this book to start, followed by another set of carefully selected artifacts, including the improvement system, safety system, and workplace organization. Audit One should only be coached when the team is ready and able to use the tool as a way to see the current improved status and opportunities for improvement. The system will be coached in the pilot hall, by the CI Team as well as the Senior Team.

Case-by-case, excited and transformational senior leaders who are early adopters of the daily management system will align their direct reports with the daily management system. This is positive momentum that is encouraged and can be supported by the CI Team. A team of mid-level leaders led by a Senior Leader is a great way to align the expansion of both pilot halls and pilot leadership tools to make it easier for Senior Leaders to learn. The emphasis and focused coaching, though, is always on the Senior Team and pilot hall.

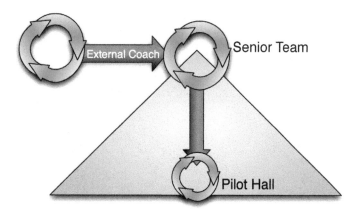

Figure 1.6. Moving from the organization's Senior Team to alignment and coaching a frontline pilot hall. Introducing the foundations to the pilot hall through Lean culture change artifacts creates alignment with the Senior Team and a model area to go and see.

Continuous Improvement Team. The ***Continuous Improvement Team (CI Team)*** is an internal group of coaches to learn, train, and then coach the new management system. Once fully established, the target size of the CI team is equivalent to one person on the CI team per every 100 employees. Once the steering committee and the Senior Team(s) decide on the standards of the management system, the CI Team becomes the keeper of those standards, applying problem solving where necessary and proposing changes to the standards to the steering committee. Establishing and growing this team will be a part of the management system's master plan.

During the pilot hall coaching and other frontline coaching, but before the tiered system of huddles, scorecards, and problem solving is all aligned, the CI team acts as the connection between the Senior Team and the pilot hall(s). Figure 1.7 demonstrates that the relationship of the external coach to the Senior Team is similar to that of the CI team to the pilot hall. In addition, the CI team may elevate problems from the pilot hall directly to the Senior Team, until all connecting teams are engaged in the new management system.

There is an ancient proverb that says, "Give a man a fish and you feed him for the day. Teach a man to fish and you feed him for a lifetime." When it comes to problem solving, some organizations have chosen a model wherein a few experts solve problems. The continuous improvement team, though they might be expert problem solvers, take the role of an internal coach, teaching others how to be problem solvers. Focused internal problem-solving efforts, without coaching support within a Lean management system, are similar to those external efforts from consultants who have promoted an event-based improvement program while neglecting the culture.

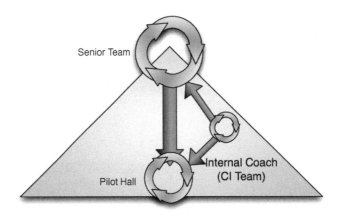

Figure 1.7. An internal coach aligning the Senior Team and frontline pilot hall as the daily management system is being aligned. Until the middle of the organization is engaged in the daily management system, the internal coach is the link between the pilot hall and Senior Team.

Communicating and Sequencing the Plan

Once the Senior Team generally understands the journey, has made a long term commitment to the journey, and has a general plan for the pilot hall, the plan will be established and communicated to the organization. The intention, strategy, and steps of deployment are known as the **Communication Plan**. This book only contains a small fraction of a multi-year journey. With that understanding, the Senior Team will communicate:

- *The reasons why the organization has chosen this pathway.*

- *The primary daily management system artifacts.*

- *The emphasis on culture, leadership, and values.*

- *The general steps the organization will take in the journey.*

- *That no one will lose their job from this system and journey.*

- *That everyone must be patient.*

- *That executive leadership is learning and leading the new culture.*

The communication plan is renewed annually and generally covers the same topics, including positive change that has occurred over the previous year. In subsequent years the communication plan will also include top improvement winners, current status of the corporate 6-year balanced scorecard, top problems from the Senior Team from the previous year, top problems anticipated for the next year, and annual planning cycle plans, as well as other information as needed.

Ultimately, the goal of this system is to create value for:

- *Customers*. Patients, families, payers, providers, etc.

- *Employees*. Staff, physicians, volunteers, leaders, etc.

- *Community*. Businesses, families, government, etc.

"Having high-level business targets [6-year corporate scorecard] broken down to more specific targets for each department [cascaded scorecard and scoreboards], with well-developed plans for action [master plans and detailed plans], and the rapid-fire kaizen [problem solving and improvement system], will allow the separate efforts to add up to meaningful results for the business" (Liker & Convis, 2012, p. 148) (contents in brackets added).

Proposed Sequencing and Next Steps

A daily management system consists of many different interconnected artifacts, so understanding the proposed sequencing for the Senior Team and pilot hall(s) is essential when adapting the Transformation Curve. Sequencing for Senior Teams and pilot halls is proposed in Tables 1.1 and 1.2 respectively.

Table 1.1. Proposed sequencing for Senior Teams

Sequencing for the Senior Team
Why? (Appendix A)
Daily Huddle (Chapter 2)
Problem Solving One (Chapter 3)
Balanced Scorecard (Chapter 4)
Monthly Meeting (Chapter 4)
Steering Committee (Chapter 1)
Master Planning (Chapter 5)
Communication Plan (Chapter 1)

Table 1.2. Proposed Sequencing for Pilot Halls

Sequencing for the Senior Team
Why & How (Communication Plan and Master Plan)
Daily Huddle (Chapter 2)
Improvement System (Chapter 6)
Balanced Scorecard (Chapter 4)
Safety System (Chapter 7)
Workplace Organization (Chapter 7)
Unit-Based Leadership Team (Chapter 4)
Problem Solving One (Chapter 3)
Monthly Meeting (Chapter 4)

A "company's culture is a result of its management system . . . culture is critical, and to change it, you have to change your management system" (2010, p. 4).

—David Mann, *Creating a Lean Culture*

Summary: Culture, Leadership, and Daily Management

1. **Change culture incrementally**. If you believe that the majority of employees and the organization have the values necessary for Lean, don't have extensive resources, and have already started positive transformations, incremental culture change may be your best approach.

2. **Start with leadership**. Like any change initiative, once you begin or refocus your lean journey, start with culture and start with Senior Leadership. Senior Leaders must not simply support kaizen events by removing barriers, but must use the daily management system first so they can apply it to the pilot hall and lead the rest of the organization through Lean transformation. Learning the daily management system means using the artifacts described in the book, grasping the foundations, and practicing the 3Gs/3Ps.

3. **Lay the groundwork for alignment**. This includes but is not limited to creating/recasting the organization's priorities (e.g., Safety, Quality, Service, Talent, Cost, and Daily Management, or People, Quality, Service, Finance, and Growth), establishing the organization-wide 6-year balanced scorecard, and creating/drafting policies for the improvement system and safety system.

4. **Use a daily management system**. Understanding and using the daily management system, first at the leadership level, then at the pilot hall, gives greater understanding of the standards of the system so that leaders can adapt the system standards to achieve the desired culture.

5. **Understand the foundations, artifacts, and the *why***. The foundations of continuous improvement are P-D-C-A, visual management, and roles and responsibilities. The foundations are intertwined into each artifact of the daily management system. The Senior Leadership team needs to learn the artifacts both in theory and in application by using the system and understanding the purpose of each artifact and the interconnections. Note: much of this understanding will come as a coach helps establish the pilot hall in conjunction with the Senior Team.

6. **Create the master plan for implementation/learning**. Create a master plan (introduced in Chapter 5) for Lean transformation with the Senior Team and the pilot hall. The plan will include specific activities, responsible persons, timing, and follow-up and help the team agree to necessary steps for resource allocation and coaching.

7. **Communicate**. Once the Senior Leadership team is beginning to understand and lead by example using the daily management system, communicate to the organization expectations of the journey, why the organization has chosen this pathway, and that leadership is actively leading the change.

Chapter 2
Daily Huddle

This chapter will introduce your team to:

- *Huddle standards within a daily management system.*

- *Artifacts for facilitating and leading huddles.*

- *Aligning huddles in a tiered daily management system.*

- *A case study integrating service excellence into daily management using huddles.*

- *Example daily huddle agendas.*

Why a Daily Huddle?

The **Daily Huddle** is a short, stand-up meeting that engages a team to make and sustain positive improvement through face-to-face communication. As a structured daily communication between team leader and team member, the huddle is conducted in front of a balanced scoreboard as a visual management tool to aid in more efficient and effective communication. The purpose of the huddle is to recognize outstanding behavior and positive improvements, to develop and understand problem-solving techniques, to check processes via leading indicators, and to communicate a proactive plan and expectations for the day. Aligned, tiered huddles serve as a standard for communication and a standard daily check throughout the organization.

Huddle Standards Within a Daily Management System

Huddle standards provide a framework and insight into the agenda, in order to keep the huddle consistent through the organization, but adapted to meet the desired culture of the unit. The goal is for all staff members to be involved in at least one huddle each day. Leaders may engage in one huddle with their team members and a second huddle with their leader. The recommended standards, which provide a quick reference for training team members on the purpose and expectations of the daily huddle, are as follows:

- ☐ *Same time, same place.*

- ☐ *Everyone, every day.*

- ☐ *Follow vitals and prompts.*

- ☐ *Stand at the balanced scoreboard.*

- ☐ *Short (5-15 min).*

- ☐ *Keep it positive.*

- ☐ *Problem-solving sheets and improvements for problems.*

- ☐ *No problem discussion.*

- ☐ *Updates and follow-up on previous problems and ideas.*

- ☐ *Proactive daily outlook/schedule.*

1. **Same time, same place.** It's important for the huddle to be held at the same time and the same place, in order to have predictability and begin to create a daily habit for all employees. Though there's never a perfect time, team leaders who have a "we'll get to it if there's time" mentality will struggle with sustainability and change because "there's never enough time" or "something else came up." Having a consistent place is just as important, because the location of the huddle will build uniformity and predictability. Generally, when starting out, this standard is more important than trying to shift the time each day to accommodate everyone.

2. **Everyone, every day.** Not all staff will be able to attend each and every huddle due to the need to care for patients. Direct, hands-on patient care that needs to be completed as soon as possible always takes priority over the huddle. However, anything that can wait for 5 or 10 minutes, such as putting a non-urgent order into a computer, registering a routine patient, or making follow-up phone calls to a physician office, can wait. Being "too busy" with non-immediate and non-urgent concerns is not a valid excuse for missing any huddle for team leaders or members. In a busy environment, it's easy to find an excuse to miss the huddle; however, if deployed properly, team members will begin to appreciate the valid reasons why they must attend the huddle.

3. **Follow the vitals and prompts.** Create and update the daily huddle prompt sheet to encourage positive communication and discussion about improvements to problems. Managers will use these standards to coach team members and engage everyone into continuous improvement. Also, the priority order of the prompts is one way for an organization to put espoused values into practice (e.g., talking about safety before finance).

4. **Stand at the balanced scoreboard.** Whether the team is a frontline caregiver team, a team of unit managers, or a Senior Team, the standard is to stand at the balanced scoreboard, which is introduced in Chapter 5. Standing helps keep the meeting short and focused on problems, improvements, and visuals on the scoreboard. One study noted that sit-down meetings were 34% longer than stand-up meetings (Bluedorn et al, 1999, p. 277)

5. **Short 5- to 15-minute meetings.** Although the huddle is essential for positive and effective communication throughout the organization, it still takes caregivers away from direct patient care. Therefore, keeping the huddle efficient and effective is critical. If all the other standards are followed, keeping the meeting short should not be a problem. This does not mean to cut the huddle short once 5 minutes are up; it means to follow the standards and provide coaching to keep your huddles both efficient and effective.

6. **Keep it positive**. Continually share and communicate the positive improvements and stories that occur at both the unit and organization level. When coaching problem statements, coach to the facts and process-driven statements, not people-driven statements (i.e., pointing blame). Do not allow negative individuals to overpower the rest of the team. Immediately focus complaints towards the problem-solving process. Select prompts that will shine light on individuals at the huddle by sharing positive employee-patient service excellence stories and positive improvement stories.

7. **Problem-solving sheet or improvement form for every problem or idea.** Generally, if the problem or idea is important enough to report at a huddle, it's important enough to have a problem-solving sheet or improvement form as a means of communication and documentation. Writing it down will increase the chances of the problem being solved. In general, Senior Teams will focus on enforcing problem solving, while frontline pilot halls will first focus on generating ideas using the *improvement system* (explained in Chapter 7). Documentation of the problem or idea is critical, as it is the first step in both the problem-solving process and the improvement process.

8. **No problem discussion.** Once the sheet is started, do not dwell on the problem at a huddle or talk about potential causes of the problem. Encourage fact management and direct observation—neither of which can be done at the huddle. If this happens, the leader will ask staff members to work together to solve the problem outside of the huddle and report back at the next huddle to the team, using the problem-solving sheet or improvement system. Though teams may use the huddle time to discuss improvements or modify existing ideas for implementation, loose problem discussion is not acceptable.

9. **Follow up and communicate.** Communication is critical. When there is an update to a problem-solving sheet or improvement in process, communicate often. Communicate with team members so they know and understand the problem-solving process, where the problem-sheets are going, and what the expectations are based on the organization's maturity with problem solving. As improvements are being piloted, implemented, and documented, the employee who owns the improvement will keep the team updated on status and impact. (This will be discussed more in Chapter 7, *Improvement System*.)

10. **Proactive daily outlook.** Use the huddle as a way to communicate the outlook and plan for the day—for example, communicating the number of patients in the Emergency Department, the day's census, planned vendor visits for the day, needed changes to Operating Room schedule, etc. Creating visual management tools to help manage the day and support the huddle will be implemented on a case-by-case basis.

Artifacts for Facilitating Huddles in a Daily Management System

The **Huddle Prompt Sheet**, or huddle agenda, is a simple, standard set of questions that the leader of the huddle asks on a daily basis to spark teams to communicate problems and potential solutions. The huddle prompt sheet generally covers what happened on the previous shift, as well as problems that may be encountered during the upcoming shift or day. The standard questions and prompts create a simple way for any team member to facilitate a huddle. The purpose of the prompt sheet is to encourage staff to bring problems within their and their manager's sphere of influence to the surface, and also to recognize their peers' positive improvements. This creates an environment that is focused on problem identification and problem solving every day.

An organization may have a few standard prompts on each and every huddle prompt sheet. For example, "Were there any employee injuries or accidents yesterday?" Each unit, though, should customize and adapt the prompt sheet as needed. As new initiatives begin and are being standardized throughout a unit, functional area, or organization, the huddle prompt sheet should be updated to serve as a communication tool. Generally, the huddle questions will become more proactive as the new management system evolves. Table 3.2 is an example of an Executive Team's daily huddle prompt sheet.

The **Huddle Record Sheet** is a handwritten account of the daily huddle. Generally, one team member will lead the huddle, and another team member will take notes on the huddle record sheet. Table 3.3 shows an example of a daily huddle record sheet, filled out after an Inpatient leaders' daily huddle. Team leaders may take separate notes to ensure actions are elevated and followed up appropriately. The huddle record sheet is used to help close the loop from one day to the next, serves as a record for those who are not in attendance, and becomes a stat sheet to bring to tiered huddles for further communication.

Both the huddle record sheet and the huddle prompt sheets are kept in a team area for easy accessibility for team members. Having these tools in a common area will make it easier for team members to lead the huddle when the team leader is not present. The standard location for the huddle prompt and record sheets is on the problem-solving board, introduced in Chapter 4. As actions are being checked from huddle to huddle, problem solving is initiated, and notes are elevated to the next tier, the organization should adopt a standard for when the huddle sheets are to be discarded.

Paul D. Hubbard, a quarterback in 1892 for Gallaudet University, a Deaf college, is credited as the first person to lead a huddle after he realized that the opposing players could read his sign language (Gannon, 1981, p. 272).

Table 2.1. Example Senior Team Huddle Prompts

Senior Team – Daily Huddle
People
Check-in: How is everyone today?
Are there people we should recognize for something they did yesterday?
Any employee complaints, grievances?
Quality
Any external concerns that may impact the health of our community?
Any inaccuracies in information that may impact quality, throughput, billing, etc.?
Any medication errors or near medication errors?
Any mistakes that could lead to quality-of-care issues with our patients?
Any patient complaints (formal or informal)?
Any patient falls or other patient safety issues?
Any serious/sentinel events?
Were there any hospital-acquired infections or potential infections?
Were there any readmissions to the ED or inpatient units?
Service
What is a recent example of an employee using our service excellence standards?
Any major issues with vendors or suppliers?
Any problems with throughput (length of stay, discharge, etc.)?
How long did it take from the time the ED physician decided to admit a patient to an inpatient bed to the time the patient actually left the ED for that bed yesterday?
How long did patients wait to be seen by a physician in the ED yesterday?
How many ED patients left without being seen by the ED physician yesterday?
Finance
Any unplanned expenses?
Did we use any float or pay staff overtime yesterday?
What is today's census?
Growth
Any Centennial Building Project update?
Any update on physician recruitment?
How many admissions in the medical center yesterday?
How many first cases started on time yesterday?
How many outpatient no-shows yesterday?
Actions and Follow-Up
Are there any outstanding action items?
Review yesterday's action items.

Table 2.2. Example Daily Huddle Record Sheet

Daily Huddle Record Sheet			
Date: 7/1/13 # RNs: 8 # Physicians: n/a Facilitator: Meg			

People

There was an employee injury yesterday, Vickie is following up with Pete to conduct root cause analysis using a problem-solving sheet (PSS)

Quality

The 6th floor had a fall without injury, see PSS on board

Service

Joe walked a lost patient from the cafeteria to the 6th floor

Dr Doe was batching patients in the ED, which lead to 7th floor receiving 3 patients at the same time. Dr Phillips is following up with him via problem-solving

Finance

There are 3 one-on-ones

Growth

4 out of 7 patients were d/c within 2 hours of the order; the other 3 are awaiting transportation

Action & Follow-Up Items

7th floor employee injury—start problem solving sheet

Dr Phillips w/ Dr Doe about batching

Starting and Aligning Daily Huddles in a Daily Management System

In both the pilot halls and the Senior Team, expect that the huddle will be operationally focused and reactive at first. Just getting people together each and every day using a standard agenda is the initial target state. As other system components such as problem solving, the improvement system, and balanced scorecard are introduced, the huddle will be more focused on improvement and proactive in nature. By continually coaching problem solving and adding proactive prompts to the huddle sheet as problems are solved and countermeasures implemented, the huddle will become transformational.

Senior Team Expectations. At the Senior Leadership level, expect that huddles will initially take 20 to 40 minutes, sometimes longer. Generally, lengthy huddles are due to leaders not defining and documenting problems well prior to the huddle (which will be coached). Typically, the Senior Team is not accustomed to hear about as many problems as they will begin to hear about during the huddles. As the problem solving is applied more robustly prior to the huddle, leaders will arrive at the huddle with problems already contained, root causes identified, and improvements in motion.

Pilot Hall Expectations. When deploying the system at the pilot hall, expect huddles to go quickly because staff "don't have time for a huddle" and because in many cases they have been plagued with the same or similar problems for decades. As the improvement system and problem solving are introduced, the pilot hall huddle will become more focused on positive improvements rather than simply information sharing. This will also cause people to begin thinking differently about the problems they have always experienced on a daily basis. But again, just getting people together at the same time and the same place, using the same agenda, is the initial target. The Continuous Improvement Team may facilitate the communication between the pilot hall and the Senior Team by elevating necessary problems and improvements, so leaders can support problem-solving efforts on a daily basis.

WARNING: Using huddle prompts to identify problems and not containing and solving those problems will lead to a negative transactional huddle versus a positive transformational huddle. A **_Transactional_** huddle can be described as a meeting where problems and information are shared, but no action is taken or communicated. A **_Transformational_** huddle is one where countermeasures and improvements are presented formally and agreed upon, and where, in addition, the total impact of past improvements is communicated to keep discussion positive and focused on further improvement. Use the standards and other tools in this book to keep meetings transformational.

How to Start Daily Huddles

Note that starting a daily management system is not linear and all artifacts within this book (Phase 1 Level A of the Transformation Curve) should be understood by leadership from a high level before starting daily huddles, so the artifacts can be aligned into a single management system, not used as disparate tools. Also, pre-work will be necessary from the Senior Team prior to introducing huddles to the pilot hall like establishing the organization's priorities, 6-year scorecard, improvement system policy, and safety system policy. These are necessary steps to align the daily management system pilot hall and the rest of the organization. General steps for starting a daily huddle are:

1. **Create the huddle prompts.** Adapt the standard huddle prompt sheet provided to meet the needs of your unit or department. Ensure the huddle prompts follow the organization's priorities, so that huddles start with the most important issues first, like safety. Keep it positive by adding prompts that will bring positive actions from team members to light, especially in the pilot hall. Table 2.2 on page 27 shows example huddle prompts.

2. **Select a time and place for the huddle.** For some, this step can be the most difficult step in initiating a huddle. When selecting a time, consider when the huddle can have the greatest staff attendance and have the least impact on patient care. Don't be afraid to pick a time and adapt as the team progresses. There is never a "ideal time" for a huddle, and many team members will resist the thought of a daily huddle/meeting. Pick a time and place, and stay consistent in order to build a habit of meeting on a daily basis and sharing information aligned with organizational/departmental goals.

3. **Introduce the standards.** When starting the huddle, if possible, train team members about the process and the system connections, such as problem solving, the improvement system, and other artifacts of the daily management system. If formal training is not possible or will significantly delay daily improvement, use the bullet points in this chapter to review and discuss the huddle standards with the team. Generally problem solving (Senior Team) and and the improvement system (pilot hall) should be introduced simultaneously in order to facilitate problem solving discussion and idea development.

4. **Share responsibilities for facilitating.** When the huddle begins to become a habit for the team, begin to share facilitating responsibilities. The purpose is to give team members ownership of the process, give them a chance to lead, and hardwire the team habits, so that huddles continue regardless of the team leader's presence. Note, though, that the team leader needs to be present, engage, and lead the huddle during his/her time at the organization. Creating

a schedule designating who leads the huddle when will also help hardwire the process of huddles on nights, weekends, and other times.

5. **Encourage and lead problem solving and improvements.** When a problem surfaces during the day, encourage team members to reflect on the problem during the huddle and to fill out the first quadrant of the problem-solving sheet (this is introduced in Chapter 3, *Problem Solving One*). Be sure to enforce problem-solving sheets at the huddle, or it could quickly turn into an ineffective complaint session. Follow up and coach employees, when necessary, in order to keep the meeting efficient, effective, and meaningful. Coaching and encouraging the improvement system at the huddle keeps the huddle positive, transformational, and focused on improvement.

6. **Obtain daily reports.** When starting a daily huddle, many of the prompts will be transactional versus transformational. As these transactional questions are aligned with the balanced scorecard, discussed in Chapter 4, it becomes clear what types of daily reports and daily information it is necessary to share at huddles. Many teams, though, may not have reports available, so asking the question at the daily huddle provides the same information, and begins to align the team around facts that align with the organization's priorities and goals. For example, "Were there any safety incidents/accidents in the last 24 hours?" is transactional, whereas "How will we improve employee safety today" is transformational. The artifacts in later chapters such as *problem-solving sheets* and *improvement forms* will help guide transformational discussion based on facts.

7. **Incorporate into Leaders' Standard Work.** As a leader, establish standards for preparing for huddles on a daily basis, attending huddles, and being an engaged leader/member of huddles.

8. **P-D-C-A.** As you implement other artifacts of the management system, ongoing updates and improvements of the questions is essential to keep the huddle a structured, but an ever-improving process. Begin to visualize high-priority huddle questions and problems in the form of metrics, indicators, and support (see Chapter 4, *Balanced Scoreboard*).

Huddle Standard Work Activities:

Daily: Prepare for the daily huddle (gather data, stats, etc.)

Daily: Close the loop before attending the next layer of huddles.

Daily: Attend the next layer of huddles.

Tiered Huddles in an Organization-Wide Daily Management System

In order to get the right information to the right person to ensure quick and appropriate follow-up, huddles must be layered appropriately. Generally, information goes up and then back down if necessary, though problems should be solved with the most appropriate people at the lowest level possible.

Elevating problems is especially important when starting the new management system, to ensure that proper follow-up is happening. Figure 2.1 is an example of how huddles may be tiered in a typical community healthcare system. Once fully deployed, information and problems will flow upward to the Senior Leadership. It is recommended, however, that huddles start at the Senior Leader level so that learning is cascaded and coached first through a pilot and then through the rest of the organization, along with the rest of the new management system.

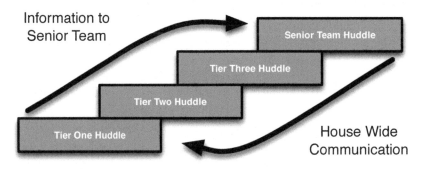

Figure 2.1. The timing of tiered huddles links communication from frontline employees to Senior Leadership and back again. When huddles are implemented throughout the organization, the Senior Team should have high-level information to coach daily improvement and lead operations.

Tier One Huddles. This huddle is generally a start-up or change-of-shift huddle discussing patient flow problems from frontline staff, checking adherence to process standards via leading indicators, communicating issues from the previous shift, and communicating the general plan of the day. This is usually done during the frontline huddles, incorporating, but not replacing specific hand-off and bedside reporting for patients. Huddles should be first thing in the morning; however, some concerns may necessitate huddles later in the day. "The first-tier team leaders' meetings are, among other things, the primary vehicle for supporting and extending bottom-up participation in improvement suggestion systems" (Mann, 2010, p. 87).

Tier Two Huddles. Individuals at this layer of huddles include the Emergency Department Manager, each Inpatient Manager, Case Management Director, Medical Services Director, and others. This is a value-stream-level meeting, which is usually done to discuss flow problems between units, discharge problems, bed placement problems, patient flow problems, and concerns that need to be elevated from frontline huddles. Leaders at this layer should be especially interested in value-stream-level metrics/indicators to drive performance. An example of tiered huddles is seen in Figure 2.2.

Tier Three Huddles. In tier three huddles, the Senior Vice President of Patient Services meets with the Director of Surgical Services, Director of Medical Services, and other team members as needed to ensure process adherence, coach elevated problems, and select problems to pass on to other Senior Team members. Depending on the organization size, tier three and tier four may be within the same huddle tier.

Tier Four Huddles. In the example, this huddle is the Senior Team's daily huddle. After auditing process and following up on frontline problems, they can use this time to ensure that the others have followed up on the actions from the previous day, and to communicate any actions that must take place for the current day and upcoming days. Once fully deployed, this huddle will have much more streamlined information, but deployment starts with learning the process.

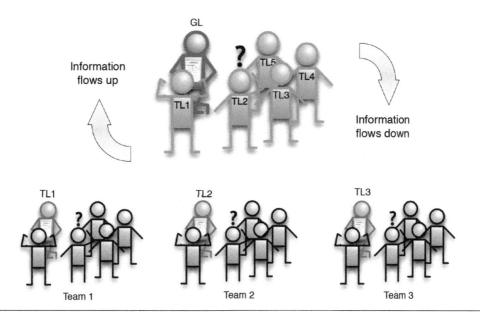

Figure 2.2. Tiered daily huddles allow for information flow on a daily basis.

"The second- and third- (and fourth- where applicable) tier meetings have a dual focus. . . 'run the business'. . . and improve the business. . . Assessment [is] based on data captured on visual controls (i.e. the balanced scoreboard), assignment for corrective action and/or improvement (i.e. problem solving sheets), accountability for having completed the previous day's assignments" (Mann, 2010, p. 87).

Baldrige Connections

Safety *6.2c(1).* The huddle supports accident prevention by keeping safety at the forefront each day through proactive safety questions. It also helps support accident investigation by surfacing safety problems both proactively and reactively when aligned with the problem-solving process (NIST, 2013, p. 23).

Communication *1.1b.(1).* The huddle serves as one mechanism for Senior Leaders to "communicate with and engage the entire workforce" (NIST, p. 7). With a brief meeting that occurs every day and with everyone in the organization participating, it becomes very easy to communicate and engage everyone.

Organizational Culture *5.2a.(2).* The huddle is one way that the organization will "foster an organizational culture that is characterized by open communication" (NIST, p. 20). At the end of each huddle, managers ask for follow-up and whether any one-on-one discussions are needed.

Knowledge Management *4.2a.(1).* The huddle is one standard for daily knowledge transfer. Tiered huddles create the mechanism to "collect and transfer workforce knowledge" up and down the organization (NIST, p. 17).

Listening to Current Patients and Other Customers *3.1a.(1).* The problems and results that arise out of everyday patient interactions are integrated into huddle prompts in order to ensure that actionable information is elevated or passed along to the appropriate level of the organization. This is one mechanism, organizationally, to listen to "patients and other customers to obtain actionable information and to obtain feedback on healthcare services" (NIST, p. 13).

Career Progression *5.2c.(3).* The huddle process and other components assist with the development of future leaders. Requesting that staff members lead the huddle is one small step in the leadership development process, as conducting the huddle is a form of leading. Also, where appropriate, a lower-tier huddle facilitator/leader can fill in or accompany the team leader to the next tier's huddle.

Best Practices *4.1c.(1).* Tiered huddles are one way that best practices are easily and informally shared throughout the organization on a daily basis. By sharing recognition, positive stories, solved problems, and improvements, individual team members can use the same ideas to improve their work areas.

Assessment of [Workforce] Engagement *5.2b.(1).* Attending a huddle and observing whether a team is quickly running through prompts or engaged in positive improvement discussion is "an informal assessment method. . . to determine workforce engagement" (NIST, p. 20).

Summary: Lean Culture Change Using Daily Huddles

The daily huddle at the Senior Team level can begin immediately after learning about Phase 1 Level A of the Transformation Curve. The daily huddle in the pilot hall begins after a master plan is created and the Senior Team is prepared to support coaching/alignment of the pilot hall.

☐ The daily huddle is a short, stand-up meeting that engages a team to make and sustain positive improvement through face-to-face communication.

☐ Initial artifacts of the daily huddle include the daily huddle prompt sheet and the daily huddle record sheet.

☐ The daily huddle prompt sheet is an adaptable list of standard questions to ask on a daily basis, providing the agenda for daily huddles.

☐ The daily huddle record sheet is a temporary account of the meeting, which is used to update team members as well as track daily actions outside the problem-solving sheets and the improvement system.

☐ These artifacts are placed in a common area so that any team member can access them and facilitate the huddle. An example of this is introduced in the next chapter, *Problem Solving One*.

☐ Expect that the Senior Team huddle will extend past the target time of 15 minutes at first, and use the tools in later chapters to help focus discussions and encourage Senior Leaders to come prepared.

☐ Expect that pilot hall frontline huddles may be very brief and met with resistance. Focusing on the positive and encouraging discussions around improvements helps win people's hearts and engage them in daily improvement faster. Enforce the standards of same time, same place, but provide the coaching necessary for the pilot hall's daily huddle to be successful.

☐ As huddles become integrated into the organization, each team/group leader should expect to attend two huddles on a daily basis—the huddle s/he leads as well as the huddle s/he participates in.

☐ Senior Leaders should expect to be visible in a coaching role at the pilot hall huddle(s) as well as at other times, described in later chapters, within the pilot hall(s).

**Memorial Regional Medical Center, Bon Secours Health System:
One Hospital Adapting and Deploying Ritz-Carlton's Daily Huddles**

The Ritz-Carlton Leadership Center was formed in 1999 after the organization won their second Malcolm Baldrige National Quality Award. Partnering with the Leadership Center in 2007, Memorial Regional Medical Center (MRMC) developed a strategy to adapt the "System of Smiles" and transfer best practices from Ritz-Carlton to the Medical Center. At MMRC, leadership was actively engaged in the process, everyone was trained, and unit-based service excellence champions helped drive the new service standards. "The best practices that the hospital closely copied were the Credo Card, key success factors, the Daily Huddle communication tool, wow stories, on-boarding process, and measurement process" (Guindon-Nasir, 2010, p. 154).

Daily huddles were deployed as a new communication tool in all units throughout the hospital in May 2008, using the title of "Called to Serve" for the daily huddle worksheet. Huddles were a mechanism for communication, education, participation, and empowerment. This was a way that every manager could communicate face-to-face with each employee and engage them in service excellence and change initiatives on a daily basis.

At first, many employees resisted daily huddles at MRMC because they "felt they did not have the time to stop and meet for 10-15 minutes every day when they could be saving lives" (Guindon-Nasir, p. 175). Taking time out of an already busy schedule of answering phones, call bells, patient requests, and so forth, seemed counterintuitive even to the the best employees of MRMC. "The employees eventually embraced the Daily Huddles and leveraged them to their benefit. . . and. . . they have come to love them" (Guindon-Nasir, p. 177).

The huddles at MRMC were a combination of unit-specific and organization-wide improvements, problem recognition, and service excellence stories. "Many of the wow stories are read during the Daily Huddle, which allows employees to hear about a fellow employee who has created a wow experience for an internal or external customer, and gives them the opportunity to challenge themselves to raise their own level of service excellence" (Guindon-Nasir, p. 199).

Memorial Regional Medical Center of Bon Secours Health System adapted the "System of Smiles" to fit their desired new culture using the daily huddle as one mode of communication. After three years, satisfaction throughout the hospital increased, including a rise in employee engagement scores from 3.98 in 2006 to 4.52 in 2009 and an increase in physician satisfaction scores from 39% in 2006 to 87% in 2009 (Guindon-Nasir, p. 74).

Table 2.2. Example Daily Huddle Record Sheet

IRMC 6th Medical—Huddle Prompts
People Employee injuries/incidents/near misses/problems/anyone feel unsafe? (If yes, was problem-solving sheet started?) Physician/Volunteer problems? How is staffing today?
Quality Safety problems (**falls**, med errors, restraints, suicidal patients, CVA/TIA patients)? (If yes, was a problem-solving sheet completed?) Any serious events (return to the OR, complication from surgery, complications related to care, or other patient occurrences that we didn't expect)? Transfers to higher level of care? **Foleys** that need to be removed today? Are they necessary? What action needs to be taken? Actionable patient complaints? Patients with PIN #s? Any issues with difficult patient transfers or need for PT/OT consults on any of our patients? Any patients restrained or been medicated (chemical restraint)?
Service Delays in discharge? Length of Stay or patient placement issues? Nurse-to-nurse hand-off issues? Any OFIs with patient handoffs? Any problems identified with cleanliness, laundry, missing supplies, maintenance, IS?
Finance How many 1:1s? Are all evaluated and necessary? Any unplanned expenses? Any 302s, etc., we have questions/concerns about?
Growth Follow-up—Any follow-up action items from previous huddles? Any problem-solving sheets that need follow-up or staff communication? Has anyone had any idea for improvement using the improvement system?
Any follow-up action items from previous huddles? Any good/great things we need to recognize? Anything for the good of the order? Any other issues you would like to discuss?
Note. Prompts adapted from a medical unit.

Chapter 3
Problem Solving One

This chapter will introduce your team to:

- *Firefighting versus root cause problem solving.*

- *Problem-solving objects, verbal expressions, and activities.*

- *Problem Solving One in a daily management system.*

- *A case study about daily problem solving and cultural change.*

- *Example problem-solving sheets and problem-solving boards.*

Why Root Cause Problem Solving?

Problems, including serious patient safety events, near misses, delays in care, and mistakes in information/communications are happening every second of every day in healthcare. In fact, preventable serious events are a leading cause of death in the United States (CQHCA, 2000, p. 26). In many cases, "it is only after a patient dies or suffers a serious injury that the type of mistake and the factors contributing to it are subject to serious scrutiny" (Spear, 2005, p. 5). Therefore, having a formal system to recognize, communicate, and solve problems before they become serious patient safety events is an essential part of a daily management system.

Problem Solving One introduces a standard method to learn problem solving, solve problems one by one, and build problem-solving capability and capacity. It is focused on building individual problem solving—learning the problem-solving language, process, and expectations. More frequent and rapid problem solving is the expectation—not necessarily slow-moving, high-impact problem solving. Operationally, Problem Solving One gives leaders a standard process, language, and framework to teach and coach improvement. The human development aspect of Problem Solving One is to teach the verbal expressions and activities of a problem-solving culture, including developing and testing countermeasures, and balancing organizational development and operational improvement.

The initial purpose of the Senior Team using Problem Solving One is to learn and adapt the common language and process to lead the organization through Lean culture change using problem solving. In the pilot hall, the initial target is to just do problem solving, which initiates a cycle of coaching and learning to test, implement, and check countermeasures to problems. It is a standard coached throughout the organization and is the basis of more advanced problem-solving artifacts. Important concepts when learning the problem-solving process include:

- ☐ *Be patient.* Teaching an organization to become a learning, problem-solving organization takes time.
- ☐ *Use fact management.* Fact finding and problem solving go hand in hand in developing people.
- ☐ *Start with simple problems.* Start with simple problems to learn the problem-solving process by doing.

"Preventable adverse events are a leading cause of death in the United States" (CQHCA, 2000, p. 26).

Firefighting Versus Root Cause Problem Solving

When coaching a daily management system to organizations, especially healthcare, many new learners immediately note they "solve" problems every day and "solving problems" is a main part of their job. Within a daily management system, this is not true problem solving. True daily problem solving, compared to the problem solving many non-Lean organizations are familiar with, can be described as first order versus root cause problem solving.

First Order Problem Solving is firefighting, temporarily fixing, containing, or working around problems, with the chances being that the problem will resurface. *Root Cause Problem Solving* is finding and changing the *Root Cause* or underlying reason the problem occurred, so that the problem never happens again. Root cause problem solving involves patience, going to see, and asking questions to deeply understand the facts and causes of the problem.

Example first order solutions from a great firefighter are: "We didn't have our linens yesterday, so I 'borrowed' some from the the other unit. . . problem solved!" Or, "Just before surgery we didn't have all the right supplies. I searched and found what we needed for the case to start on time. . . problem solved!" Root cause solutions or *Countermeasures*, however, address the root cause of the problem. Tables 4.1 and 4.2 explore first order versus root cause solutions.

Table 3.1. First Order Problem Solving Examples

Problem	First Order Solution
Dr. Smith didn't receive the lab results yet.	Resend the results to Dr. Smith ASAP.
The microscope the ophthalmologist used in the operating room was dim.	Go find a functioning microscope for this surgery and buy a new light for the next.
We couldn't find 704's telemetry pack.	Use a telemetry pack from a different room.

Table 3.2. Root Cause Problem Solving Examples

Problem	Root Cause	Countermeasure
Dr. Smith didn't receive the lab results yet.	There's no standard process for updating physician information.	Create a standard for updating fax numbers with our internal physicians.
The microscope Dr. Roberts used in the operating room was dim.	No standard process for finding/removing preventative maintenance items.	Create a standard process for locating preventative maintenance items.
Unit RN could not find the telemetry pack for room 704.	The standard location for the telemetry pack is too large.	Standardize location of packs to fit one pack, not two.

Using Fact Management for Problem Solving One

Problem solving must be done based on facts. In order to find facts, one should go to where the work is being done and observe what is actually happening. In Japanese, the terms used to describe this are: Gemba, Gembutsu, and Genjitsu, with Lewis' version in Table 3.3 as go see, get the facts, and grasp the situation.

Go and See, Get the Facts, Grasp the Situation. Lewis Americanized this concept to the ***3Gs***: "Go See, Get the Facts, Grasp the Situation." Problem solving needs to be done at the ***Gemba***—the actual place where the problem occurred and was first recognized. The focus needs to be on ***Gembutsu*** (the actual thing, not heresy or speculation), and based on ***Genjitsu*** (the actual facts that surround the problem and causes).

Table 3.3. The 3Gs

Japanese 3Gs	Translation to 3As
Gemba	Actual place
Gembutsu	Actual thing
Genjitsu	Actual facts
"Go See. Get the Facts. Grasp the Situation."	

Genchi Gembutsu—Go Observe. When hearing about a problem, most likely only a small fraction of the facts that surround the problem are understood and told. In order to fully grasp a problem, coach problem solving, or be a role model following the problem-solving standards, fact finding through direct observation and other techniques is necessary to truly understand what's happening or not happening. Direct observation is not going to where the work is done, asking a few questions, and hurrying back to the office. True direct observation takes time, patience, and passion. Remember the ***3Ps***: People, Passion, and Patience.

"Focus on the Process, Not the Person." Focus on process problems, not people problems. Most problems are process problems, not people problems. Most perceived people problems are because of poor processes. If a person is not following a standard, ask why to understand the root cause(s) of the problem.

"Prescription before diagnosis is malpractice." —Unknown

Problem Solving One Objects, Verbal Expressions, and Activities

Problem Solving One artifacts serve as both human development and operations improvement tools. Developmentally, these objects give a way for leaders to teach and coach problem-solving skills to team members in the organization. This increases both individual capability and the problem-solving capacity of the organization. Operationally, artifacts are used to communicate and solve problems. The concepts introduced in this section are the *problem-solving sheet, problem solving one process*, and the *problem-solving board*. The purpose of these artifacts is to standardize the communication around problems between frontline team members, team leaders, the Senior Team, and others.

Problem Solving One Process

The **Problem Solving One Process**, shown in Figure 3.1, demonstrates how a problem is recognized and root cause identified. The **Point of Recognition** is the initial awareness of the problem. This takes little or no investigation, it is simply a realization or recognition that a problem has occurred. Example points of recognition may include a patient fall, medication error, or surgical case cancellation. The **Point of Occurrence (PoO)** is the step, time, location, etc. where the problem originated, and should be found prior to creating a Problem Statement. The **Problem Statement**, generated from facts found at the point of occurrence, is a clear factual account of the problem, which may include who, what, when, where, and generally why. This statement helps to focus the root cause analysis using the 5 *Whys*. The **5 Whys** are a method of asking why to get from the point of occurrence to the root cause. Examples of the problem recognition process are shown in Figures 3.2–3.4.

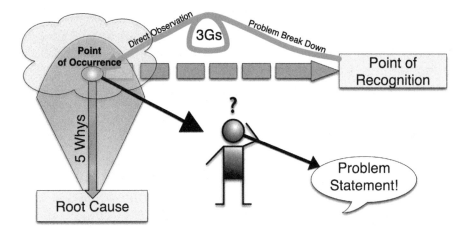

Figure 3.1. The Problem Solving One process. Creating a problem statement by first recognizing, breaking down, and observing the problem to identify the point of occurrence (right to left). The 5 Whys are then used from the problem statement to identify the root cause.

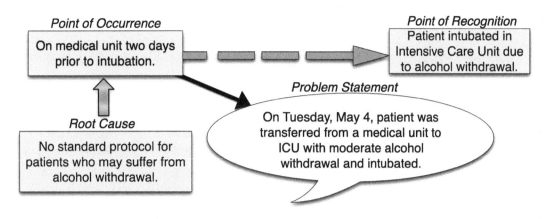

Figure 3.2. An example of how not having a withdrawal protocol to recognize and treat symptoms of alcohol withdrawal can lead to a patient being intubated in the intensive care unit.

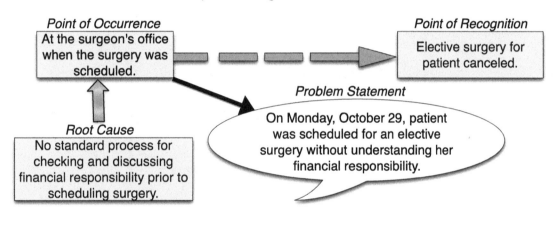

Figure 3.3. An example of how not having a standard process for discussing financial responsibility at the same time a surgery is scheduled can lead to a canceled surgery.

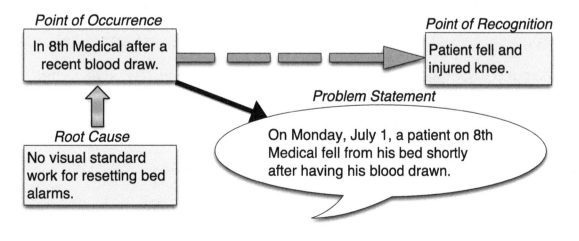

Figure 3.4. An example of how not having visual standard work for resetting a patient bed alarm can lead to a patient falling.

Problem-Solving Sheet and Flow

The **Problem-Solving Sheet**, overviewed in Figure 3.5, is a standard tool used to facilitate and communicate the status of problems within the Problem Solving One process individually, departmentally, and organizationally. This tool is not a piece of paper that replaces face-to-face communication. It provides a common pathway to recognizing, clearly stating, and solving problems. Later, more advanced artifacts will be introduced that build upon the problem-solving sheet.

This 8.5 x 11" sheet of paper, shown in Figure 3.6, is used by anyone in the organization to recognize and solve problems using a common language, framework, and follow-up method. Problem-solving sheets are used to solve one problem at a time and double as a way to teach individuals how to do problem solving, and create, implement, and check countermeasures based on root causes. Basic flow and use of the problem-solving sheet is as follows:

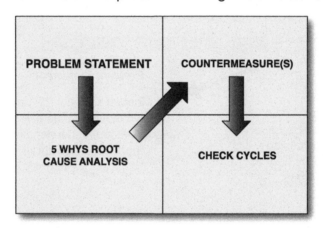

Figure 3.5. Overview of the four quadrants of the problem-solving sheet.

1. First Quadrant (Top Left). Using the Problem Solving One process, identify the problem being solved. Include the recognition, containment, and target.

2. Second Quadrant (Bottom Left). Using the 5 Whys and 3Gs, analyze the facts to determine the most appropriate root cause.

3. Third Quadrant (Top Right). Identify the countermeasures—long-term solutions, who is going to implement them, and when.

4. Fourth Quadrant (Bottom Right). Visualize how and how often the recurrence of the problem or cause will be checked, along with the future outlook.

"Every system is perfectly designed to get the results it gets."
—Paul Batalden, M.D.

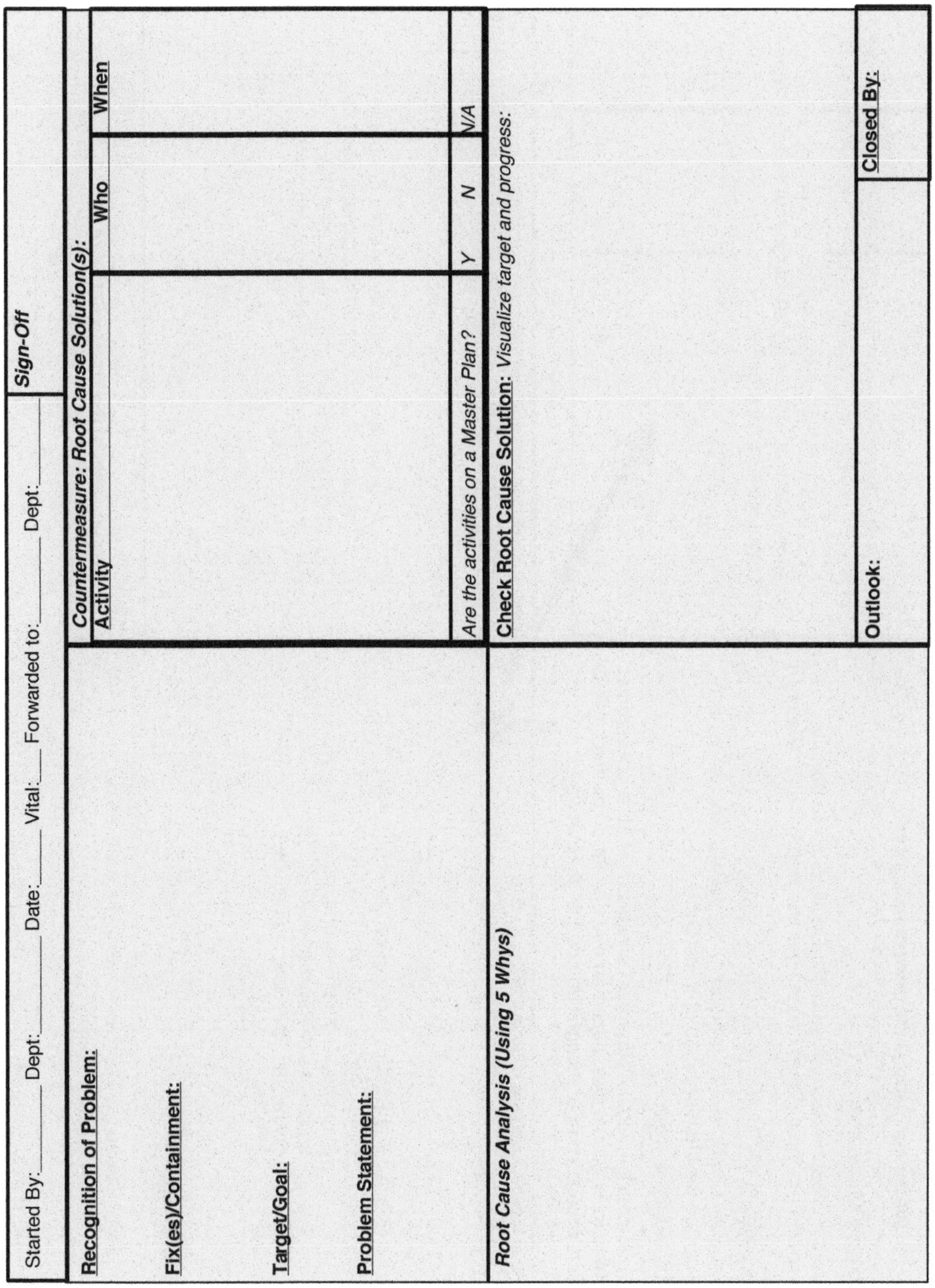

Started By: _____ Dept: _____ Date: _____ Vital: _____ Forwarded to: _____ Dept: _____		*Sign-Off*

Recognition of Problem:

Fix(es)/Containment:

Target/Goal:

Problem Statement:

Root Cause Analysis (Using 5 Whys)

Countermeasure: Root Cause Solution(s):

Activity	Who	When

	Y	N	N/A
Are the activities on a Master Plan?			

Check Root Cause Solution: *Visualize target and progress:*

Outlook:

Closed By:

Figure 3.6. A blank problem-solving sheet.

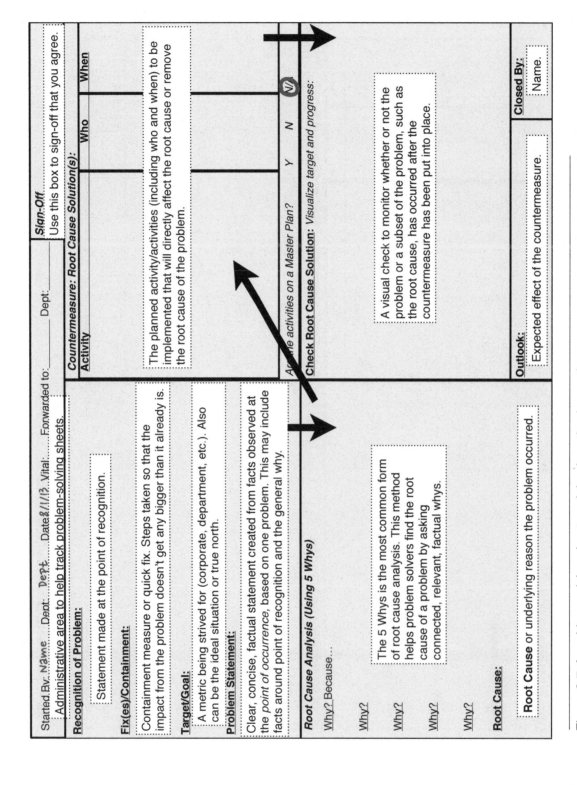

Figure 3.7. A problem-solving sheet explained section by section.

Started By: JC Dept: 8M Date: 7.1 Vital: Q Forwarded to: _____ Dept: _____ **Sign-Off** *Kathy Kelly Joe*

Recognition of Problem:

Patient fell and injured knee.

Fix(es)/Containment:

Post fall safety huddle, neurology checks, treat knee.

Target/Goal:

Zero patient falls.

Problem Statement:

On Monday, July 1, a patient on 8th Medical fell from his bed shortly after having his blood drawn.

Root Cause Analysis (Using 5 Whys)

Why? Patient stirring for at least 10 minutes in bed without his nurse hearing his bed alarm.

Why? The bed alarm was not activated.

Why? The phlebotomist accidentally bumped and deactivated the alarm and did not reactivate it.

Why? He did not know how to reset the bed alarm.

Why? No visual standard work for resetting bed alarms.

Countermeasure: Root Cause Solution(s):

Activity	Who	When
1.) Create visual standard work on resetting the bed alarm.	Kathy	July 5
2.) Review fall prevention purpose and standard work for resetting bed alarms at laboratory huddle.	Kelly	July 15
3.) Review fall prevention purpose and standard work for resetting bed alarms at other ancillary department huddles.	Joe	August 1

Check Root Cause Solution: *Visualize target and progress:*

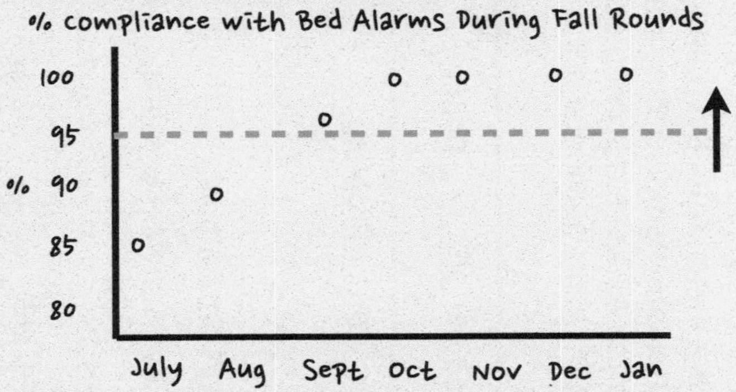

% compliance with Bed Alarms During Fall Rounds

(Chart: y-axis % from 80 to 100; x-axis months July, Aug, Sept, Oct, Nov, Dec, Jan)

Outlook: △ | **Closed By:** Kathy

Figure 3.8. An example completed problem-solving sheet.

First Quadrant (Top Left). Using the problem-solving process, write the point of recognition and the problem statement from the point of occurrence (see examples in 3.2–3.4 for clarification). Describe the **_Containment Measure_**—the step(s) taken to fix the problem and/or ensure it does not get any larger. The **_Target_** can be a metric from the balanced scoreboard or the ideal situation. Ensure that the administrative information (name, department, date, etc.) is filled out when starting a problem-solving sheet. Figure 3.9 shows an example first quadrant of a problem-solving sheet.

Started By: _JC_   Dept: _8M_   Date: _7.1_   Vital: _Q_ Forwarded

Recognition of Problem:

Patient fell and injured knee.

Fix(es)/Containment:

Post fall safety huddle, neurology checks, treat knee.

Target/Goal:

Zero patient falls.

Problem Statement:

On Monday, July 1, a patient on 8th Medical fell from his bed shortly after having his blood drawn.

Figure 3.9. An example first quadrant of a problem-solving sheet.

Checks for Finalizing the First Quadrant:

- ☐ Top left administrative information, including name, department, priority, etc., is filled in and clear.
- ☐ The problem recognition is written as a short, clear statement.
- ☐ The containment is written and in place or implemented if possible.
- ☐ The problem statement is articulated in a clear factual account of what happened, including general cause if possible.

"A problem well stated is a problem half solved." —Charles F. Kettering

Second Quadrant. This quadrant is used to describe and think through root cause analysis. ***Root Cause Analysis*** is understanding facts by asking questions to best determine the underlying reason why a problem occurred. Ideally, changing the root cause should ensure the problem never happens again for the same reason. If the root cause is related to a missing, incorrect, or insufficient standard, process, or protocol, generally it is actionable. Finding and stating an actionable root cause is essential in developing countermeasure(s).

The ***5 Whys*** are the most common form of root cause analysis. Asking connected, relevant, factual whys, starting with the problem statement and answering each question, helps identify the root cause. The answers to the 5 Whys are not necessarily found easily, and identifying the answer to each why may be its own fact finding experience. Other tips for conducting the 5 Whys include: use facts, not possibilities; focus on the process (not the person); answer the whys on the problem sheet; and ensure the root cause can be changed. An example root cause analysis on a problem-solving sheet is shown in Figure 3.10, and a more detailed 5 Whys analysis is shown in Figure 3.11.

Root Cause Analysis (Using 5 Whys)

Why? Patient stirring for at least 10 minutes in bed without his nurse hearing his bed alarm.

Why? The bed alarm was not activated.

Why? The phlebotomist accidentally bumped and deactivated the alarm and did not reactivate it.

Why? He did not know how to reset the bed alarm.

Why? No visual standard work for resetting bed alarms.

Figure 3.10. An example second quadrant of a problem-solving sheet.

WARNING: Do not try to jump to the root cause. Finding the root cause may take some time to ask questions and find factual answers. The root cause found after questioning (5 Whys) is typically very different from a superficial cause.

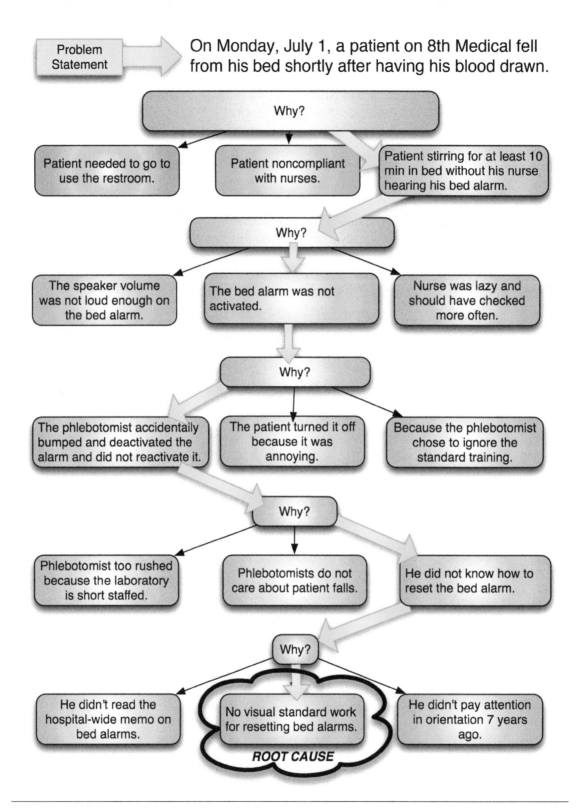

Figure 3.11. Example using the 5 Whys and fact finding in order to find a root cause.

Checks for the Second Quadrant:

Ensure there is a clearly articulated and written problem statement before starting root cause analysis and filling out the second quadrant.

☐ Answers to the whys are listed in the second quadrant—not questions.
☐ All answers to the whys are connected to each other and factual.
☐ Removing the root cause will ensure the problem does not happen again for the same reasons.
☐ If multiple problems are discovered during root cause analysis, multiple problem-solving sheets are started.

Third Quadrant. The third quadrant is used to list the countermeasure(s), who is responsible for implementing the countermeasure(s), and when it will be implemented by, as shown in Figure 3.12. A countermeasure is an action or long-term solution that directly impacts or removes the root cause of a problem. Generally, countermeasures should be implemented one experiment at a time in order to grasp the true impact of each one. Countermeasures may include creating a standard, piloting the standard, and standardizing or expanding.

to:_____ Dept:_____	Sign-Off *Kathy Kelly Joe*	
Countermeasure: Root Cause Solution(s):		
Activity	**Who**	**When**
1.) Create visual standard work on resetting the bed alarm.	Kathy	July 5
2.) Review fall prevention purpose and standard work for resetting bed alarms at laboratory huddle.	Kelly	July 15
3.) Review fall prevention purpose and standard work for resetting bed alarms at other ancillary department huddles.	Joe	August 1

Figure 3.12. An example third quadrant of a problem-solving sheet, listing the countermeasures.

"By repeating why five times, the nature of the problem as well as its solution becomes clear."

—Sakichi Toyoda

Creating the problem statement and identifying the root cause informs the creation of the countermeasure. Countermeasures are a "P" (Plan) in the P-D-C-A cycle and involve creating new standards, updating existing standards, and changing the way work is done—all informed by the root cause of problems.

Checks for the Third Quadrant:

Once a root cause is identified, a countermeasure must be identified, along with who and when. The root cause and countermeasure should be clearly linked.

☐ Ensure countermeasures impact or remove the root cause.
☐ Include who will complete the action and when the action will be completed.
☐ Speak with the person responsible for implementing the countermeasure before writing it down. Once s/he has agreed, sign off.
☐ Ensure there is a pilot and expansion of the countermeasure if needed.

Fourth Quadrant. The fourth quadrant is for visualizing the *Check Cycle*—a graphical representation of the total effect of the countermeasure compared to the plan. Generally a check cycle will have a timeframe, or period for which the effect of the countermeasure will be tracked against the target, or the expected result. The check cycle may visualize the recurrence of the recognition of the problem, root cause, or the most efficient and effective place in between to measure to ensure that the problem's root cause has actually been impacted by the countermeasure(s) as planned. A simple example check cycle is seen below in Figure 3.13. Another example embedded within the fourth quadrant is shown in Figure 3.14. Once the check cycle has been completed, symbols in Figure 3.15 are used to communicate the future outlook of the problem/countermeasure. If the outlook needs improvement, a new problem-solving sheet may be started proactively.

Were bed alarms activated?

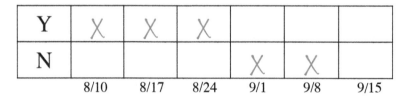

	8/10	8/17	8/24	9/1	9/8	9/15
Y	X	X	X			
N				X	X	

Figure 3.13. An example check cycle checking bed alarm activation in August/September.

"The famous tools of the Toyota Production System are all designed around making it easy to see problems, easy to solve problems, and easy to learn from mistakes. Making it easy to learn from mistakes means changing our attitude toward them. That is the lean cultural shift."
                                        —John Shook, *How to Change a Culture* (2010, p. 9)

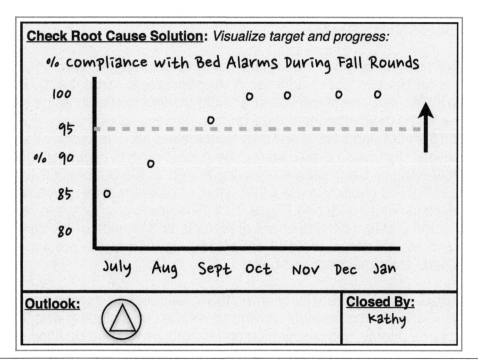

Figure 3.14. An example fourth quadrant of a problem-solving sheet.

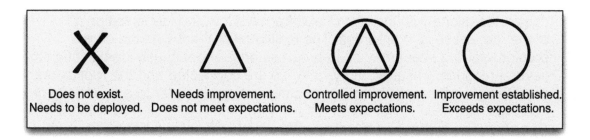

Figure 3.15. Outlook symbols to predict the future outlook of the problem.

Checks for the Fourth Quadrant:

Ensure that there is a clear, simple, and visual way to see whether or not the countermeasure is working as planned.

☐ Use a simple, visual graph that tracks whether or not the countermeasure is working as planned.
☐ Include a target line and targeted direction of the results, so anyone unfamiliar with the problem can understand its status.
☐ When the check cycle is complete, the problem is closed out and outlook predicted.
☐ Once monthly master plans are introduced, ensure activities get on a monthly master plan if necessary.

The Problem-Solving Board

The problem-solving board is a standard board to manage problem-solving sheets. It is broken into four quadrants: **A. Recognize; B. Analyze; C. Resolve; D. Confirm**. The purpose of the board is to aid leaders in checking the status of problems and the development of their team's problem-solving skills. It is a tool used at the Senior Leader level and with frontline teams. The problem-solving board, shown in Figure 3.16, also stores the huddle prompt clipboard, huddle record clipboard, and blank problem-solving sheets at the bottom of the board. Some organizations choose to use other types of problem solving boards like the examples in Figure 3.20 and Figure 3.21. The one-word names for each quadrant of the problem-solving board are simple and provide quick training on the floor, and are not meant to be all-encompassing for how the problem-solving board is used. They are described below.

A. **Recognize**. This quadrant is for when the initial problem-solving sheet is started. Generally the problem-solving sheet header, including who, date, department, priority, and recognition of the problem, should be filled out prior to placing the sheet in the A quadrant. Ideally, the problem should be contained, and the target identified as well. Ensure there is a clear factual problem statement before moving the problem-solving sheet to quadrant B.

B. **Analyze**. This quadrant is for when the problem statement has been completed, along with the rest of quadrant A. Now, the identification of the root cause is in progress. The individual or team working on the problem-solving sheet may be in progress on the root cause identification for several reasons. Ensure that the 5 Whys are connected and the root cause is something the team member can actually change in order to move to the next quadrant.

C. **Resolve**. This is the third quadrant of the problem-solving board. Once the problem-solving sheet has a root cause identified, a countermeasure to resolve the problem at the root, including the who and when, can be determined and listed on the problem sheet. The problem should remain in quadrant C until the countermeasure has been implemented and confirmed via the check cycle. Some problems may be checked for several weeks or longer, so having many sheets in this quadrant is not unusual, and provides a visual sign to coaches that teams are identifying countermeasures.

D. **Confirm**. This quadrant is for problems that have an implemented countermeasure, which has been confirmed via the check cycle. The sheet remains here for a period of time in case the problem or root cause happens again, or if the problem-solving countermeasure needs to recorded into the improvement system.

Leaders should check the problem-solving board at least weekly in order to keep problems moving and provide coaching where necessary—the "C" in the P-D-C-A cycle, and one element of leaders' standard work.

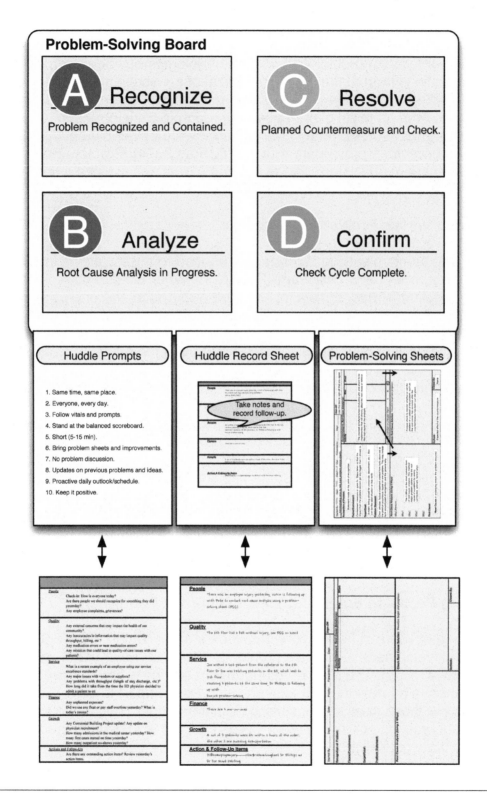

Figure 3.16. An example problem-solving board helps teams manage problem-solving sheets (top) and provides a location to store huddle prompt and record sheets (bottom).

Problem Solving One in a Daily Management System

Past implementation of problem-solving methodologies has been primarily based off of observations from mature Lean organizations—observing A3s. An A3 is used to report on large-scale problems and rapid improvement events (among other things). After an initial event-based approach to transformation, one healthcare organization's primary goal shifted toward developing people to solve problems in order to improve performance (Barnas 2014). Problem Solving One in a daily management system shares the same goal and creates a tiered system to elevate and coach problems on a daily basis.

A3 Thinking Versus Problem Solving One

One way that problem solving has been introduced to organizations is in the form of an A3, also known as a *One Page Report*. Whether used to communicate a proposal, problem, status, project, or for another purpose, the one page report is without a doubt an essential part of organizational Lean transformation. However, the most appropriate sequencing of one page reports in organization-wide transformation is very often misunderstood and used too early. This artifact comes later in the Transformation Curve after more frequent problem solving—focusing on changing behaviors.

In order to achieve "A3 thinking," behaviors must change—and an A3 report should be typically reserved for larger-scale problem solving, not one by one for more frequent problem solving. The sequence proposed and coached by Lewis to transform many organizations begins with simple and frequent problem solving (i.e., Problem Solving One), and expands using more advanced artifacts, such as the one page report, after the skill is developed. Problem-solving basics must be learned and put into action frequently in order to build muscle memory before an organization adopts an A3 as a standard problem-solving tool to report out on (for example) Kaizen events, multiple problems, or large-scale problems.

Developing People to Solve Problems to Improve Performance

During the later years of Lean at one healthcare organization, a new goal was stated: "to develop people, to solve problems, and to improve performance" (Barnas, 2014, p. 11). The sequence of problem solving is first to develop people by giving them a framework, artifacts, process, and support to solve problems; second, to put those skills to use solving problems, regardless of the impact of the actual problem solving. In other words the goal is to develop people, with the primary objective being to learn how to solve problems and develop countermeasures. Then, once individuals understand problem solving, they begin using those skills to solve real problems. Other artifacts such as the balanced scorecard's top problems help focus and prioritize problem-solving efforts to improve department, value stream, and overall organizational performance.

Basic Theory of Problem Solving One

The artifacts of Problem Solving One, including the problem-solving language, problem-solving sheet, boards, and coaching cycles, when coached and followed up, begin to change attitudes about problems and help drive Lean culture change. Problem Solving One creates a way for everyone in the organization to learn problem solving and solve problems.

Leaders engaged in coaching cycles will use the problem-solving sheet as a guide to ask questions along the pathway of root cause analysis. As Senior Leaders and other leaders, especially in the pilot hall, transform into coaches, it's important to learn the Problem Solving One process so leaders can teach it, coach it, and otherwise support it by staying at least one step ahead of the pilot hall and organization. Doing problem-solving sheets on simple problems is essential so that leaders can learn the process and solve problems along the way—no matter how small the problem may seem.

One by one problem solving via the problem-solving sheets, reported on and elevated through huddles (and other activities discussed in later chapters), builds problem identification and solving into daily operations and communication in all tiers of the organization. Coaching cycles from leadership and frequent use of the problem-solving sheet build problem solving capacity (more people can solve problems besides just the CI Team) and capability (individual skill set increases). Frequent one by one root cause problem solving builds personal and organizational muscle memory so that the organization performs P-D-C-A on problems. Problem solving, then, becomes embedded in the culture.

The purpose of problem solving in this phase of a daily management system is cultural change. Many and frequent problem-solving sheets, under the guidance of a coach, begin to build capability and capacity aligned with daily operations. This begins to shift the culture from firefighting to root cause problem solving, all while giving ownership to team members to develop countermeasures, especially in the pilot hall, supported and coached by the Senior Team.

Problem solving may sound intimidating, confusing, and time-consuming to some at the early stages of culture change and Lean transformation, so starting problem-solving sheets and having a plan to check and follow up via weekly check cycles and monthly balanced scoreboard meetings helps an organization act its way to a new way of thinking. Yes, training is important, but more important are the coaching cycles and problem-solving support on a daily basis.

"It's easier to act your way to a new way of thinking than to think your way to a new way of acting" (Shook, 2010, p. 5).

Steps for Starting Problem Solving One

Generally, huddles should be in place, or at least just getting started, prior to introducing Problem Solving One. Problem solving may be introduced earlier in Lean culture change for the Senior Team compared to later (after the improvement system) in the pilot hall(s). Below are steps for aligning Problem Solving One in a daily management system.

1. **Align with huddles**. Before starting problem solving, huddles should already be in place. Some team leaders will choose to introduce problem solving after the huddle has sunk in and others will choose to introduce problem solving right away. Either way, a primary purpose of the huddle is reporting out on problems and countermeasures via problem-solving sheets as well as improvements (introduced in Chapter 6, Improvement System). Transactional information sharing (e.g., "Were there any incidents/accidents yesterday?") provides the mechanism to introduce problem solving to a particular problem surfaced at the huddle.

2. **Introduce problem-solving sheets**. Provide training if possible, but simply introduce problem-solving sheets as the mechanism to communicate problems. Being a role model for the daily management system and Lean culture change means that the leaders introduce problem-solving sheets by reporting out on problems during the huddle via the problem-solving sheets. Initially, and even after time, problem-solving may be met with resistance, so be ready to coach and hold team members' hands throughout the process.

3. **Put pencil to paper.** Encourage team members by helping them start problem-solving sheets. Many times this means doing problem solving with the team member. Reiterate that the standard, to begin, is to simply start a sheet using the top left quadrant. Team members must be coached on creating problem statements before expecting to perform detailed root cause analysis, implement countermeasures, and visualize check cycles. Putting pencil to paper and attempting to start a problem-solving sheet is a huge step, and it doesn't matter if it's done correctly or not! Writing the problem down is a necessary first step in the problem-solving coaching model.

4. **Celebrate problems**. Problems are opportunities to improve. Celebrate when team members surface and identify problems both at the huddle and throughout the day. Celebrate when problems are brought to the huddle, and don't necessarily worry about the quality of the problem solving when starting. During daily work, celebrate when team members identify problems as problems. Do not "punish" them by making them start a problem-solving sheet (more work). Sit down with them, coach, and use the problem-solving sheet to ask questions and guide the conversation towards a problem statement,

root cause, etc. Publicly celebrating when a problem is identified is a step in Lean culture change. In addition, coaching and supporting the team member in actually solving (or at least containing) the problem is great way to lead the system, be a role model, and coach.

5. **Go and see**. Coach problem solving by asking questions and going to where the problem occurred. Use opportunities whenever you can to go and see to truly understand the problem. Do this under the guidance of a coach if you aren't comfortable (the coach can be your one-up).

6. **Use the problem-solving board**. Use the board to manage problem-solving sheets. On the human development side, study/check the board to learn where your team needs coaching. Checking the progression of problems visually using the board helps to see the status of an individual problem, as well as to see the status of problem solving as a team (e.g., are there more problem-solving sheets in the top left quadrant of the board—recognition—or the top right quadrant—countermeasures/checks). Adding at minimum a weekly check cycle around the problem-solving board provides a coaching and check cycle to follow up and coach problem solving, which adds confidence and capability to the daily management system.

7. **Problem selection for monthly balanced scoreboard review**. Using the monthly balanced scoreboard meeting, introduced in Chapter 4, Balanced Scoreboard, provides a standard monthly check on the top problems. The monthly scoreboard meeting is a time to sift and sort through all the problem-solving sheets and select the top problems to ensure the appropriate amount of attention is given to them until they are solved.

8. **Next steps**. Continue to learn and coach problem solving on a daily basis to gain organizational capacity and individual capability in the skills of problem solving. Later, more advanced artifacts will be introduced, such as Problem Solving Two, process maps, fishbone diagrams, and other tools.

Problem-Solving Standard Work Activities:

Daily: Come to the huddle prepared to present problems and countermeasures as well as to follow up on and coach problems.

Weekly: Check the status of problems to help team members move problems through the system.

Monthly: Audit the problem-solving board to remove or elevate problems.

Problem Solving and Tiered Huddles

As huddles are aligned throughout the organization, first from the pilot hall to the Senior Team via the CI Team, problem solving begins to elevate through huddles. During the initial phases of problem solving, expect that problem-solving sheets may rise to the group or Senior Leader level without being solved. As Figure 3.17 demonstrates, when problems are brought up or reported out during the huddle, the team leader (TL) and/or group leader (GL) should ask themselves, Should I challenge the team member to solve this problem, should I solve the problem myself, or should I pass along/elevate the problem?

The better the organization becomes at enforcing and coaching problem solving using the foundations (P-D-C-A, visual management, and roles and responsibilities) closer to the frontline, the more problems will be solved prior to elevation to the Senior Team. This takes reinforcement of the system through coaching cycles by leaders. In addition, "any improvement must be made in accordance with the scientific method [P-D-C-A], under the guidance of a teacher [coach], at the lowest possible level in the organization" (Spear, 1999, p. 98).

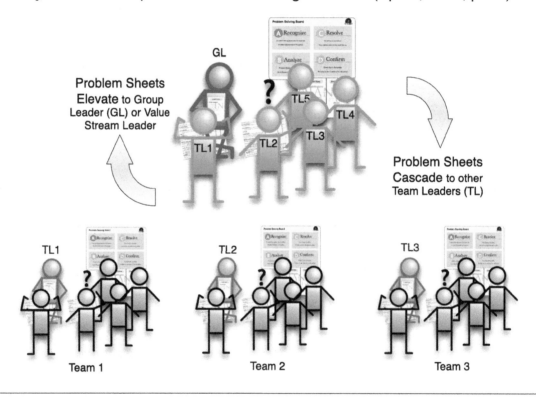

Figure 3.17. Tiered huddles and problem solving. Once huddles and problem solving become an organizational standard, a pilot hall (Team 1) may have a daily huddle with the group leader (GL), and elevate or hand off a problem via a problem-solving sheet to another team (Team 2). Huddles help facilitate this communication and further follow up on the status of the problem.

Roles and Responsibilities

The following roles and responsibilities are for both the daily huddle and Problem Solving One. Some team leaders may be leading teams of individuals who are also team leaders. Roles and responsibilities become more defined as other artifacts of the Transformation Curve are implemented. The following consists of roles, responsibilities, and general advice as huddles are just starting.

Team Members

Be patient. In many cases, this is not only a new process for team members, but also for managers and even Senior Leaders. Trust the problem-solving process and do not expect every problem to get solved. The system encourages ownership of problems, filtering of top problems, and quick turnaround of high-priority problems. But it's a work in progress for everyone—be patient.

Use the system. If a team member doesn't know the status of a problem that was brought up prior, ask about its status. Also, write clear, factual statements on problem-solving sheets so that they are easy to read by anyone. Take the problem as far as possible, and ask for coaching when ready. Use the daily huddle to communicate problems via problem-solving sheets to other team members and leaders. Don't expect to tell team leaders about a problem without writing it down, and then expect them to solve it today. Use the system.

Own the problem. The huddle is not a time to verbally communicate issues to team leaders and expect managers to do the root cause analysis and implement a countermeasure. Especially in the beginning, focus on problems that can be solved; find the root cause, and pilot, implement, and check countermeasures.

Focus on problems in your span of control. To become a learning organization, each individual must learn the problem-solving process and be engaged with communication within the huddle. Though notifying team leaders of problems outside your span of control is important for problem identification, it does not necessarily build problem-solving skill during this phase. Work on the fundamental and seemingly simple problems individually so problems can be owned and solved at the individual and department level.

Trust the process. Communication and problem solving can be difficult, so continue to be patient and trust the process. Expecting that large-scale, cross-functional problems will be solved just because they were written down on a piece of paper and discussed at a huddle is unrealistic—the system takes time, and large-scale problems also take time, but the process works. Trust the system, know the standards, and own the problem if possible.

Team Leaders

Celebrate. Problems are opportunities to improve—celebrate each one, especially in the beginning. When team members bring problems to the huddle via problem-solving sheets, celebrate by thanking the individual and give feedback and follow-up as quickly as possible. A positive attitude toward problem identification is critical to the success of becoming a transparent and problem-solving organization.

Communicate. When a team leader takes responsibility for a problem, follow up and follow up frequently. Even if the problem isn't solved, or there's a major hurdle that limits problem solving, communicate the status at the huddle to team members. Most team members care about the organization and the patients, and want to know the status of problems and other items that they have brought up during the huddle. Keep good notes and follow up accordingly.

Challenge. Challenge team members to start problem solving, follow up with root cause analysis, and propose countermeasures on their own (under the guidance of a coach). Do not just accept problems. Challenge staff to solve problems and support them with the appropriate coaching.

Walk the talk. Don't challenge team members and encourage problem solving without walking the talk. Come to the huddle prepared and using problem-solving sheets. When elevating a problem, ensure that it is passed on, taking the analysis as far as possible, then expect the same from team members.

Coach. Provide coaching to staff members with regards to problem solving outside of the huddle. When enforcing problem-solving sheets, be sure to support staff, especially if they have had minimal training. Coach by being a role model, modeling the system, and following the standards, using the huddle as a daily communication mechanism about the status of problems. A team leader should also provide coaching, and be coached in order to provide better coaching.

Use the 3Gs. Never assume what the problem is. While coaching or following up on a problem, always use the 3Gs: go and see, get the facts and grasp the situation.

Tip: Leading a huddle, when a problem is brought up, ask yourself:
1. *Should I challenge the team member to solve the problem?*
2. *Should I solve the problem?*
3. *Should I elevate the problem to the next level?*

Baldrige Connections

Action Plan Modification *2.2b.* Problem solving within a daily management system, aligned to the long-term goals and annual objectives, provides one way for everyone in the organization to modify and add to action plans on a daily, weekly, and monthly basis. (NIST, 2015, p. 12)

Complaint Management *3.2b(2).* Problem solving applied to patient complaints allows team members to identify countermeasures to "avoid similar complaints in the future" (NIST, p. 15).

Performance Analysis and Review *4.1b.* Especially when applied in the context of the monthly balanced scoreboard meeting, problem solving helps team members and Senior Leaders "respond rapidly to changing organizational needs and challenges" in the operating environment (NIST, p. 16).

Organizational Learning *4.2a.(2).* The problem-solving approach is first and foremost about developing people to solve problems. The problem-solving sheet is a simple yet powerful artifact to teach individuals and teams how to create a problem statement, conduct root cause analysis, and how to check the countermeasures actually affecting the problem. This provides one way to use "knowledge and resources to embed learning in the way [the] organization operates" (NIST, p. 18).

Knowledge Management *4.2a.(1).* The problem-solving process is one way for employees to "collect and transfer workforce knowledge" on an individual level, and when applied organizationally with other artifacts, this creates a robust knowledge gathering system. Problem solving is a standard way to begin to collect knowledge around problems, which leads to the development of further organizational knowledge and standards (NIST, p. 18).

Organizational Culture *5.2a.(1).* Problem solving, and the coaching cycles that surround problem solving, help empower the workforce and encourage open communication about problems.

Continuous Improvement *4.1c.(3).* Problem solving, and the cycles that surround problem solving, are the basis of continuous improvement. Problem recognition and identification is essentially the first step to solving problems at the root so they never happen again.

Learning and Development System *5.2b.(1).* Problem solving and the coaching cycles around problem solving "support organizational performance improvement, organizational change, and innovation" (NIST, p. 20).

Summary: Lean Culture Change Using Problem Solving One

Problem Solving One introduces a standard method to learn problem solving, solve problems one by one, and build problem-solving capability and capacity.

☐ Problem Solving One serves as the foundation for more advanced problem-solving artifacts.

☐ The 3Gs are: go see, get the facts, grasp the situation.

☐ The point of recognition is the initial awareness of the problem.

☐ The point of occurrence (PoO) is the step, time, or location where the problem originated.

☐ The problem statement, generated from facts found at the point of occurrence, is a clear, factual account of the problem, which may include who, what, when, where, and generally why.

☐ The 5 Whys are a method of asking why to get from the point of occurrence to the root cause of a problem.

☐ The root cause is the underlying reason the problem occurred.

☐ The problem-solving sheet is a standard artifact used to facilitate and communicate the status of problems.

☐ A containment measure is the step(s) taken to fix the problem and/or keep it from getting any larger.

☐ The target is a desired metric or the ideal situation.

☐ A countermeasure is an long-term solution/action that directly impacts or removes the root cause of a problem.

☐ A check cycle is a graphical representation of the total effect of the countermeasure compared to the plan.

☐ The problem-solving board is an artifact to manage problem-solving sheets.

☐ Leaders will add daily problem solving to leaders' standard work.

☐ Check the problem-solving board at least weekly to advance problems.

American British Cowdray (ABC) Medical Center, Mexico City
Daily Problem Solving for Cultural Change and Operational Improvement

ABC Medical Center, in Mexico City, began a daily management system in mid-2011 as a primary tool for continuous improvement throughout the health system, starting with cultural change first. The organization's operational priorities and action plans were aligned around Safety (patient safety and safety of all medical collaborators), Quality (clinical quality and service for patients and families), Productivity, Human Talent, Costs, and Operational Excellence.

Using the daily management system, these priorities were reviewed and incidents were reported on during a 15-minute daily meeting/huddle. As ABC has continued with the daily management system, the number of suggestions has risen consistently year after year since the introduction of the system. The daily meeting and the use of the problem-solving sheet resulted in some groups achieving a collaborative improvement atmosphere and some groups who were still in a resistance phase. In an attempt to understand the impact after roughly two years of implementation, ABC conducted a survey throughout the organization with staff involved in daily meetings.

The results of the survey included both positives and opportunities for improvement. The difficulties identified, according to respondents, included lack of training and proficiency in the use of the problem-solving tools, and discipline around the analysis and monitoring of improvement activities and countermeasures. Some responded that the daily huddles and problem solving were a deficiency to the organization. Most, though, responded that daily huddles and problem solving had positively impacted the organization.

Benefits received by the staff included improved communication and timing of troubleshooting, and an increased recognition of problems as opportunities for improvement. Relationships of mutual trust and respect among partners had a positive rating among 85% of the respondents, which ABC considers a great stride towards a culture of mutual trust and respect as the underlying value.

Overall, the results suggest that the collaborators recognize the value of operational excellence in daily work, and that the necessary reinforcement must be aimed at training to achieve greater standardization and commitment, and to overcome resistance to change. ABC notes that though problem solving is perceived as difficult, it is the discipline of the daily meetings and the ongoing coaching from the leaders that will lead to understanding and success of culture change using Lean culture change tools.

(Hernandez & Handal, 2014)

Example Problem-Solving Sheet from Surgical Services

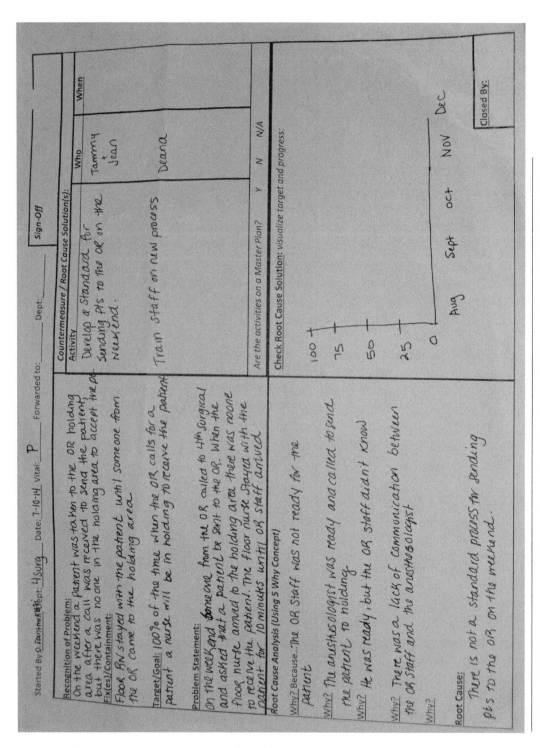

Figure 3.18. An example problem-solving sheet developed by Deana Szentmiklosi during daily management system training, used later to inform creating a standard process for patients being sent to the Operating Room.

Example Problem-Solving Sheet from Maternity and Obstetrics

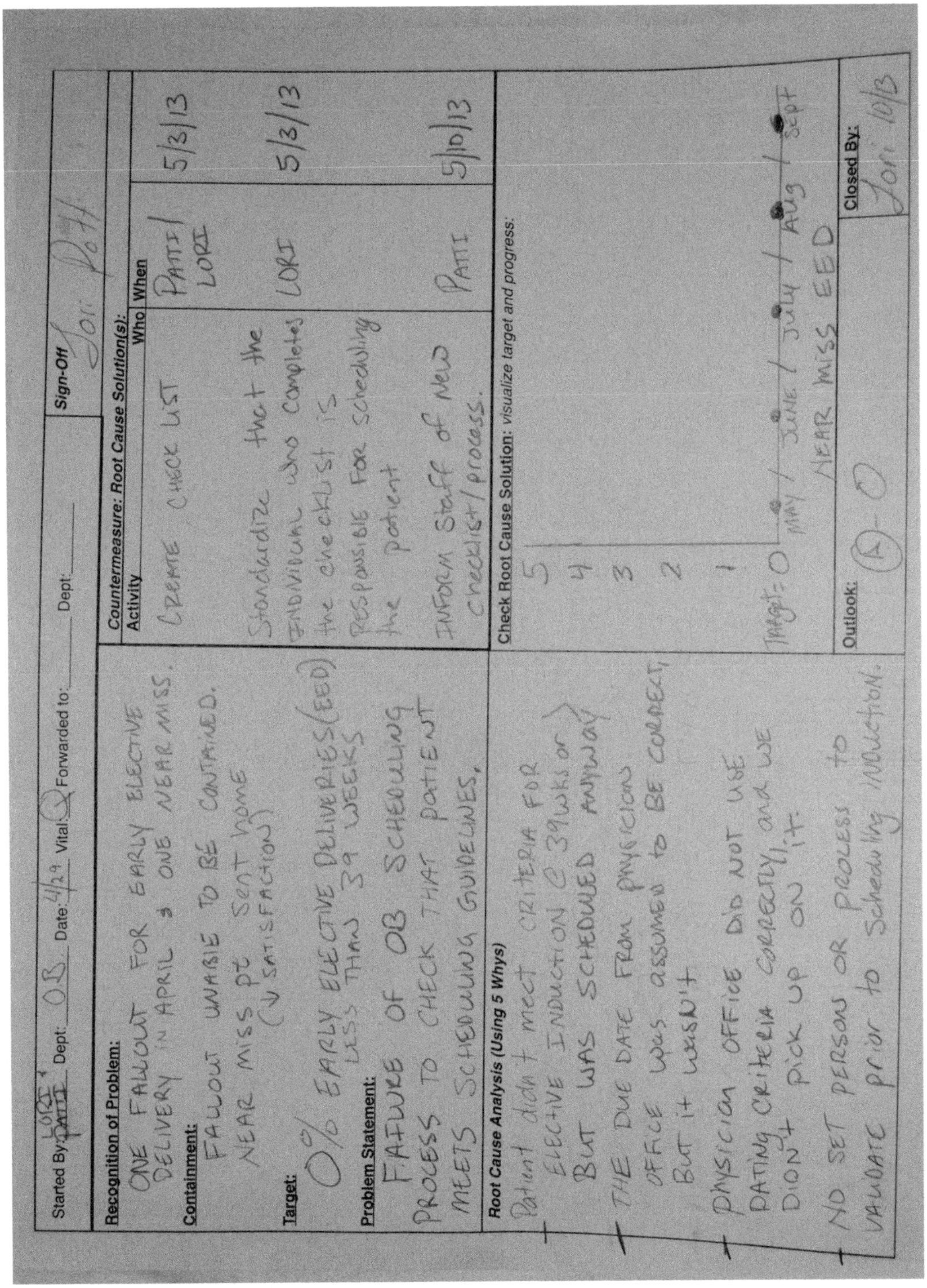

Started By: LORI / PATTI   **Dept:** OB   **Date:** 4/29   **Vitals:** ☑   **Forwarded to:** ____   **Dept:** ____   **Sign-Off:** Lori Patti

Recognition of Problem:
ONE FALLOUT FOR EARLY ELECTIVE DELIVERY IN APRIL & ONE NEAR MISS.

Containment:
FALLOUT UNABLE TO BE CONTAINED. NEAR MISS PT SENT HOME (√ SATISFACTION)

Target:
0% EARLY ELECTIVE DELIVERIES (EED) LESS THAN 39 WEEKS

Problem Statement:
FAILURE OF OB SCHEDULING PROCESS TO CHECK THAT PATIENT MEETS SCHEDULING GUIDELINES.

Root Cause Analysis (Using 5 Whys)
Patient didn't meet criteria for Elective Induction @ 39 wks or but was scheduled anyway

The due date from physicians office was assumed to be correct, but it wasn't

Physician office did not use dating criteria correctly, and we didn't pick up on it.

No set person or process to validate prior to scheduling induction.

Countermeasure: Root Cause Solution(s):

Activity	Who	When
Create check list	PATTI / LORI	5/3/13
Standardize that the individual who completes the checklist is responsible for scheduling the patient	LORI	5/3/13
Inform staff of new checklist / process.	PATTI	5/10/13

Check Root Cause Solution: *visualize target and progress:*

5

4

3

2

1

Target = 0   MAY / JUNE / JULY / AUG / SEPT

NEAR MISS EED

Outlook: Ⓐ - Ⓞ

Closed By: Lori 10/13

Figure 3.19. An example problem-solving sheet by Lori Hennessey (rewritten for training purposes), which improved a process between a physician's office and the OB/Maternity Unit at IRMC.

Example Problem-Solving Board

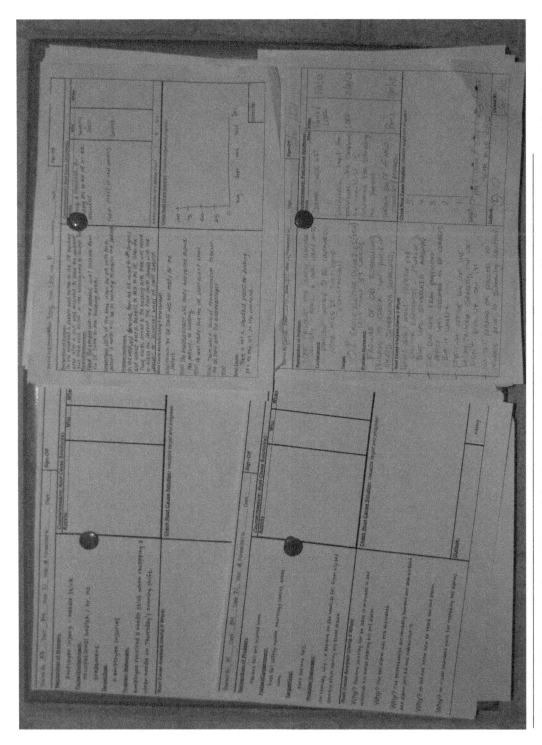

Figure 3.20. An example problem-solving board using a simplified cork board to manage problem-solving sheets following the same standards presented in this chapter.

Example Problem-Solving Board

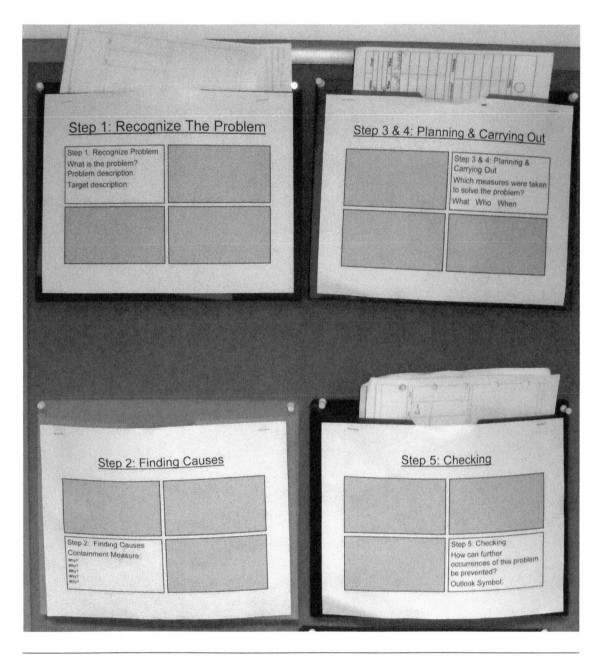

Figure 3.21. An example problem-solving board from Forbes hospital in Monroeville, PA to accompany the case study in Chapter 4.

Chapter 4
Balanced Scoreboard

This chapter will introduce your team to:

- *Aligning 6-year targets with annual objectives.*

- *Aligning annual objectives with daily management.*

- *Leadership teams and the monthly scoreboard meeting cycle.*

- *Tiered scorecards, leadership teams, and monthly check cycles.*

- *A case study of a pilot hall improving clinical results.*

Why a Balanced Scoreboard?

The Balanced Scoreboard is a visual management improvement tool that is the centerpiece of the daily management system, established from the 6-year scorecard (BSC). A transactional purpose of the balanced scoreboard (see Figure 4.1) is to communicate the mission, vision, values, long-term goals, and annual objectives of an organization. The main role of the balanced scoreboard is as a transformational alignment tool, as it is used to visualize specific objectives and metrics, key processes, indicators, and top monthly problems specific to the leadership team that is maintaining the scoreboard. It is a framework to align and visualize annual targets with daily management. Figure 4.1 shows the alignment of the scorecard and scoreboard tools with daily improvement. "Daily management focuses the team on hashing [introduced in Chapter 5, Annual Planning] goals through the review of the prior day's performance and meetings to discuss the goals versus the target as the day goes on" (Liker & Convis, 2011, p. 171). Standardized cycles around the scoreboard include the huddle, monthly scoreboard meeting, and annual plans.

Figure 4.1. Aligning vision to daily improvement cycles.

Having a balanced scoreboard helps teams to focus not on one or two vitals, but on all vitals each and every day. The balanced scoreboard vitals, or priorities, if selected and communicated in the right way, create a value system because of their particular order. In the example used throughout this chapter, the order represents respectively employee safety, patient safety, patient satisfaction, and then finances. The respective order of the vitals is a value system used to select problems and align organizational effort. The vitals below originate from Sherman's Creating the New American Hospital (1993), and were made popular by the Studer Group. Regardless of how the exact priorities (column headers) are selected, the methods of how metrics are selected and cascaded align with organizational priorities for daily improvement.

Table 4.1. The Studer Pillars (Plus the Daily Management System)

People	Quality	Service	Finance	Growth	DMS

Aligning World-Class Performance with Annual Objectives

The corporate 6-Year Scorecard is a tool to organize the top organizational priorities, objectives, and targets, aiming toward achieving world-class organizational operations. It is a preliminary tool that aids in creating the balanced scoreboard, which ultimately aligns daily problem solving with the 6-year plan. The 6-year scorecard is cascaded and aligned throughout the organization and used to visualize balanced scoreboard metrics. The scorecard also serves as the foundation to begin the annual planning process of developing action plans to achieve objectives and targets (discussed in Chapter 5). Figure 4.2 is an example of a organization-wide 6-year balanced scorecard. Figure 4.4 is an example of a blank scorecard. The definitions and steps for establishing the 6-year scorecard are as follows:

1. **Vitals**. Transcribe the organization's vitals or priorities. In the example (Figure 4.2), these are People, Quality, Service, Finance, Growth, and VIP. Lewis-proposed standards are Safety, Quality, Productivity, Human Development, Cost, and Operational Excellence.

2. **Long-Term Goal**. Articulate the long-term goal, which is a statement that is unchanging for the next several years. This statement should be broad enough to include everyone in the organization (e.g., clinical areas, primary care offices, billing department, and human resources department), so that they can align with the statement in their day-to-day work.

3. **Metrics**. Decide on the top one to three metrics at the highest level that will be monitored on both the scorecard and scoreboard, and will be cascaded throughout the organization. If the team or organization is lacking in implementation, follow-through, or general focus, choosing one metric per vital may be key. If the organization is already focused and excels in implementation and sustaining improvements, it may be possible to choose two or three metrics per vital. The team or organization can always refresh the scorecard in upcoming years' implementation, follow-through and sustainment increase.

4. **Baseline**. The baseline reflects where the organization is currently at, or a more appropriate average over some period of time. Find the baseline for the metrics that have been chosen. A baseline can be fiscal year to date, average over the past several months, or last year's annual result. Just be consistent and choose the most appropriate baseline.

5. **World-Class Metric**. The world-class metric is critical to put in perspective where the organization needs to go in order to be a world-class organization. This does not take the place of true north metrics or target zero metrics. The world-class metric should be in alignment with true north, while at the

same time creating a realistic waypoint between current state and true north. A world-class target is not an average, top-quartile, or even the best target that is known today. The world-class target is the best and most appropriate number that will be valid and the best in six years.

6. **Annual Targets**. Once the team clearly understands the six-year world-class target, the current baseline, and the gaps, it sets targets each year, known as the annual targets.

7. **Responsible and Support (R/S)**. The R and S represent the leaders who will be primarily responsible for leading, coordinating, facilitating, and checking the progress of the efforts to achieve the annual objective.

8. **Annual Objective**. The annual objective is a clear link between the long-term goal and the metric. The annual objective is specific to the team (in the example, the organization's Senior Leadership team). The annual objective will later drive annual planning to brainstorm, select, and implement actions to achieve the objective. Ensure the annual objective is SMART, as described below.

Table 4.2. Creating SMART Objectives (adapted from Doran, 1981)

Key questions for creating SMART objectives		
S	Specific	Is the objective clear and specific enough to create a concrete plan for achieving it?
M	Measurable	Is the objective able to be measured on a frequent basis (daily, weekly, or monthly)?
A	Agreed-upon	Have all the necessary teams agreed to the objective?
R	Realistic	Do the necessary teams agree that the objective is able to be achieved in the given timeframe?
T	Timed	Is there a clear target date to achieve the objective?

"[T]he measurement used determines what one pays attention to. It makes things visible and tangible. The things included in the measurement become relevant; the things omitted are out of sight and out of mind."
—Peter Drucker, The Practice of Management (1954, p. 64-65)

Priority	Long-Term Goal	Annual Objective(s)	R	S	Metrics	Baseline	2015	2016	2017	2018	2019	2020	World-Class
PEOPLE	To have the safest, healthiest, most engaged workforce in the healthcare industry.	To strengthen our systematic approach to employee safety and thereby decrease the OSHA recordable rate to 4 or less.	JK	SVP	OSHA Total Recordable Rate	5.6	4	3.5	3	2.5	2	1.5	1
QUALITY	To become a high-reliability organization, eliminate preventable serious events, and creat a defect-free care and work environment.	To improve patient safety by reducing preventable serious events to a rate less than .8.	BAB	CV	Serious Event Rate	1.2	0.8	0.6	0.4	0.3	0.25	0.2	0.17
SERVICE	To ensure the highest levels of patient-centered care that cultivate loyalty and engagement.	To increase patient satisfaction by exceeding expectations. This will be evidenced by 75 percent of scores on average 90% or higher.	CV	BAB	Percentage of Satisfaction Scores 90% or Higher	50%	60%	70%	80%	85%	90%	90%	90%
FINANCE	To sustain a financially viable organization while delivering the most affordable, high-quality healthcare in the industry.	To reduce length of stay from 4.2 to under 4.	DP	RG	Average Length of Stay	4.2	4.00	3.90	3.80	3.70	3.60	3.50	3.50
GROWTH	To achieve and sustain market relevance.	To obtain market-dominant shareholders greater than 55% inpatient and greater than 45% outpatient.	LVS	MR	Market Share (Inpatient and Outpatient)	45%	50%	55%	60%	65%	70%	75%	75%
DMS	To create and sustain the best performance improvement system in the healthcare industry.	To integrate and deploy a DMS, evidence by Senior Team and the pilot hall achieving an 80% or higher on Introduction Audit 1.	BB	SL	Introduction to Audit 1 Score for Senior Team	0%	80%	100%	100%	100%	100%	100%	100%

Figure 4.2. An example 6-year balanced scorecard.

Cascading and Aligning 6-Year Scorecards

During its initial cycle(s), aligning the scorecard is very much a cascading process, whereas in future years it may be more of an aligning process. Each team in the organization must be able to support the 6-year balanced scorecard. If the scorecard cannot be cascaded from top to bottom, each individual will not be able to support it. Although the process is described as starting with the Senior Team and cascading to frontline teams, the metrics on this scorecard should not just be departmentalized, but be value-stream and patient-centered.

Table 4.3. Methods for Cascading 6-Year Scorecard Metrics

Method	Description	Examples	
		Organization	**Unit/Department**
#1 – Adopt	Use the same measure from the corporate 6-year scorecard.	Audit One	(Medical Unit) VIP Audit One
#2 – Adopt	Use a similar measure that directly aligns with the corporate scorecard.	OSHA Reportable Injury Rate	(Telemetry Unit) Number of Employee Injuries
#3 – Adopt	Use a different measure that supports the annual objective on the corporate scorecard.	Serious Event Rate	(Facilities) Response Time to Patient Work Order
#4 – Adopt	Use a measure that aligns with the long-term goal rather than the corporate scorecard metric and/or objective.	Defect-Free Care (Long-Term Goal)	(Obstetrics) Low-Risk Prime C-Section Rate

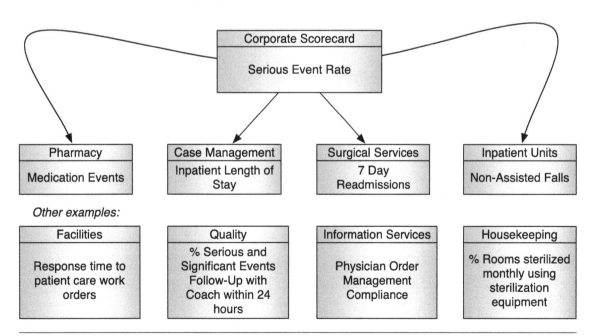

Figure 4.3. Example cascaded metrics aligned with the corporate 6-year scorecard.

Priority	Long-Term Goal	Annual Objective(s)	RS		Metric(s)	Baseline2	015	2016	2017	2018	2019	2020W	orld-Class
PEOPLE													
QUALITY													
SERVICE													
FINANCE													
GROWTH													
DMS													

Figure 4.4. Blank 6-year balanced scorecard used as a worksheet to align teams with the corporate 6-year scorecard.

Aligning Annual Objectives with the Daily Management System

The **Balanced Scoreboard** is a visual management tool used to visualize corporate communication, annual targets, leading indicators for processes, and top problems. One purpose of the balanced scoreboard is to show facts visually; that way, for those reviewing, performance is not in question, but rather problems and improvements to performance. The board measures 4 x 7 ½ feet and is typically mounted in a common team area near the problem-solving board. The vital, long-term goal, and annual objective from the organization-wide scorecard are transcribed as the organization-wide communication on the top of each scoreboard, as seen in Figure 4.5. The current year's targets from the scorecard are shown graphically at a higher frequency (weekly or monthly) on the objective/ metric row on the scoreboard, again seen in Figure 4.6. The adapted columns are aligned by priority, and the rows are aligned as described below. The standard balanced scoreboard layout from Lewis is seen in Figure 4.12 (end of the chapter).

- Priority Headers
- Objectives and Metrics
- Leading Indicators and Support
- Top Monthly Problems

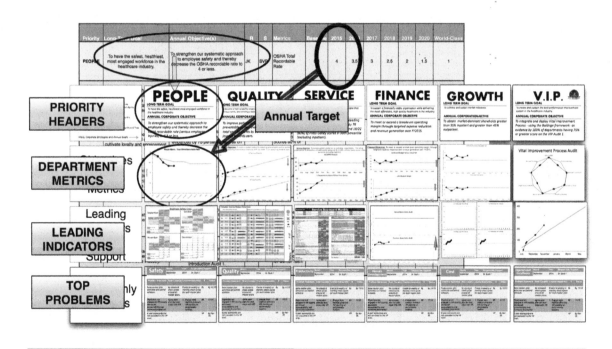

Figure 4.5. Aligning the current/upcoming annual target from the 6-year BSC (top) to the balanced scoreboard's metric row. In the pilot hall, the scoreboard will showcase department/unit metrics, indicators and top problems

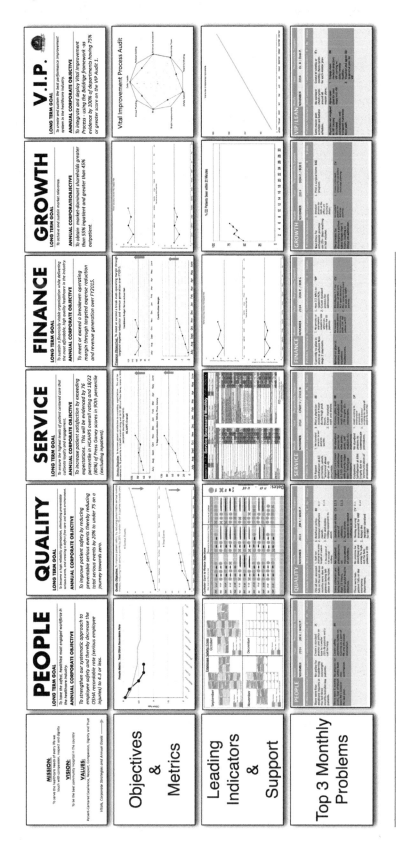

Figure 4.6. Example balanced scoreboard.

The First Row: Corporate Communication and Vital Headers

The first row on the balanced scoreboard is reserved for corporate communication and remains standard for each team throughout the organization, i.e., every scoreboard has the same information for alignment purposes. An example is Figure 4.8.

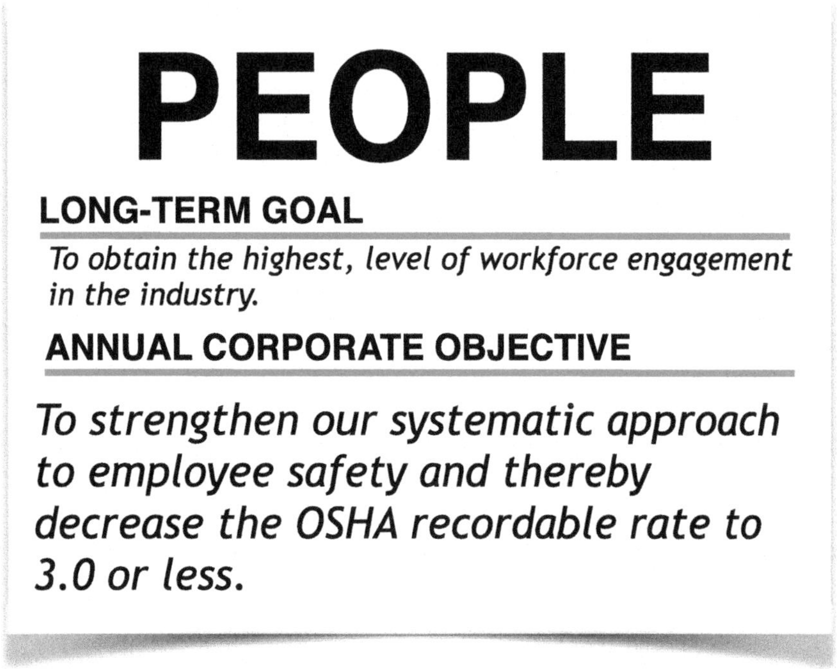

PEOPLE

LONG-TERM GOAL

To obtain the highest, level of workforce engagement in the industry.

ANNUAL CORPORATE OBJECTIVE

To strengthen our systematic approach to employee safety and thereby decrease the OSHA recordable rate to 3.0 or less.

Figure 4.7. Example scoreboard column header stating corporate objectives.

The Second Row: Team Objectives and Metrics

This row contains the annual team objectives and metrics for each vital from the team's scorecard. Generally, this row should be updated monthly for group leaders and more frequently (even daily) for team leaders. As a metric approaches the frontline, it should be measured more frequently. Note: it is recommended to use pencil or markers as much as possible, especially when updating metrics as opposed to electronic.

> "Frequent measurement is most importantly a way to reinforce positive behavior. . . . By measuring often, process improvement increases and the hospital becomes a better organization."
>
> —Quint Studer, *Hardwiring Excellence* (2003, p. 65)

The Third Row: Watch Numbers, Leading Indicators and Support

Watch Numbers are all of the applicable metrics that a team needs to monitor or watch. Watch numbers serve as a simple tracking mechanism to aid in top problem selection and ongoing process monitoring, once the process has been hardwired. Focus should not be placed on the watch numbers, as they are primarily used to aid in the top monthly problem and indicator selection process. Watch numbers are placed behind the leading indicators/support row header or within the support row as needed.

Leading Indicators are a visualization of key process drivers that may show, for example, whether or not the process is being followed. Leading indicators should generally be simple "yes" or "no" questions. Anyone should be able to look at the balanced scoreboard's leading indicators and, in a few seconds, be able to tell their purpose. They can be used at frontline scoreboards as well as executive-level scoreboards. Depending on the frequency of the process, leading indicators may turn over daily, weekly, or monthly. An example of a leading indicator is at the bottom of Figure 4.8. Once a leading indicator is no longer necessary, it may be moved to a watch number to monitor less frequently.

Support Metrics are any numbers, graphs, or other visual data that assist in giving more detail to a top metric or give further information in regards to a top problem. They should be used to track important numbers and processes on a day-to-day basis and also to support the monthly meeting in order to tell a story relevant to top problems. Support may include a Pareto diagram, fishbone analysis, process map, or other tools.

Leading Indicator and Support Row: People and Operational Balance

The leading indicator/support row on the balanced scoreboard has two primary purposes. The first is a focus on the positive. The scoreboard is an improvement artifact and a team will select top problems and showcase metrics, indicators, and support that highlight the positive results of problem-solving activity. Selecting "Top Problems" that the team is not engaged in solving will lead to demoralization and slow moving culture change. The Senior Leadership Team and the CI Team should not expect each team throughout the hospital to grasp the meaning of true leading indicators right away. However, it is the responsibility of the Senior Leadership Team to grasp which teams should be monitoring which leading indicators that will impact the organization-wide BSC. Focusing on the right leading indicators at the right level will impact results. This is the second primary purpose of the leading indicator/support row. It is the leader's responsibility, through coaching cycles, to ensure that this positive showcasing of improvement and results driven approach are balanced.

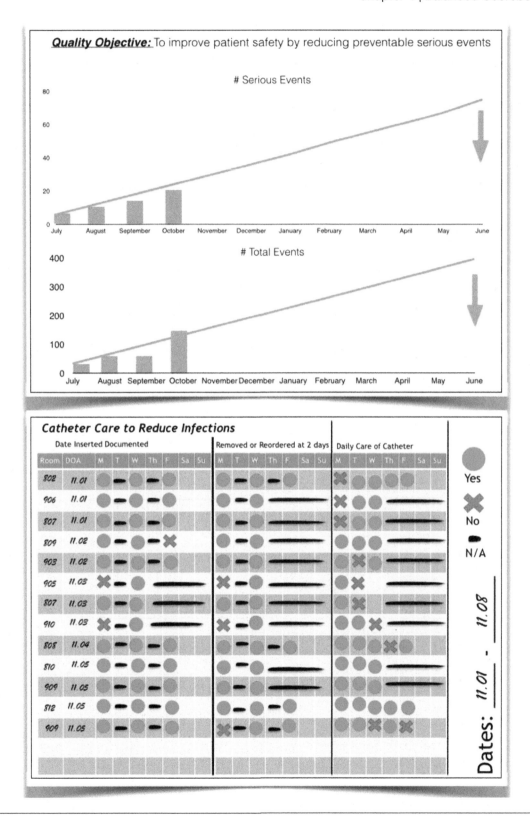

Figure 4.8. Example metrics and leading indicators.

The Fourth Row: Top Problems

The fourth row on the balanced scoreboard is for visualizing the top problems and their respective problem-solving sheets. Figure 4.9 shows an example of the top problem list for quality and the top three problems. The following sections explain more about the monthly meeting and top problems.

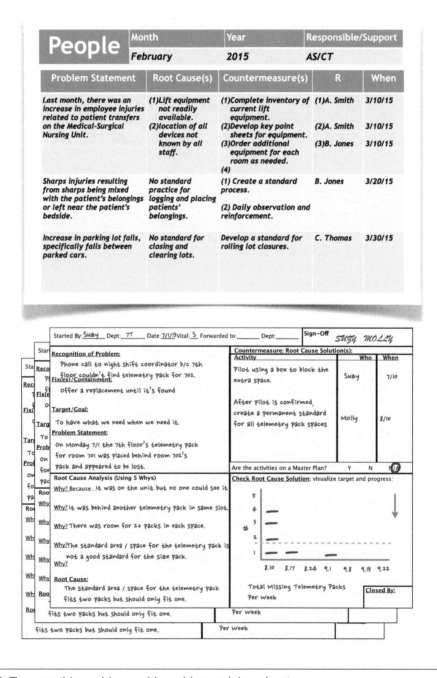

Figure 4.9. Top monthly problems with problem-solving sheets.

Leadership Teams and the Monthly Scoreboard Meeting Cycle

The **Leadership Team** is a core group of people responsible for coaching and/or solving top problems, maintaining the balanced scoreboard, preparing for and conducting the monthly balanced scoreboard meeting, overseeing the top implemented idea winners, leading annual planning sessions, and other responsibilities. "Each unit or clinic identifies the leadership team responsible for review of the unit's work. . . they complete PDSA [P-D-C-A] cycles on big issues that cannot be solved by a frontline worker. Such issues may include cross-departmental or system concerns of major safety and quality problems that could affect the entire hospital" (Toussaint, 2013, p. 9-10).

Like huddles, leadership teams are also tiered. The daily management system's purpose is developing people, solving problems, and leading in a consistent, standardized approach. The leadership team becomes a primary group to teach and coach that standard way to manage and lead for everyone in the organization, including charge nurses, directors, and Senior Team members. Though the roles and responsibilities are similar from tier to tier, the focus of problem solving may be different depending on the maturity of problem-solving skills in the organization and the particular team. Ad hoc members will be added to leadership teams when cross-departmental problems lie outside the normal span of control of its members until the problem is solved. Below are two examples of the individuals comprising leadership teams, the first a frontline team and the second a team of team leaders.

Table 4.4. Functional Leadership Team

Inpatient/Medical Services Leadership Team
Medical Services Director
Telemetry Manager
Medical Floor Manager
Emergency Department Manager
Shift Coordinator(s)
Case Management Manager
Finance Advisor
Quality Advisor

Table 4.5. Unit-Based Leadership Team

Emergency Department Unit-Based Leadership Team
Director (Physician)
Assistant Director (Physician)
Manager (Nurse)
Coordinator (Nurse)
Charge Nurses
Unit-Based Educator (Nurse)
Finance Advisor
Quality Advisor

The Monthly Scoreboard Meeting Cycle

The Monthly Balanced Scoreboard Meeting Cycle is a standard check on the previous month and should morph into a proactive look at the next month as well. It takes the pulse of the unit/organization and serves as a time to check the status metrics, indicators, top problems, improvements, and overall performance of the unit or units the team leads. The monthly meeting cycle typically consists of two meetings, the scoreboard preparation meeting and the scoreboard review.

The **Scoreboard Preparation Meeting**, the first of two meetings, is specifically for the unit-based leadership team to understand the current situation via top metrics, indicators, all the problem-solving sheets, and any other sources of information. During this time the leadership team decides which problems they need to elevate as top problems. They may also discuss other things, such as changing indicators or starting new problem-solving sheets. The monthly meeting cycle serves as a check in the P-D-C-A (Plan-Do-Check-Act) cycle for annual planning, scoreboard metrics, and top problems.

The **Scoreboard Review**, the second meeting, typically involves a Senior Leader or another leader higher in the organization than the team leader. The scoreboard review is a time when the unit-based leadership team presents the current metrics, indicators, top problems, and top improvement winner to a leader or group of leaders. The purpose of this meeting is to elevate top problems and for the group leader to understand all of the department's problems as an aid to selecting top problems.

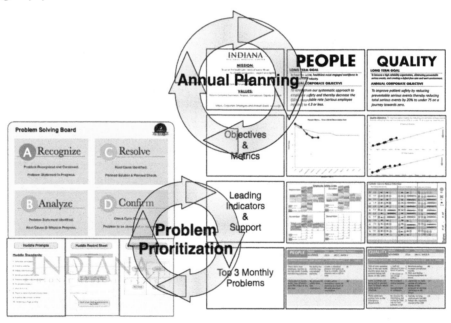

Figure 4.10. The monthly meeting cycle aligning daily and yearly cycles.

Top Problem Selection and Meeting Preparation

The purpose of the preparation or top problem selection meeting is to gather the leadership team, ensure the metrics and indicators are up-to-date, select the top problems to focus on for the upcoming month, and check the status of top problems from last month. Later, this time will be used to select top improvement winners and check the status of master plan implementation. Below are a number of methods teams can use to help facilitate top problem selection. Using any or a combination of these methods is acceptable:

Sift and sort through problem-solving sheets. One way to select top problems is to remove all of the problem-solving sheets, place them into a pile for each vital, and begin to identify top problem candidates. For example, pass the sheets around the room, with individuals proposing a top three candidate. All the other sheets go back on the problem-solving board, and the unit leadership team then discusses and selects the top three problems for each vital.

Unit/area leaders propose top functional problems. Using the medical services team as an example, each manager can bring the top three problems from his/her functional area as potential top problems for the medical services team.

Responsible/Support propose top problems. The R/S for each vital can also propose top problems for his/her vital by sorting through problem-solving sheets, which may include grasping other top problems selected on other units. This selection method generally works better for unit-based leadership teams and not as well for management teams.

New problem-solving sheet is started based on metrics or indicators. Sometimes there are problem-solving sheets that need to be started based on the metrics, indicators, or problems that may have occurred and that were identified throughout the month but that no one has yet started solving.

**WARNING:** Using the balanced scoreboard to focus on large-scale unresolved problems with little to no progress month after month will lead to demoralization. Focus on the positive and use the scoreboard as an improvement artifact to showcase improvements that have been made using the problem-solving process. Daily problem recognition and daily testing of countermeasures makes selecting top problems and top countermeasures much easier and more positive. As the team leader, when the team is selecting top problems for the scoreboard, ensure that they are focused and narrow enough so that the improvement is showcased—not the problem.

Table 4.7. Proposed Standard for Monthly Balanced Scoreboard Meeting

Team Leader: Key Points for Conducting Scoreboard Review
1. Introduce all attendees at the huddle/monthly meeting.
2. Conduct the daily huddle, ensure clear break before the monthly meeting.
3. Start the monthly balanced scoreboard review.
4. Read the organization's mission, vision, and values to the group.
R/S: Key Points for Conducting the Scoreboard Review
1. Review the corporate strategy and annual corporate goals for People.
2. Review unit goals and metrics for the previous month for People.
3. Review indicators and support metrics for People from previous month.
4. Review the top 3 problems, and their problem-solving sheets, for People.
5. Ask for questions/comments from group and Senior Leaders.
6. Repeat steps 5-10 for Quality, Service, Finance, Growth, and VIP.
Team Leader: Key Points for Finishing the Scoreboard Review
1. P-D-C-A the meeting—what does the team need to start/stop/continue?
2. Recognize the top monthly improvement implementer.

Having simple standards around conducting the monthly balanced scoreboard review helps alleviate the stress of team members and aids in preparation for presenting the scoreboard information in a setting that may have Senior Leaders and other frontline staff. Table 4.7 above is a proposed standard for conducting a monthly balanced scoreboard review for teams. These standards serve as key points to prepare for during the actual balanced scoreboard review. Adapt the standards where necessary, and keep the standard in a location that is easily accessible by team members (e.g., behind one of the scoreboard row headers).

"Every manager had a monthly scorecard developed and maintained by the advisory team to help keep track of progress against drivers. The scorecard's vital few metrics help us focus deeply to solve problems and improve performance."
—Kim Barnas, *Beyond Heroes* (2014, p. 29)

R/S getting ready for the preparation meeting:

- ☐ Metrics/indicators for the previous month are updated.

- ☐ Potential top problems are selected.

- ☐ Other needed monthly reports are prepared.

Team leader questions for selecting the top problems:

- ☐ In what direction are the metrics/indicators moving and why?

- ☐ What information are the other monthly reports telling the team?

- ☐ What is the status of the previous top problems?

- ☐ What are the proposed current top problems?

- ☐ What are the root causes and countermeasures?

- ☐ What top problems will help showcase our daily improvement?

- ☐ What top problems require support from leadership to solve?

Group leaders' checklist for scoreboard review:

- ☐ Keep it positive. The balanced scoreboard review meeting is a time for teams to showcase their problem-solving skills and improvements.

- ☐ Give positive feedback—either directly or by asking questions that will lead to positive answers.

- ☐ Ask questions to help lead team members to problems and improvements they may not have uncovered during the preparation cycle. Socratic questions also help gauge the level of preparation, problem-solving understanding, and alignment of the team.

- ☐ When providing direct coaching, either through Socratic questioning or planned improvements, a general rule of thumb is to provide three positive coaching comments for each direct coaching comment or improvement opportunity.

- ☐ Ask and follow through on, "How will I help this team succeed?"

Establishing and Aligning Scorecards in a Daily Management System

Before using the balanced scorecard/board in the pilot hall, ensure that the Senior Team has established or at least drafted a 6-year balanced scorecard with a focused number of metrics. The pilot hall especially should be able to align and impact the 6-year scorecard, which helps communicate the long-term plan and the overall vision of the organization and the pilot. Steps for establishing scorecard, scoreboard, leadership team, and monthly meeting are as follows:

1. **P-D-C-A the daily huddle and problem solving**. Ensure the huddle is meeting expectations. By this time, the huddle is being led by different staff members, not just the team leader. Problem-solving skills are beginning to be developed, as evidenced by a large number of problem-solving sheets on the problem-solving board. If the weekly problem-solving board checks are not yet established, the monthly meeting becomes a great way to close the loop and showcase improvement.

2. **Establish the leadership team**. Create the unit-based leadership team following the guidelines set forth in this chapter. Ensure members are clear on timing, attendance, and frequency of the meetings.

3. **Align scorecards**. Using the cascading and aligning standards and the organization's 6-year scorecard, establish the 6-year scorecard for the pilot hall(s) with the unit-based leadership team.

4. **Designate and visualize R/S**. R/S for each priority needs to be established so roles and responsibilities are clear. Designating, supporting, and coaching R/S for each priority disseminates improvement responsibilities to the frontline, increases engagement, and sidelines the concept that managers are responsible for all metrics on a unit. Use members on the unit-based leadership team to establish R/S and visualize it on the scoreboard.

5. **Set the scoreboard**. Obtain a physical balanced scoreboard or create one following/adapting the standards. Generally, all pilot hall scoreboards should look the same so that team members, team leaders, and Senior Leaders can quickly navigate the scoreboard and focus on the content, not spending time looking for the content.

6. **Visualize 1-year metrics on the scoreboard**. From the 6-year balanced scorecard, visualize the annual objectives and next year's metrics/targets. This begins to align daily activity with the long-term 6-year plan. Some teams/ organizations may choose to visualize a smaller timeframe for metrics, e.g., quarterly. Regardless, ensure they align with the long-term plan.

7. **Prepare for the monthly balanced scoreboard review**. With the unit-based leadership team, prepare for the monthly meeting by updating the current status of metrics, and selecting and visualizing top problems. Select problems that are gaining traction and will help showcase the team's individual improvements, not the faults/problems of other departments.

8. **Conduct the first monthly meeting**. Conduct the first monthly meeting as practice with either the Continuous Improvement leader or a Senior Leader. Remember, everyone is learning and coaching a new system. During the monthly meeting leaders, especially Senior Leaders, need to use the 3Ps before the 3Gs—have passion, patience, and recognize people.

9. **P-D-C-A**. Build P-D-C-A into the monthly meeting by asking, "What do we need to start, stop, and/or continue?" in regards to the daily management system and the monthly balanced scoreboard meeting. This serves as a precursor to the audit introduced in Chapter 8.

10. **Communicate and celebrate**. If all team members cannot attend the monthly meeting continually communicate and celebrate the progress of top problems by (for example) having short reviews at daily huddles, newsletters, etc. Remember, the balanced scoreboard is an improvement tool/artifact and helps teams see and communicate positive changes within the unit.

11. **Standardize cycles**. Standardize the time for preparation and conducting the monthly meeting. Schedule necessary members of higher leadership for the monthly meeting many months in advance and staff even further in advance. Begin to also wrap more frequent P-D-C-A cycles around top problems—for example, checking top problem status every Tuesday. Also, ensure a coach is available to guide this process. It is a great time to learn and continue progressing in the Lean management system.

Balanced Scoreboard Standard Work Activities:

1. *Daily*: Use necessary information to update the balanced scoreboard metrics/indicators prior to the huddle.

2. *Weekly*: Check the status of top problems and note progress made since the last checkpoint (keep it positive).

3. *Monthly*: Prepare for the monthly balanced scoreboard meeting.

4. *Monthly*: Conduct the monthly balanced scoreboard meeting, reporting out to the unit-based leadership team's one-up and unit.

5. *Yearly*: Update, recast, and re-communicate the 6-year balanced scorecard.

Tiered Scoreboards, Leadership Teams, and Monthly Check Cycles

When the balanced scoreboard and check cycles are deployed throughout the organization, it creates a system of aligning goals, targets, and objectives from the Senior Team to frontline teams. This also creates a mechanism to elevate and align top problems from one unit, to a value stream or functional leader, to the Senior Team. The system of check cycles integrated with the daily management system both develops leaders and aligns problem-solving efforts. Figure 4.11 shows some benefits of tiered balanced scoreboards in a Lean management system.

Senior Team Focus. As the daily management system is learned and being lead by Senior Leadership, the balanced scoreboard is a catch-all for problems of both the pilot hall and teams that have not yet started with the daily management system. It is critical that the Senior Team standardizes check cycles so that problems that are elevated either from the pilot hall or other areas are solved in a timely manner.

Pilot Hall Focus. Establishing an aligned balanced scorecard and check cycles creates both a place and a designated time to go and see teams engaged in the management system at the monthly meeting. Most importantly, standard coaching and check cycles begin to teach Senior Leaders how to coach P-D-C-A, as cycles become standardized.

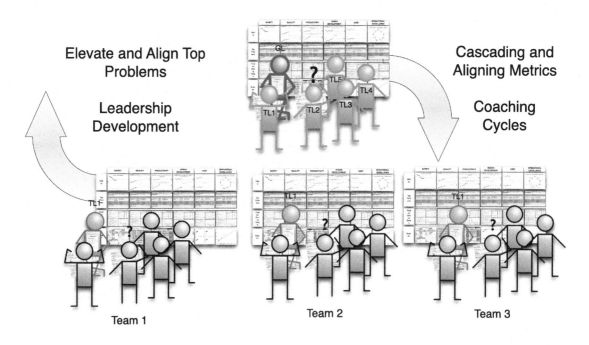

Figure 4.11. Aligned scoreboards and check cycles help align metrics, top problems, leadership development, and coaching cycles throughout the organization.

Roles and Responsibilities

Priority Owner/Responsible. Also known as the "R-person" for the priority. This person is responsible for the maintenance of the priority, including but not limited to making graphs, updating metrics and indicators, updating the template for the top three problems, proposing top problems for the priority, and reporting out on the vital during the monthly balanced scoreboard review.

Priority Support. This person, also known as the "S" person, supports the priority "R" and takes his/her place during the process if the owner is absent, unavailable, or needs additional assistance. Note that the team leader is always a support person regardless of whether they are designated an S-person or not.

Problem-Solving Sheet Owner. This is the person who is seeing the problem-solving process through. In some cases they started the actual problem-solving sheet; in other cases, the problem-solving sheet was forwarded to them. The problem-solving sheet owner should be a member of the leadership team.

Countermeasure Owner. This is the person responsible for implementing the countermeasure. This person may or may not be the problem-solving sheet owner. If not a member of the unit leadership team, the problem-solving sheet owner checks with the countermeasure owner to ensure implementation. There may be more than one person responsible for implementing countermeasures.

Team Member. Team members will continue to be an active participant in problem solving, the improvement system, and the overall daily management system. Trust your leadership team, and if you're interested in being a member of the unit-based leadership team, speak with your team leader. For those team that team, communicate with other team members and get their input. When available, use other team members to help solve problems. If you're a team member on the leadership team, you are representing your fellow members.

Team Leader. Be an active member of the leadership team and encourage active participation. Ultimately, you are responsible for improvement, balanced scorecard maintenance, problem solving, etc. Roles/responsibilities, including the leadership team, are established to help you lead.

Group Leader. Go and observe monthly meetings, listen, celebrate, and coach. If you have input on top problems or other improvements to the scoreboard, go and see the team leader prior to the report out meeting. The balanced scoreboard is an improvement tool, not a control tool, so use the monthly meeting as an improvement and celebration meeting, focusing on the positives more than the improvements still necessary.

Baldrige Connections

Vision, Values, and Mission *1.1a(1)*. Senior leaders deploy vision and values to the workforce using the leadership system. In addition, the unit-based leadership teams include key stakeholders and partners, i.e., physicians or in some cases external suppliers or patient representatives. This helps creates both communication and an alignment with the vision (NIST, 2015, p. 7).

Communication *1.1b.(1)*. The scorecard and scoreboard are tools to help align the vision of the organization with daily management and improvement. It is one mechanism for the senior team to "communicate with and engage the entire workforce" (NIST, p. 7).

Action Plan Modification *2.2a.(6)*. The balanced scoreboard's top problems serve as a mechanism to "implement modified action plans if circumstances require a shift in plans and rapid execution of new plans" (NIST, p. 12). The monthly meeting cycle, including selecting and solving top problems, is a key mechanism in making adjustments and improvements to problems based on the action plans that are made evident using the daily management system.

Measurement Agility *4.1a(4)*. Using the balanced scoreboard cycle, and particularly the appropriate leading indicators, ensures that the "performance measurement system can respond to rapid or unexpected organizational change" (NIST, p. 16).

Performance Analysis and Review *4.1b*. This Senior Team's monthly balanced scoreboard meeting is a mechanism to "review organizational performance. . . [using] key organizational performance measures." The problem-solving cycles engrained in the monthly meeting provide analyses "to support these reviews and ensure that conclusions are valid" (NIST, p. 16).

Learning and Development System *5.2b.(1)*. The tiered leadership teams' engagement in the daily and monthly cycles for improvement is one way that the daily management system is a learning and development system. This process "supports the organization's needs and the personal development of workforce members, managers, and leaders" (NIST, p. 20).

Career Progression *5.2b.(3)*. Just as huddles are tiered, so too are scoreboards and leadership teams. This not only creates a funnel for metrics, top problems, and improvements, but also a leadership system for creating, developing, and furthering leaders both personally and professionally. Unit-based leadership teams are a great way to build future leaders and "carry out succession planning for management" (NIST, p. 21).

Summary: Lean Culture Change Using a Balanced Scorecard

Generally, the organization should have a 6-year scorecard established in order to align the organization, Senior Team, and pilot hall towards a common set of focused metrics.

☐ The corporate 6-year scorecard is a tool to organize the top organizational priorities, objectives, and targets, aiming toward achieving world-class organizational operations.

☐ Keep the 6-year scorecard focused on a few metrics—not to exceed 3 per priority (18 metrics max total).

☐ Objectives on the scorecard need to be SMART—Specific, Measurable, Agreed-upon, Realistic, and Timed. This helps with clear communication when cascading, measuring, and reflecting upon goals.

☐ Visualize the one-year targets of the 6-year scorecard on the balanced scoreboard, an artifact used to visualize corporate communication, annual targets, leading indicators for processes, and top problems.

☐ Use the balanced scoreboard meeting as a positive meeting showcasing improvements from the team and reinforcing the daily management system. This is essential at both the Senior Team level and the pilot hall level.

☐ Establish leadership teams on each unit as the primary individuals responsible for maintaining the scoreboard, selecting and coordinating top problem initiatives, and being the first to learn new artifacts of the daily management system.

☐ Align scorecards throughout the organization (Senior Team and pilot hall first), so that each team is striving toward similar, connected targets. Eventually, monthly meetings will also be tiered by timing throughout the month.

☐ Establish a monthly balanced scoreboard meeting cycle consisting of the scoreboard preparation meetings with the Senior Team first, then the unit-based leadership team within the pilot hall.

☐ Check top problems on a weekly basis to increase communication and awareness of the progress towards solving the problems.

☐ At least annually, reset the balanced scoreboard based on the next year's aligned objectives and metrics.

Forbes Regional Hospital, Allegheny Health Network
Improving Heart and Vascular Service using a Daily Management System

Through weekly training and coaching, the Heart and Vascular Center (HVC) at Forbes Regional Hospital near Pittsburgh, PA learned the objects of a Lean management system they call Operational Excellence (OE). "The OE model is rigorous in execution while promoting the flip in culture from 'problems are punished' to 'problems are blessings.'" (Culig et al 398).

Over a two year period during the ramp-up of a new cardiac catheterization and cardiac surgery program, the team began daily huddles, established a balanced scoreboard, and solved problems on a daily basis using the problem-solving methodology. The team's balanced scorecard priorities were Safety, Quality, Productivity, Human Development, Cost, and Organizational Excellence. The team performs "daily, rigidly orchestrated 10-minute meetings during which all participants stand. Each problem from the previous 24 hours is presented on a problem-solving sheet" (p. 395).

First, the principles were coached with the HVC's management team, followed by the cardiothoracic intensive care unit (CTICU) and cardiac catheterization laboratory as pilot halls. Using tiered huddles and problem solving on a daily basis, the CTICU and laboratory were able to both solve and elevate problems to the HVC's management team. "As quickly as possible, an early action plan is developed by the team and includes the person who has experienced the problem" (p. 395). Through a daily management system, leadership, and ownership by the cardiac surgeon, the HVC team and teams aligned with HVC became problem solvers. The culture shifted to a positive culture recognizing, discussing, analyzing and solving problems.

"It takes months for personnel to learn how to use problem-solving sheets. The daily structured meetings create the safe environment to dispassionately and objectively study defects to create trials for solutions" (398). The team use these and other components of a Lean management system as well as best practices including aligned huddles, collaborative rounds, surgery standards, visual management, and standardized hand-offs. The daily huddles are a way to communicate the new standards, and problem solving is a way to improve upon those standards.

Results after two years, 409 heart operations, and 923 problem-solving sheets included that "the risk-adjusted incidence of major adverse events has decreased by 50% as compared with that for the region," and a cost savings of $884,900 (p. 399). The team noted that rather than focusing on cost to reduce cost, focusing on safety and quality resulted in quality care, high levels of patient satisfaction and engagement, and reduced cost as well.

Balanced Scoreboard Using Lewis' Standard

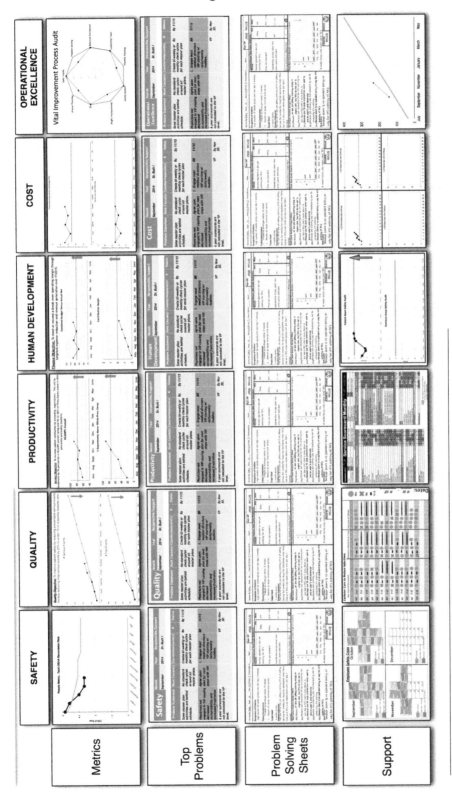

Figure 4.12. An example balanced scoreboard using Lewis' standard format.

Balanced Scoreboard from Indiana Regional Medical Center

Figure 4.13. An example balanced scoreboard from Indiana Regional Medical Center's Medical Services units.

Balanced Scoreboard from Forbes Hospital

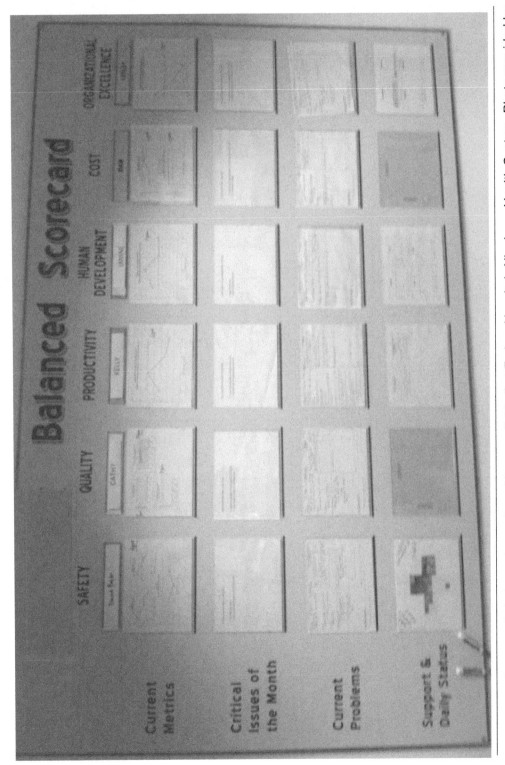

Figure 4.14. An example balanced scoreboard from a pilot hall at Forbes Hospital, Allegheny Health System. Photo provided by Dr. Michael Culig.

Example Balanced Scoreboard from Excela Health (i.e. CI Board)

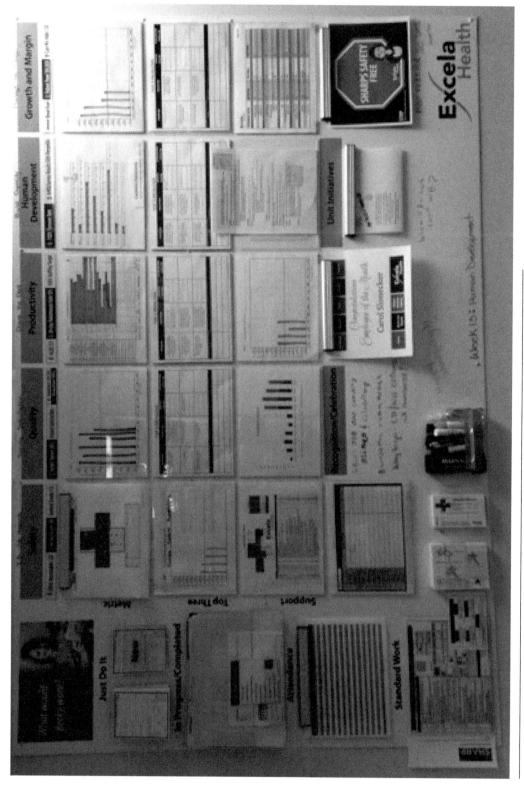

Figure 4.15. An example balanced scoreboard from Excela Health in Greensburg, PA.

Example Top Level Metric from IRMC Senior Team

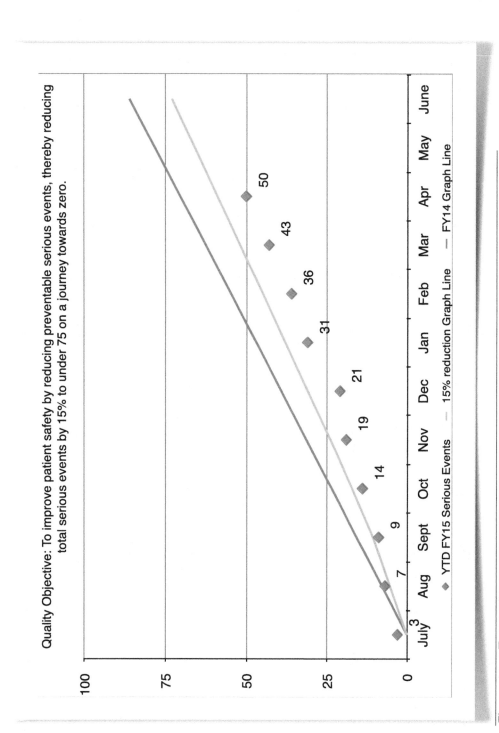

Quality Objective: To improve patient safety by reducing preventable serious events, thereby reducing total serious events by 15% to under 75 on a journey towards zero.

Figure 4.16. Top quality metric, visualizing the number of serious events (red diamonds), this current year's target (green line), and last year's performance (blue line). Dr. Bruce Bush, Chief Medical Officer and "R" for Quality, uses the balanced scoreboard and this graph to update the Senior Team, Board of Directors, Patient Safety Committee, and others on the status of performance compared to the target.

Example Top Problems

People	Month: February	Year: 2015	Responsible/Support: AS/CT	
Problem Statement	Root Cause(s)	Countermeasure(s)	R	When
Last month, there was an increase in employee injuries related to patient transfers on the Medical-Surgical Nursing Unit.	(1)Lift equipment not readily available. (2)location of all devices not known by all staff.	(1)Complete inventory of current lift equipment. (2)Develop key point sheets for equipment. (3)Order additional equipment for each room as needed. (4)	(1)A. Smith (2)A. Smith (3)B. Jones	3/10/15 3/10/15 3/10/15
Sharps injuries resulting from sharps being mixed with the patient's belongings or left near the patient's bedside.	No standard practice for logging and placing patients' belongings.	(1) Create a standard process. (2) Daily observation and reinforcement.	B. Jones	3/20/15
Increase in parking lot falls, specifically falls between parked cars.	No standard for closing and clearing lots.	Develop a standard for rolling lot closures.	C. Thomas	3/30/15

Figure 4.17. An example top problem template for the balanced scoreboard containing modified problems from Indiana Regional Medical Center's VP for Organizational Development Dr. James Kinneer.

Chapter 5
Annual Planning

This chapter will introduce your team to:

- *Annual planning and Hoshin kanri.*

- *Aligning world-class targets with daily activities.*

- *Creating, checking, and adjusting master plans.*

- *Tiered annual planning.*

- *A case study about goal selection and daily management.*

Why Annual Planning and Hoshin Kanri?

Chapter 5 introduced the 6-year balanced scorecard, a tool to establish, align, and cascade metrics throughout the organization. **Annual Planning** is a process for recasting the 6-year scorecard and establishing plans to achieve each scorecard objective and improve the organization's performance. Hoshin kanri is used to describe mature Lean organizations' processes for utilizing the 6-year scorecards, balanced scoreboards, leading indicators, and annual plans throughout the organization. Hoshin kanri is "the process of setting consensus goals for long-term improvement and deciding on the best allocation of effort and resources to reach those goals" (Liker & Convis, 2011, p. 42). Table 5.1 shows the definition/translation of Hoshin kanri (Hutchins, 2008, p. 3).

Table 5.1: Hoshin kanri defined

Ho	Shin	Kan	Ri
Direction	Focus	Alignment	Reason

Creating Concrete Plans To Achieve Targets

Peter Drucker, in The Practice of Management (1954), states that "'some of the most effective managers I know' go beyond only deploying quantitative targets downward. He briefly describes how these managers engage in a two-way dialogue with the level below them in order to develop written plans for the activities that will be undertaken to reach the targets" (Rother, 2009, p. 67). Eventually, everyone will be engaged in annual planning; however, the development of the initial annual plans is lead by leadership, who learn and establish the annual planning cycle. Though deploying targets and metrics is important in the annual planning process, the most critical, and often missed, component to annual planning is the development of specific, documented, agreed-upon plans to achieve objectives. This chapter proposes a standard for the Senior Team to lead the creation of those specific plans for achieving objectives, hitting targets, and establishing beginning stages of organizational routines for creating, negotiating, checking, and adjusting those plans.

> "Hoshin kanri is the process of setting goals and targets and, most important, the concrete plans for reaching those targets."
>
> —Jeffrey Liker & Gary Convis (2011, p. 42)

Aligning World-Class Targets with Daily Activities

The **Annual Planning Cycle**, visualized in Figure 5.2, is a yearly organization-wide improvement cycle. One Lean culture change tool in this cycle is a master plan. A **Master Plan** is a tool used to visualize the master schedule, annual master plan activities, and timelines. The general format is seen in Figure 5.1. Each annual objective from the corporate 6-year scorecard has a master plan.

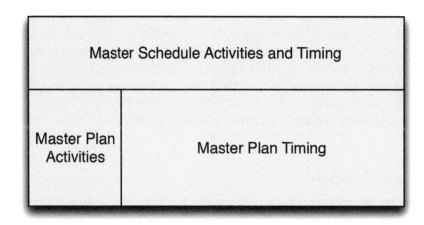

Figure 5.1. Master plan layout overview.

Dimensions of the Master Plan

The master plan contains master schedule activities, master plan activities, responsible and support persons, planned checkpoints, start dates, end dates, and other details necessary to achieve the objective of the plan. Examples of linked plans are shown in Figure 5.2 and a master plan in Figure 5.3.

Master Schedule Activities. Previously planned activities or events that keep team members from completing master plan activities are included in master schedule activities, as is their timing. These generally cannot or should not be moved. Examples include a planned new building opening, the launch of a new service line, a team member's vacation, a leadership retreat, or other events.

Master Plan Activities. Specific steps or actions that are planned and needed in order to achieve an objective. Master plan activities have an R- and an S-person, who are responsible (R) and support (S), for completing the activity.

Detailed Plans and Project Plans. These plans have the same structure as master plans. Detailed plans may be generated for selected master plan activities. Project plans are used case by case and may or may not be directly connected to the 6-year scorecard.

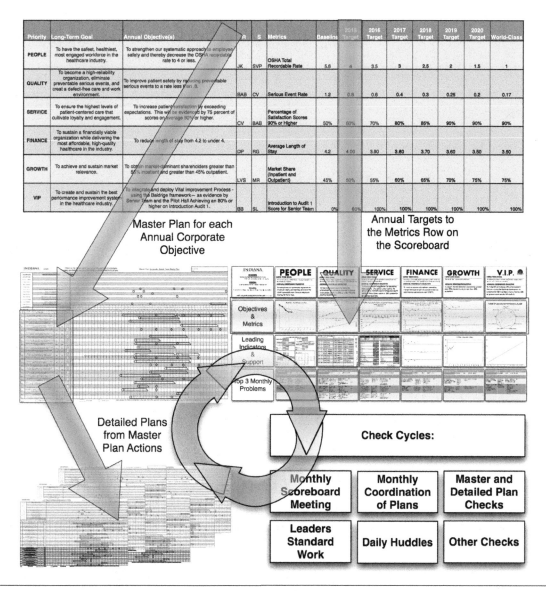

Figure 5.2. The Plan-Do-Check-Act cycle of annual planning.

Note. The organization's 6-year scorecard has the annual objectives and annual targets aligned with world-class targets. Each annual objective has a master plan with activities on how the objective will be achieved. Case by case, master plan activities will have more detailed plans.

In addition, the upcoming year's annual targets are visualized on the balanced scoreboard's metric row. Leading indicators, support metrics, daily huddles, problem solving, and monthly meetings ensure teams are aligned with the 6-year scorecard and world-class performance.

Lean Culture Change

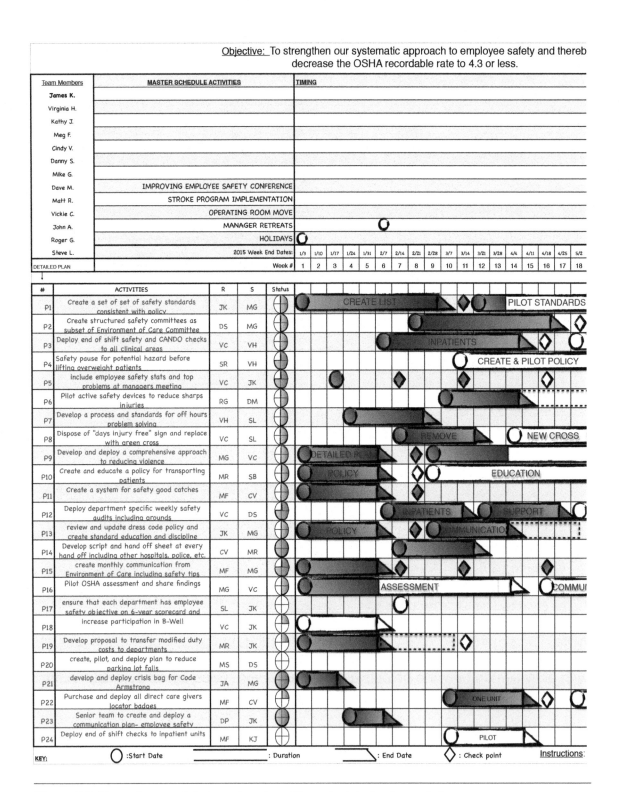

Figure 5.3. Example completed master plan, 17 weeks into implementation.

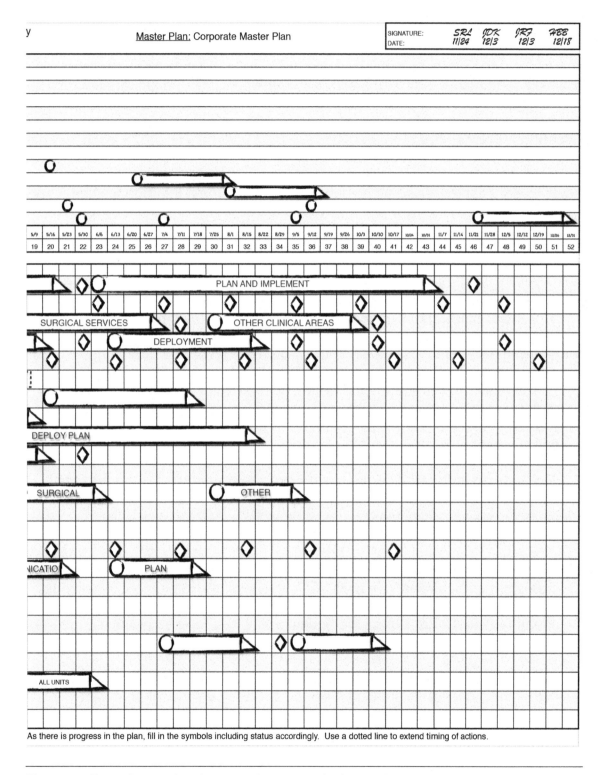

Figure 5.3. Example completed master plan, 17 weeks into implementation *(continued).*

As annual planning becomes an organization-wide initiative, true Hoshin begins to take place. Leaders are engaged in the process of cascading 6-year scorecards, and master plans, for each objective. "At each level where the Hoshin kanri process is active, a senior leader works with the leaders beneath her to create a plan for achieving a specified goal" (Liker & Convis, 2011, p. 167).

Creating Master Plans

Although master plans can be directly tied to each 6-year scorecard, it may take several years to create and align master plans throughout the organization, whereas cascading the scorecard may be a faster process. The first year, the organization may only establish one master plan for each corporate objective, meaning there may be six master plans total. The following steps show how to create one master plan as it relates to a corporate multi-year scorecard:

1. **Select the objective.** Start with an annual objective from the 6-year scorecard. Since annual planning is creating concrete plans to achieve objectives and targets, each objective essentially will have its own master plan with a detailed list of actions to achieve the objective. Grasp top problems and best practices. SWOT (Strength, Weakness, Opportunity, and Threats) Analysis, and other forms of information gathering, may be necessary at this step. Understanding past problems, potential future problems, and the problems that are currently facing the organization is a critical step before brainstorming improvement ideas.

2. **Brainstorm innovative ideas to achieve the objective.** During the initial stages of brainstorming there may innovative ideas, best practices, and ideas the organization has discussed previously. At this stage, all ideas are acceptable and should vetted, typically in a group setting.

3. **Sort ideas and list as actions.** Once all ideas have been vetted during brainstorming sessions, use a PICK Chart (Possible, Implement, Challenge, and Kibosh) as a simple, visual way to prioritize. Figure 5.6 shows an example PICK Chart. During the brainstorming, place each proposed activity into a quadrant on the PICK Chart, using input from the group.

4. **Select ideas for implementation.** Generally, all low-expense and high-impact quadrants should be selected. Case by case, high-impact and high-expense activities are selected and integrated into the budgeting process.

5. **Negotiation.** Negotiation is a process that takes place formally and informally until the master plans and budgets are agreed upon and approved. Check

cycles, after plans are established, are also a form of ongoing negotiation if the plans need to be changed or timelines need to be extended.

6. **Master scheduling**. Visualizing the master schedule helps the team understand the current situation for the team and organization. Grasping the master schedule is necessary in order to plan improvement activities around master schedule activities.

7. **Create timelines for improvement activities.** Clearly state the improvement activities, with responsible and support. Visualize the start dates, end dates, and check points for each improvement activity.

8. **Negotiate and confirm the plan.** The final negotiation is another informal process; the master plan may be passed around in a meeting, with face-to-face discussions between different leaders, or other informal processes. It is important that the right people are able to see the plan, understand the resources and required budget, and give any final input. Yes, the plan may be flexible, but the more thorough the plan the easier the check.

9. **Sign-off.** When the master plan is finalized by the responsible person (R) and team members agree to the planned activities, the executive team signs off on the plan on the top right hand corner, symbolizing approval and support.

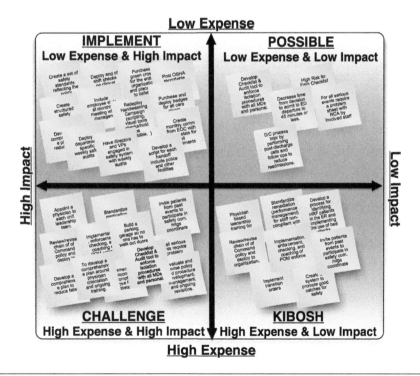

Figure 5.4. A PICK Chart, separated into four quadrants, is a simple way to help select the most appropriate improvement activities to plan on a master plan.

Checking, Implementing, and Adjusting Master Plans

1. **Check the plan.** Having standard check cycles is essential to following through with any plan. Within the master plan, planned check cycles are visualized using the diamond symbol; however, especially in the beginning of annual planning, having standardized check cycles is essential to implementing activities on the master plan. In many cases, because the new management system has not fully integrated daily activities, translating annual activities to monthly plans and to daily activities is not second nature. Therefore, having frequent check cycles helps to keep plans at the forefront at least every other week or monthly.

2. **Align with monthly and daily activities.** As the concept of creating and checking concrete plans for improvement is being utilized on an annual basis, the annual plans are translated to monthly plans using a form that looks like the annual plan but that is designed around the 30/31 days of the month versus the 52 weeks of the year. The monthly plans for each leader or department, which integrate both annual planning activities and monthly countermeasures to top problems, are used to plan daily activities. As a result, annual plans, as opposed to firefighting, will begin to drive the daily schedules.

3. **Update the status and adjust if agreed upon.** Though the master plan may be time-consuming to create, it is a Lean culture change tool that quickly visualizes the current state of the annual plan. The status symbol, illustrated in Figure 5.5, shows the current status at 75% of the individual activity (circled in green). Also, using the current week number as baseline, whether or not the planned activities are being worked on as per the plan can be easily visualized.

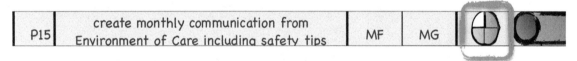

| P15 | create monthly communication from Environment of Care including safety tips | MF | MG | | |

Figure 5.5. Master plan activities with responsible, support, and status.

4. **Adjust the plan.** Adjusting the plan will always be necessary, especially during the first phase of annual planning. Strive to hit the timelines, but if necessary and agreed upon, they can be extended. Figure 5.6 shows a simple way to extend timing while preserving the original planned dates.

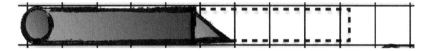

Figure 5.6. Master plan activities after plan timing extended.

Tiered Annual Planning

As the Senior Team creates, visualizes, checks, and coordinates plans, annual activities align to monthly activities, and these monthly plans inform weekly and daily activities. These cycles begin to build a P-D-C-A mindset into leaders with the initial emphasis on planning and a later emphasis on checking. Having the most appropriate activities on the master plan, aligned with frequent check and planning cycles, helps to proactively drive the organization to focus on the long-term by focusing on the most appropriate daily activities.

As the daily management system is coached throughout the organization and the Senior Team continues to fine-tune master planning skills, they will have more time to focus strategically, because the plans are established and check cycles are engrained into the culture. The alignment for the Senior Team between the vision, 6-year scorecard, annual/monthly plans, and daily activities is shown in Figure 5.7. Although annual planning starts with leadership, it is eventually for everyone. As cycles are refined by Senior Leadership and coached throughout the organization, improvement activity roles/responsibilities become embedded into the daily management system.

Figure 5.7. Aligning the vision with daily activities using master plans.

WARNING: The master plan is a control tool and the balanced scoreboard is an improvement tool. Initially, ensure that the team will be successful with the master plan by selecting the most appropriate activities to achieve the objective on the 6-year scorecard that are able to be accomplished within the given timeframe. Do not add every activity that needs to be accomplished by the Senior Team. Once the master plan and P-D-C-A is learned by the Senior Team, it should be used as a control tool to control planned improvement activities and, as needed, countermeasures.

Roles and Responsibilities

Board of Directors. In most organizations, the Senior Team presents goals for the upcoming year(s), whether it is in the form of a 6-year scorecard or another format. The Board of Directors' responsibility is to ensure the organization has a plan to achieve those goals and objectives. A plan that is only articulated but without documented activities, responsible and support persons, timeframes, and check points is not a true plan. The board also ensures that there are check cycles in place and checks and adjusts the master plan(s) on an ongoing basis. Status reports help give boards quick insight into the status of the overarching master plans and complete a P-D-C-A cycle.

Chief Executive Officer. In consultation with the board and the Senior Team, the CEO sets the annual theme for improvement, which the rest of the organization rallies behind when creating aligned action plans. This is especially important as the annual planning cycle becomes more mature. The CEO's role is to help and ensure that the Senior Team leads as a team, by coordinating, communicating, implementing, and adjusting master plan activities as a team.

Senior Team. The Senior Team is responsible for communication before, during, and after annual planning. The CEO communicates the annual theme for improvement, and the Senior Team ensures the activities and overall plans are communicated to the entire organization and the areas that will be affected by master plan activities. Senior leaders will lead communication throughout the year, giving reports on the effects of implemented activities and upcoming planned activities.

Master Plan Leader. The leader who has the R for the entire master plan (a Senior Leader for corporate-level plans) has the responsibility to ensure the plan is complete and to lead the check cycles. This leader will elevate the positive improvements from the master plan, problems, and upcoming activities on an ongoing basis to other Senior Leaders and the CEO.

Activity-R. The responsible person for the activity may need to create a detailed plan using the master plan template, or at least create another informal plan. The activity-R will come to any master plan check point prepared to report on status, coordinate, and elevate problems as needed.

Activity-S. The support (S) for each activity is able to support the responsible person and also report out the status to the master plan R. If the R-person is unable to implement the activity for any reason, the S is now responsible.

Continuous Improvement Team. The CI team supports the master plan leader by facilitating any group meetings, creating the actual documents, and training others on how to create a detailed plan.

Baldrige Connections

Focus on Action *1.1b.(2)*. The annual planning process focuses on creating plans based on activities to achieve the objectives. By cascading master plans and detailed plans to monthly and daily activities, it helps "senior leaders create a focus on action that will improve the organization's performance. . . and attain its vision" (NIST, 2015, p. 7). As master plans drive Senior Leaders' schedules, the Senior Leaders are focused on action.

Strategic Planning Process *2.1a.(1)*. The annual planning process and its components align "short- and longer-term planning horizons," aligning the 6-year scorecard targets, annual plans, monthly plans, and daily activities (p. 10).

Innovation *2.1a.(2)*. The plan development process creates an environment that supports innovation, which aligns with other systems, such as the improvement system. Using facilitation techniques such as the PICK chart supports leaders in identifying "strategic opportunities and intelligent risks for pursuing" (p. 10).

Key Strategic Objectives *2.1b.(1)*. Annual planning identifies key strategic objectives, the activities to achieve the objectives, and "timetables for achieving them" (p. 10).

Action Plans *2.2a.(1)*. Annual planning provides a step-by-step process to develop action plans, which align "key short- and longer-term action plans" related to strategic objectives (p. 10).

Action Plan Implementation *2.2a.(2)*. Frequent communication (e.g., huddles) and check cycles help to "deploy action plans to the workforce throughout the organization to the workforce and key stakeholders" (p. 12).

Action Plan Modification *2.2b*. As the scoreboard is checked on a monthly basis and plans are checked and cascaded to daily activities, "if circumstances require a shift in plans and rapid execution of new plans," the frequent check and adjust cycles allow this need to be identified and plans recreated (p. 12).

Innovation Management *6.1c*. As the annual planning cycle becomes aligned with the strategic planning cycle and budgeting cycles, master plan activities help to drive the budget by preparing and planning for necessary resources as they relate to strategy and action plan deployment. This helps "make financial and other resources available to pursue opportunities" agreed upon during the annual planning cycle (p. 22).

Best Practices *4.1c.(1)*. Preparing for the upcoming annual planning cycle includes identifying "organizational units or operations that are high performing" and ensuring those best practices are shared and incorporated into other departments through annual plans (p. 16).

Summary: Lean Culture Change Using Annual Planning

Annual planning is a process that engages everyone, though not everyone may have a master plan to manage or a master plan activity on which to report. During the first cycle, the Senior Team may be the only team with master plans, but as P-D-C-A cycles are learned, master plans can be aligned throughout the organization.

☐ Grasp the objective. Whether it's from the 6-year scorecard, a detailed activity on a master plan, or a project plan, grasping and understanding the objective is the initial step.

☐ Brainstorm and select innovations. Adapting the steps outlined in this chapter, create the master plan with your designated team. This starts with grasping the master schedule and understanding the problems and best practices around the objective. Brainstorm, sort, and plan for innovative ideas to achieve the objective.

☐ Create the plan. From the selected innovations and activities, establish the timelines, responsible person, support person, and create your master plan.

☐ Negotiate, finalize, and communicate. Ensure all necessary people and teams agree with or will support your master plan. Though the plan is flexible, the work should be done upfront to ensure the plan is as accurate as possible before signing off and communicating with the appropriate teams.

☐ Cascade the plan. Depending on the master plan you are creating and the detailed activities on the plan, you may need to coach an R-person to develop a detailed plan that is aligned with the activities and dates on your master plan.

☐ Check and adjust. Establish standardized and planned check cycles around the master plan and detailed plan, and elevate any necessary actions. Planning to check is critical in supporting those who are tasked with implementation.

☐ Align annual activities to monthly and daily activities. Ensure you are using the annual master plan to determine your monthly plan and your daily schedule in advance so you and others can stay on task.

☐ Problem solving. As problems arise from your master plan and the activities you identified to achieve the objective, continue to use the other Lean culture change tools, such as problem solving and the monthly balanced scorecard meeting, to select and elevate problems that you did

Case Study: Indiana Regional Medical Center, Indiana, Pennsylvania
Master Planning: A Commitment to Systematically Execute & Adjust Strategy

Historically, most plans either fail or languish unfulfilled because of the inability to execute strategy in a timely manner. As the late management guru, Peter Drucker, once stated, "unless commitment is made, there are only promises and hopes, but no plan." IRMC was not immune to this implementation malaise after developing its strategic plans. In 2013, however, introducing a Lean transformation initiative across the enterprise, the Senior Team was introduced to the concept of master plans.

Indiana Regional Medical Center (IRMC) deploys its strategic planning process every three years, identifying the strategic imperatives that must be addressed in the new cycle going forward. In addition, the organization develops operational goals annually, which advance progress towards a best-in-practice level of attainment that is targeted within six years. The strategic plan can inform and influence how the annual goals are developed. IRMC's planning process aligns these strategic and operational goals with its five vitals—People, Quality, Service, Finance, and Growth—and then it formulates enabling strategies to achieve the stated goals.

"A master plan for implementation is critical," states Larry Sedlemeyer, SVP for Business Development & Planning, "because we have learned that absent a visible, hands-on commitment with identified resources and checkpoints, initiatives wither and gains slip away." To start, IRMC conceives a master plan for each of its five vitals. This master plan articulates a goal statement for each vital, defines a 6-year target, and identifies the major initiatives to be undertaken. These initiatives can be a combination of strategic or operational origin. If any given initiative is of enough scale or import, a (mini) master plan can be developed for it. Further, each master plan identifies the specific milestones, or partial levels of attainment, that are required over the course of a year in order for a goal to be achieved.

"Master plans provide for a consistent line of sight throughout the whole organization," Sedlemeyer says. With frequent periodic review and update, the master plan tool allows for modification of strategy when needed and enables problem-solving to occur when roadblocks are encountered or when specific milestones are not attained on time. IRMC has learned to hardwire commitment to strategy implementation through the use of master plans.

Dr. James Kinneer, Vice President for Organizational Development, reflects, "we are establishing an organizational rhythm, especially at the Senior Team level, of what seemed like disparate processes in the past. Without a robust management system work is done and improvement is made in isolation. The outcome of this aligned work which will give Senior Leaders more time to focus on strategy." Figure 5.8 is IRMC's desired process, which Kinneer and Sedlemeyer refer to as "grow, run, and fund."

(Larry Sedlemeyer & James Kinneer, 2015)

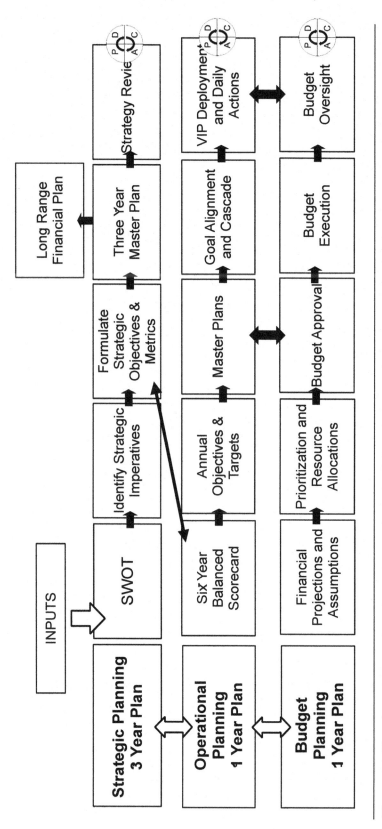

Figure 5.8. The strategic, operational, and budget planning process at Indiana Regional Medical Center, integrating the 6-year scorecard, annual master plans, and 3-year master plan(s).

Chapter 6
Improvement System

This chapter will introduce your team to:

- *The purposes and criteria of a self-implemented improvement/suggestion system.*

- *A pathway to align positive recognition with daily management.*

- *Artifacts of an improvement system including forms, boards, and activities.*

- *A case study on improving operations and employee engagement.*

- *Example improvement stories, forms, and visual management boards.*

Why a Self-Implemented Improvement System?

A suggestion system "should be a process that engages employees in fast improvement cycles, allowing them to take ownership of improving their processes instead of just lobbing complaints at their leaders" (Graban, 2008, p. 192). The Toyota suggestion system is known as "soui kufuu seido," which translates to "creative ideas suggestion system" (Miller 2003). "The Suggestion System at Toyota is famous for its team member involvement and payback in company cost savings" (Liker & Hoseus, p. 164). The system is "based on the premise that people inherently want to improve" (Meier, 2005, p. 261). One major difference in Toyota's suggestion system compared to other systems is the team leader–member relationship. Toyota leaders have an improvement kata, a framework for how to coach suggestions to acceptable implemented improvements, which is an expression of Toyota's culture (Rother, 2009, p. 28). The all-encompassing suggestion system, when fully implemented, consists of individual, team, value stream, and Vice President–led improvements (i.e., Quality Circles). This chapter outlines the creative ideas system for selfimplemented improvements, referred to as the *Improvement System.*

Purposes of the Improvement System

Engaging Team Members. The improvement system creates an outlet for employee creativity, and is designed to harness employees' ideas, innovation, and initiative. Empowering employees is much more than just asking for ideas, but giving them the framework, permission, and tools to improve.

Engaging Team Leaders. This system is just as much about engaging employees as it is about developing managers. The improvement system provides a framework for positive communication between team members and the team leader. It puts leaders in a coaching/mentoring role, and staff in a role of creating improvement while taking ownership of the improvement processes.

Engaging Senior Leadership. The improvement system creates a safe and positive environment for Senior Leaders to go, see, and learn from team members at the Gemba. It encourages positive and effective communication between Senior Leaders and frontline staff. The system also creates a simple way to learn and practice the 3Gs by rewarding and recognizing improvements.

Did you know? Approximately 700,000 ideas are generated at Toyota each year with an implementation rate of 99% (Miller, 2003, p. 4).

Criteria and Responsibilities of a Self-Implemented Improvement System

Acceptable Improvement Ideas:

☑ **Positive Impact.** The idea must create a positive impact on the process, balanced scoreboard, or overall patient experience. The individual signing off on the idea must ensure that there is not a negative impact on other departments or the overall value stream.

☑ **Minimal Cost and Simple Tools.** No improvement is too small. Some organizations may define *minimal cost* in the policy, and others will leave it to interpretation based on the resources and tools available.

☑ **Within Submitter's Area of Responsibility.** This criterion further promotes self-implemented improvements, and spells out that ideas in someone else'swork area are not acceptable in this system, though using cross-functional problem solving is encouraged.

☑ **Implemented by the Submitter.** The improvement needs to be owned and implemented by the submitter. This is not a system for suggesting improvements for someone else to implement.

☑ **Successfully Tested.** The submitter will ensure that the idea will actually work and is sustainable. There are a number of ways someone can pilot or test an idea without full deployment. Piloting is encouraged where possible.

Some Ideas Need Improvement:

☐ **"I Thought of It—You Do It."** This system is not about having an idea and expecting someone else to implement it or putting it on a manager's to-do list.

☐ **Complaints with No Idea for Improvement.** Complaints are not acceptable and should be funneled to the problem-solving system.

☐ **Changes to Regulations.** Though changes to standards, standard work, and procedures are all acceptable and encouraged, changes to regulations are not acceptable, including those of government and other accrediting bodies.

☐ **Containment/Quick Fix/Simple Corrections.** The system is not about using containments or quick fixes as an improvement. Yes, the problem should be contained, but ensure that the improvement is sustainable.

☐ **Changes Outside of Submitter's Span of Control.** If an idea is implementing a suggestion *onto* someone, rather than someone changing his or her own work, the idea needs to be modified.

Team Member Responsibilities

As an outlet for employee creativity, the improvement system aims to capture the hearts of employees. The initial purpose of this system is to engage team members in improvement activity engrained into their daily work responsibilities, as opposed to improvement being additional to the everyday work. Though necessary at times, kaizen events, improvements done during overtime hours, and dedicated time separate from planned work time create a *time to improve* and a *time to work*. For Lean culture change to take hold, improving the work must be part of doing the work. As the system is developed and communicated, this enables any team member to participate in improvement, not just ones who are given allocated time. The initial purpose of the system is engagement, and the aim is improvement quantity and an increasing participation rate. The key points for team members below outline their responsibilities.

Key Points for Team Members:

- ☐ **Learn the Criteria.** Understanding the criteria, roles, and responsibilities will help team members think of and implement great improvements. Understanding what ideas do not qualify for improvement will help team members refine ideas so that the ideas do meet the acceptable criteria.

- ☐ **Participate.** Some may say they already made improvements, and they do not want to be rewarded. Participation, however, is critical, so that implemented ideas can be documented, shared, and standardized throughout the department and organization. Even what may seem to be a small improvement should be included in this system, as it will inspire other individuals in other departments to implement a similar improvement.

- ☐ **Keep It Simple.** Some of the best improvements are simple. Though largescale, high-impact improvements are important, it is the sum of all the simple improvements that is the heart of the system. All improvements within the criteria qualify and should be implemented and documented, regardless of the perceived impact. A seemingly low-impact idea in one area may transform into a high-impact idea in another area.

- ☐ **Encourage.** Encourage others to participate in the system by giving suggestions, or coaching others to utilize the improvement system once they discover an improvement or solution to a problem. Remember, though, one of the best ways to encourage others is to participate.

- ☐ **Share Improvements.** Especially during the huddle, team members should share improvements both implemented and in process. This encourages others and demonstrates support for improvement.

Team Member Responsibilities

This system builds trust and respect between team leader and team member through positive communication of improvement ideas, support from team leaders on implementing ideas, positive recognition at huddles, and support after the improvement to communicate and standardize. Team leaders support the system by giving time, resources, coaching, recognition, and other support.

Key Points for Team Members:

- ☐ **Sign-Off or Coach.** The standard is very clear: if the improvement meets the criteria, the idea qualifies. It is not the manager's responsibility to judge whether or not they believe the improvement will be successful, sustained, or have an impact. *Don't judge, coach.* Either the improvement meets the criteria or it doesn't. It is the team leader's responsibility to coach—not to say **"No."**

- ☐ **Make Resources Available.** Whether time, money, or other assistance, the team leader makes resources available to the team members implementing improvements. Note: this does not mean that any improvement at any cost will be financially supported. Remember, one of the criteria is minimal cost.

- ☐ **Act Quickly.** Act as quickly as possible and do not procrastinate on signing off on improvements or assisting in the documentation, reward, or recognition process. Acting quickly is essential to gain and keep team members' trust in the system and in some cases to notify the group/Senior Leader.

- ☐ **Encourage.** Encourage the use of the system by suggesting that team members utilize the system. Continue to add energy, encourage team members to share improvements at the huddle, and show documented improvements from other departments. Never minimize the impact of seemingly small improvements. One improvement will not change the world, but the compilation of all improvements will begin to change culture.

- ☐ **Help Standardize.** Once an idea is implemented and shared, team leaders support the system by helping make the idea a standard, through communication and/or by updating department standards.

"Toyota production operators work with a team leader who follows the improvement kata. Within that framework, team leaders are also expected to actively obtain a certain number of suggestions from their team members. Furthermore, the team leader also helps team members fine-tune their suggestions, via mentoring, before they are submitted. This is very different from simply installing a suggestion box, so to speak, and actually has a different purpose" (Rother, 2009, p. 28).

Group and Senior Leader Responsibilities

"Daily kaizen can't happen without adding new energy to the system. This is the role of the leader in supporting daily kaizen: making sure that new energy is added" (Liker & Convis, 2011, p. 124). During the initial deployment of the new management system from leadership to the pilot hall, frequent P-D-C-A cycles may be weak or nonexistent. Starting deployment and coaching in the pilot hall is necessary so that leaders do not become spread thin, and P-D-C-A cycles for "adding new energy" do not become diluted throughout the organization.

As more areas in the organization start experiencing the new culture, Senior Leaders may go and see less frequently to any one particular area. Group leaders, as the culture is spreading, can take on the role of adding energy to the system. Then, the monthly meeting becomes the monthly check cycle to check the pulse of the area, listen to the top problems (asking, "How can I help?"), and rewarding/recognizing the top improvement winner of that area.

Key Points for Team Members:

☐ **Be Excited and Passionate.** Senior Leaders add energy to the individual, the department, and the system by bringing enthusiasm during rewards and recognition. Always notice the best in any improvement. Never minimize an improvement—though seemingly small to an executive leader, it may be a significant improvement in work flow to a team member.

☐ **Be Curious.** Ask questions and learn about the idea and the person implementing the idea. How did they think of it? What road blocks did they overcome during the implementation? What other problems exist around the improved process? Asking questions helps leaders learn about process and other problems that exist that an executive leader can help solve.

☐ **Help Standardize.** Many improvements should be shared, copied, and adapted from unit to unit. Provide ideas, resources, and check cycles to ensure that ideas, especially high-impact ideas, are standardized and shared throughout the organization.

☐ **Ask for Further Improvement.** Ask what the implementer could do to expand upon the idea even further. Ask if the implementer has any other ideas s/he is working towards. Each improvement should spark another idea.

☐ **Ask How You Can Help.** How can you support this improvement by making it a standard or sharing it with other units to copy? Ultimately, your engagement and active support is what demonstrates your appreciation.

A Pathway to Align Positive Recognition with Daily Management

The focus of other Lean transformations has been to eliminate waste, relying heavily on **Waste Walks**, or going to observe problems where the work is being done. Then, once a new process has been identified, leaders go to the Gemba to check and coach adherence to the new process that has been developed and deployed. Though elimination of waste and accountability to processes are essential along the Lean transformation curve, these practices are focused heavily on operational improvement. Without a balanced approach, waste walks and "holding people accountable" casts a shadow on the team members, i.e., the ones doing the work. Therefore, nurturing the culture by focusing on the positive actions and improvements is essential in the early stages of a Lean transformation. Reward, recognition, and coaching help leaders focus on the positive, and having a standard process for the flow of improvements helps to embed the positive actions and coaching into the daily management system.

An Improvement Pathway Defined

The pathway and process for conceiving, implementing, rewarding, and recognizing ideas needs to be streamlined as much as any other process, with clearly identified roles, responsibilities, and timing. Though this will change over time and be integrated into leaders' standard work, a clearly defined process helps the improvement system and positive recognition become embedded into the culture. This pathway, summarized in Figure 6.1, helps to standardize positive recognition and embed it into the culture. These steps serve as a baseline process to guide leaders to reward, recognize, coach, and encourage improvement on a daily basis. Example artifacts of the improvement system include Figure 6.2, an improvement form, and Figure 6.3, a management board.

Figure 6.1. The general pathway from idea to recognition. Though this is a fluid process of coaching and refinement, these steps help leaders integrate the improvement system into the daily management system.

Step 1: Idea Generation and Documentation. Once an idea is generated, whether the individual thinks of the idea themselves or the team leader encourages the team member to capture an already discussed idea, it is documented using an improvement system form. These forms have been adapted by many organizations, but should remain simple, visual, linked to the balanced scorecard, and not confused with problem-solving sheets. Example forms with documented improvements are shown in Figures 6.2 and 6.7–6.9.

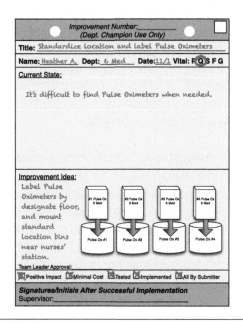

Figure 6.2. Example improvement system form. This form should be adapted by the organization, kept simple, and have built-in check points to help coach the process.

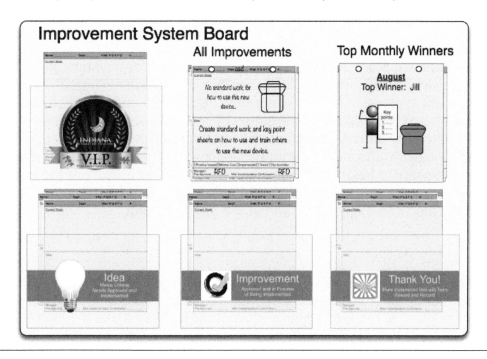

Figure 6.3. Example improvement system board. This board should be adapted, kept simple, and integrated with the huddle. Some organizations/teams will not need a board to manage improvements. Another example improvement board is shown in Figure 6.10.

Step 2: Coaching and Communication. As the huddle becomes an embedded daily communication and coaching opportunity, it provides a forum to share improvement ideas along the implementation continuum. Documenting ideas promotes swift and meaningful discussion to keep huddles transformational yet prompt. Depending on the type of improvement, the implementer may or may not brief the team leader prior to the huddle. Regardless of how and where the team leader is presented with the idea, it is his/her responsibility to coach and support the team member in their implementation idea, so that it can be presented again at the huddle as an implemented improvement.

Step 3: Testing and Implementation. Some improvements are implemented much quicker than others, and do not need to go through rigorous testing. Most should be simplified, if possible. A unit-based improvement system board may help manage the in-process ideas and improvements. The improvement system board, seen in Figure 6.3, is a standard visual board that helps teams with the overall management of ideas. This becomes part of the huddle and an area for leaders to go and see which ideas are in process and which ideas have been implemented. The example board is integrated with the monthly meeting cycle, when top monthly winners are selected and recognized during the meeting.

Step 4: Improvement Documentation and Sharing. In order to capture improvement stories and spread the positive impact of the improvement system, it is critical to document and share improvements at different forums, including the huddle, monthly meetings, organization-wide forums, rewards ceremonies, etc. Documentation allows for leaders to go and see and recognize individuals for their contributions. Many artifacts of this new management system, including problem-solving sheets, master plans, and the improvement system forms, are completed using pencil in order to decrease complexity and increase face-to-face communication. Electronic documentation of implemented improvements, however, can allow for more efficient sharing throughout an organization, especially those organizations with multiple locations. An electronic system may also be necessary to track financial rewards. Paper and pencil are the main method of initial documentation so that improvement discussion continues to be easily integrated into the daily huddle at the frontline level.

WARNING: Electronic systems to track rewards, showcase implemented improvements, and notify leaders of improvements to inform their standard work (i.e., going to the Gemba) are exceptional ways to make the improvement cycle more efficient. However, having an electronic system to submit and communicate about ideas typically lacks the daily communication and coaching of the idea necessary by the team leader. The huddle and face-to-face conversations outside the huddle should be the primary mode of idea communication and refinement.

Step 5: Reward and Recognize. Reward, recognition, and sharing occur for each and every improvement. This may change over time, depending on the maturity of the management system. The reward and recognition from group leaders and Senior Leaders should occur for each improvement until it is integrated into daily standard work for the leader. The improvement cycle is visualized in Figure 6.4. Tiered rewards and recognition are explained in the next section.

Key Points for Team Members:

☐ Go and see the improvement and the person who implemented it.

☐ Sincerely thank the individual (and reward if applicable).

☐ Ask what other improvements they are working on.

☐ Listen and ask how you can help.

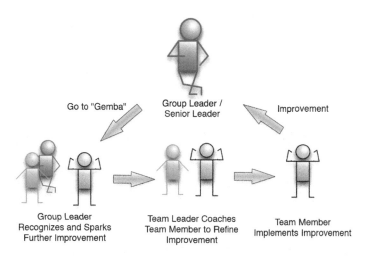

Figure 6.4. The improvement system cycle. This figure demonstrates how a group or Senior Leader goes to the "Gemba" to reward, recognize, and encourage further improvement. The team leader then coaches the team member to refine and implement the improvement.

WARNING: Though an idea should be successfully tested prior to reward and recognition, it is the responsibility of the team leader to ensure that ideas are scaled back if necessary to help with faster testing, reward, and recognition, especially in the beginning stages of the daily management system. The purpose of this phase of the improvement system is to promote creativity and ownership—not necessary rigorously tested improvements. Team leaders and group leaders can help standardize and sustain improvements.

Rewards and Recognition

Rewards and recognition occur for each implemented improvement. The implementer receives recognition from individuals within different layers in the organization, a monetary or cash value reward, and points aligned with the balanced scorecard.

Recognition Per Improvement. Each improvement is recognized by a team leader or higher leader in the organization, depending on the stage of daily management system maturity. Remember, daily improvement cannot happen without adding new energy to the system, which is the role of the leader in supporting daily continuous improvement (Liker & Convis, 2011). Over time, Senior Leaders, through frequent cycles, coach team/group leaders to add new energy to the system.

Reward Per Improvement. Each improvement that is implemented receives a reward, regardless of its impact or cost savings. Money may not be the ultimate motivator, but it helps leaders and the organization to put value and meaning to personal recognition. Some organizations choose to forgo this; others award $5 to $50 per improvement. Monetary rewards will later be used to integrate a complete organizational compensation strategy.

Points Per Improvement. Each improvement is awarded a certain amount of points, based on the priorities on the balanced scorecard, seen in Table 6.3. The points system is established in the policy, and senior leadership reserves the right to increase points as needed, based on the annual planning theme or a top problem, aligning the improvement system with an organization-wide initiative to leverage daily improvement. For example, the Senior Team may decide that for one quarter any improvements related to reducing hospital-acquired infections will be worth double or triple the points, helping all team members to focus and align with an organizational initiative at no additional cost. It becomes a mechanism to increase focus and alignment towards corporate goals, increases communication towards top problems, and doesn't cost additional money.

Table 6.1. The Point System

Vital	People	Quality	Service	Finance	Growth
Points	5	4	3	1	1

Note. Adapt the amount of points to align with values, priorities, and the scorecard. Above is an example point system and example priorities.

Why Pay for Improvements? Compensation for improvements is one of the first steps in an organizational compensation strategy that is introduced later in the Transformation Curve.

Monthly Winners. Each unit's leadership team selects a monthly winner. The form, the improvement, and the person's picture are all generally displayed on a visual board in a common area to showcase the improvement winner. The unitbased leadership team selects the unit's monthly winners during the balanced scoreboard preparation meeting, and awards the implementer immediately following the monthly balanced scoreboard review meeting. The purpose of having monthly winners by each team, area, and the organization is to have a P-D-C-A cycle around reviewing improvements and showcasing winners. When designing frequent improvement system winners, ensure the purpose is P-D-C-A.

Selecting Team-Based Monthly Winners

When selecting a monthly winner, the team considers which improvement has the greatest impact on safety, the corporate 6-Year Scorecard, and the team's objectives. Ultimately, the top improvement winner is selected as the improvement that best represents the team and has the greatest chance to be selected as the top improvement of the organization.

Selecting Group Monthly and Quarterly Winners

Groups can be divided by service line, Vice President, director, or area in the organization, depending on size and span of control within the organization. Some administrative areas, such as marketing, business development, human resources, and finance may be combined. Top area winners are chosen from the selected monthly winners from the units that are a part of the area. Quarterly winners are selected from each area, and for the organization.

Organization-Wide Winners Monthly

An overall organization winner is selected from the area winners. The Senior Team visits the winner in his/her work area, immediately before or after the Executive Team's monthly balanced scoreboard meeting. Select members from the board of directors may go and see the top organization-wide improvements on a quarterly or semi-annual basis to learn about the status improvement system and to further recognize employees. An example monthly meeting agenda with a monthly winner is:

Annual Rewards. An annual awards banquet is held and all monthly winners from the organization will be invited, along with their spouses. The top point earners will also be invited to attend. An award for the top improvement of the year will be awarded, with a grand prize equaling a significant amount in cash value. An equal prize will be given to the individuals with the most points. All Senior Leaders will be in attendance at the awards banquet.

Visual Recognition. Though the improvement system must be working substantially in the pilot hall prior to organization-wide implementation, once the improvement system has permeated the culture, having visual boards to recognize monthly improvement winners creates a way to recognize team members, a way for leaders to visually P-D-C-A the quality of improvements from an area of the organization, and timelines of monthly recognition. Figure 6.5 shows an example recognition board and 6.6 shows how recognitions can be tiered throughout the organization.

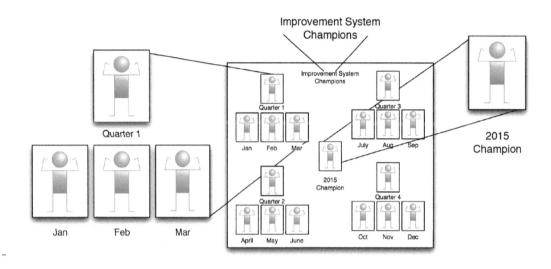

Figure 6.5. Example improvement system champion board, showcasing organization-wide monthly, quarterly, and annual winners.

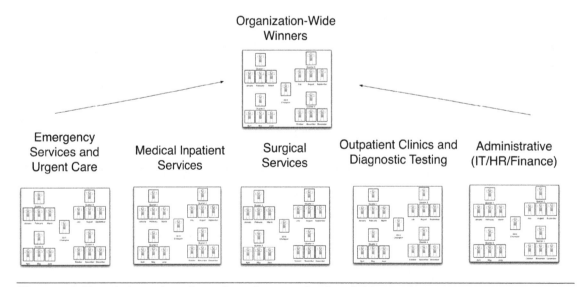

Figure 6.6. Tiered champions throughout the organization, linking to the overall champions.

120

Daily Improvement Examples

Improving Audibility of Bed Alarms. A team member in facilities management received a work order that the bed alarms were not loud enough. After investigation, he realized that the older and newer models of beds were almost the same, except the older models had only one speaker versus two, making them more difficult to hear. He then ordered and installed a new speaker on one of the older beds and tested the improvement out with a few nurses. His team leader then helped him standardize this improvement throughout the hospital, allowing nurses to hear bed alarms and prevent falls (IRMC, 2015).

Decreasing Potential for Hospital-Acquired Infections. When an inpatient with a communicable disease was brought to the diagnostic imaging department for testing, the patient sat in two to three different seats and used two different restrooms. One team member implemented the idea of designating one single chair and one restroom for isolation patients in diagnostic imaging, using visual management (i.e., signs on the door). This improvement reduced patient safety events (hospital-acquired infections) (IRMC, 2015).

Organization in Urgent Care. At an urgent care center, team members needed to lock and unlock three separate cabinets on a twice-a-day basis. As nurses needed basic supplies in these cabinets, they would often check one cabinet, only to realize that what they needed was in another cabinet. One nurse decided to consolidate the three cabinets into one cabinet, and organize and label the supplies. In a busy urgent care center, less wasted time looking for supplies results in more time to solve problems and spend with patients (IRMC, 2015).

Improved Return of Heart Monitors. A team member in the cardiology department realized that outpatients returning heart monitors were spending unnecessary time and effort returning the monitors. Previously, outpatients would need to wear the monitor for 24 hours, keep the monitor on, come to the hospital, and register, only to have someone in the cardiology department remove the monitor. The patient could then leave, go home, shower, and go about their day. Now, through this employee's improvement, outpatients are given removal instructions, a return bag, and a drive-up, drop-off location at the hospital (IRMC, 2015).

Improved Method to Distribute Radiology Contrast. A team member in patient access noticed that oncology patients needed to walk across the hospital parking lot from the oncology building to the main hospital building to pick up the contrast necessary for radiology. She suggested that she make a key point sheet and script for handing out the contrast, and work with those in the oncology building to dispense the contrast. This takes one unnecessary step out of the cancer treatment (IRMC, 2015).

Starting an Improvement System

Before initiating the improvement system within the pilot hall and/or the rest of the organization, ensure there is a a drafted policy. In addition, the Senior Team may want to test the policy and improvement system process by implementing small, simple improvements (without receiving an award). Once the system is ready to be piloted, follow the steps below to start the improvement system, either opened up to just the pilot hall(s), or the entire organization with an emphasis on the pilot hall(s):

1. **Introduce the artifacts.** The artifacts of the improvement system include the improvement forms, board, policy, rewards, and recognition. This should be done at the huddle and other forums, generally by a Senior Leader, especially in the pilot hall. (Do not copy the ones in this book, adapt them).

2. **Designate a champion.** The unit leadership team, including the improvement system champion (if applicable), should be identified. If this person is not identified, which is common for the pilot hall, the CI leader becomes the interim champion for the unit.

3. **Align with the huddle.** Integrate huddle questions to include prompts for the improvement system, asking for new ideas, asking if any support is needed to implement ideas, and having team members share implemented ideas. The huddle is also a great time for reward/recognition of individuals in front of the team to strengthen the positive outcomes of the improvement system.

4. **Leaders coach to the criteria.** Many team members may be used to suggestion systems of the past—suggesting ideas that are far outside of their span of control. Keeping close to the criteria, including implementation by the submitter, helps to reinforce the individual effort necessary for the improvement system. Ongoing coaching, especially in the beginning, helps gain traction in the right direction. Plus, self-implemented improvements are generally less time consuming to implement and have less red tape associated with them—therefore, team-member-implemented improvements help to create faster cycles of improvement, reinforcing the system.

5. **Coach and follow up quickly.** Once the improvement system process has started, follow up quickly every step along the way. Ensure you give approval and coaching to improvement ideas as soon as possible, have staff share improvements at the huddle, and record the improvements in the database so the group leader or Senior Team member(s) are notified and can reward the improvement quickly. Remember, make resources, including time, available. Do not get caught up in over-coaching improvements; keep it simple and allow staff to implement improvements, no matter how small.

6. **Establish daily and weekly cycles.** Establishing daily cycles to check/coach improvements is essential. Having at least a weekly cycle to input improvements into the tracking system, as well as having at least a weekly cycle where Senior Leaders reward/recognize improvements in the pilot hall(s), helps to add new positive energy to the system, sparking further improvements.

7. **Align with monthly meeting.** Whether or not you have a fully functioning meeting on a monthly basis, use your unit-based leadership team to select the top improvements on a monthly basis during the top problem selection/monthly meeting preparation. Immediately after the monthly scoreboard meeting has been conducted, with the appropriate members of leadership present, go and see the top implemented improvement and the person who implemented it. Reward and recognize according to the policy.

Improvement System Standard Work Activities:

Daily: Review ideas on the improvement system board prior to the huddle.

Weekly: Check the improvement system board to ensure ideas are moving through the system quickly.

Monthly: Select/reward/recognize the top monthly improvement winner.

Yearly: Reward/recognize the top organization-wide improvement system champion as well as the champion with the most points.

"Capture their hearts." The primary purpose of the improvement system within the Transformation Curve is to capture the hearts of team members through daily improvement. The improvement system is in many ways the simplest, yet most powerful artifact in the daily management system. When the process is designed properly, integrating rewards/recognition with the Senior Team, the culture will quickly shift to a culture in which problems are "opportunities for improvement."

The improvement system is the first step of an overall continuous improvement program, including team improvements, value stream improvements, and quality control circles. Leadership must first capture the hearts of team members and gain positive confidence in the daily management system in order to effectively put in place more advanced problem-solving artifacts, one of which is the cross-functional team participating in a kaizen event.

Roles and Responsibilities

Team Members. Employees utilize their creativity and innovation to solve problems and improve their work area. They complete the "improvement form" and have the implementation of the improvement reviewed by their immediate team leader in their unit. Team members need to understand that team leaders are also learning the system, and should be receptive to coaching from team leaders, system coordinators, and group and Senior Leaders.

Team Leaders. First and foremost, if the idea meets the criteria, the idea is acceptable and should be implemented and rewarded, no matter how small. Team leaders will coach improvements, suggest improvements, and look for opportunities to standardize improvements. Depending on the scenario, sometimes it's best to accept and celebrate improvements rather than overcoach to make additional improvements. Remember, this system is not about home runs, it's about engagement with the continuous improvement process.

Group Leaders. This may include Senior Leaders, depending on the size of the organization and the span of improvement system implementation. Go and see improvements as soon as possible to recognize and thank employees for their improvements. Based on the improvements that group leaders see, they should also look for opportunities to share improvements and standardize the improvements across the organization. Do not interrupt patient care when awarding and recognizing. If necessary, ask the team leader to take over for the team member so you can reward and recognize the implementer. Look for opportunities to standardize improvements to the rest of the organization. If an improvement has been approved incorrectly, coach the team leader, not the team member.

Unit-Based Improvement Coordinator. Typically a member of the unit-based leadership team, this person may be the team leader or a designee that is responsible for the unit coordination, submission, and tracking of the improvement system. The coordinator is responsible for monitoring and improving the flow of the improvements and proposing changes to the team leader as needed.

Improvement System Champion. As a member of the Continuous Improvement team, the improvement system champion is responsible for coaching the system to managers, proposing changes to the policy, and monitoring the overall performance, participation, rewards, and recognition of the improvement system. Depending on the size of the organization there may be multiple improvement system champions on the Continuous Improvement team, or the Continuous Improvement team and improvement system champion may be a single person.

Baldrige Connections

Communication *1.1b.(1).* Using the improvement system, the Senior Team takes "an active role in motivating the workforce, including participation in reward and recognition programs to reinforce high performance" (NIST, 2015, p. 7). Communication is much more than verbal, and as the Senior Team participates actively in rewards and recognition of improvements in the Gemba, it sends a positive message that continually reinforces the system.

Assessment of Engagement *5.2a.(3).* The number of improvements and overall participation rate in the system are simple, informal ways to measure workforce engagement from unit to unit and for the organization. Both the quantity of improvements and the quality of the top monthly winners from each unit are used to determine the level of engagement and improvement skills throughout the organization (NIST, p. 20).

Performance Management *5.2a(4).* The improvement system and its components, coaching cycles, and recognition cycles incorporate "workforce compensation, reward, and recognition" (NIST, p. 20). Compensation, reward, and recognition will be integrated even more as the organization continues to implement additional Lean culture change tools.

Knowledge Management *4.2a.(1).* The improvement system and its documenting, sharing, and standardizing of improvements is one way to "share and implement best practices" (NIST, p. 18). Having a central repository of all improvements creates an easy place to share implemented ideas to spark further innovation.

Learning and Development System *5.2b(1).* The improvement system includes organizational performance improvements and innovations (NIST, p. 20).Sharing, adapting, and standardizing frontline improvements on a daily basis creates a culture of performance improvement and ownership.

Service and Process Improvement *6.1b.(4).* Giving team members the authority and framework to improve "work processes to improve health care services and performance and reduce variability" promotes continuous performance improvement on a daily basis. (NIST, p. 22).

Creating a Sustainable Organization *1.1a.(3).* Having Senior Leaders engaged in positive recognition, encouragement of team leaders to coach employees, and team members owning and implementing ideas to solve problems and achieve organizational objectives creates "an environment for the achievement of your mission, improvement of organizational performance, performance leadership, and learning for people in the workforce" (NIST, p. 7).

Summary: Lean Culture Change Using an Improvement System

Before starting the improvement system in the pilot hall or throughout the organization the Senior Team and Steering Committee should have an established or drafted policy and general process for reward and recognition of improvements.

- ☐ The improvement system is meant to engage all levels in the organization, including frontline team members, team leaders, and Senior Leaders, in improvement activities integrated within the daily management system.

- ☐ Criteria for the improvement system include minimal cost, simple tools, implemented within the submitter's area of responsibility, tested, and successfully implemented by the submitter.

- ☐ Many small incremental improvements are the primary goal—not just a few large improvements—which will help engage everyone in daily improvement.

- ☐ Team leaders (managers) should be coaching improvements according to the criteria, and never saying "no" to an improvement idea.

- ☐ When improvements are implemented, Senior Leaders and other leaders need to act quickly, go and see, and reward, recognize, and learn from the improvement.

- ☐ It is the role of the leader, especially Senior Leaders during Lean culture change, to add energy to the daily management system and encourage further improvements.

- ☐ The improvement system will help change the huddle from transactional to transformational on all levels of the organization as positive improvements and improvements to existing improvements are discussed at the huddle.

- ☐ Each improvement is awarded a monetary reward, which eventually will be a part of an overall organizational compensation strategy.

- ☐ A point system is in place to give Senior Leaders the ability to increase point levels to focus problem solving and improvement efforts towards a single problem/goal at any time throughout the year at no additional cost.

- ☐ Visual management of improvement winners showcases improvements and quickly visualizes the teams following the improvement system process.

- ☐ The improvement system will later be aligned with team problem solving to further advance teamwork when team improvements are introduced.

126

**Case Study: St Mary's General Hospital, Kitchener, Ontario
Alignment Using Few Goals, Leadership Commitment, and Daily
Management**

St Mary's General Hospital's Lean culture change began in 2010, as leaders
began applying best practices learned from ThedaCare. At that time they initiated
a goal setting and communication process aligning the organization around 13
operational goals and 42 projects linked to those goals. Since that time both
the Senior Leadership team and Board of Directors have come to realize that
less is more and focus is powerful, and have thus reduced this to 3 operational
goals and approximately 20 projects. Now, senior leaders spend more time in the
Gemba (i.e., actual place) to coach daily improvement activities aligned on those
goals—and the Board is following suit.

"Limiting our goals and projects, aligned with the daily improvement system, has
positioned us to see the value of aligned work and aligned conversations
throughout the hospital," says President Don Shilton. In addition, the Board of
Directors understands the value of delivering on small numbers and the power of
the new management system. In fact, over the past year, the Board of Directors
has used huddles to begin each Board meeting. This 15-20 minute update on
the hospital's operational goals, aligned with other Lean tools, has created a
systematic transformational approach to continuous improvement, engaging
the Board. The conversations at this huddle include status of operational goals,
top contributors to current performance, and countermeasures to improve
performance. In addition, the Board is now also discussing improvements at their
own huddle—as they have accepted the challenge to own and implement at least
one improvement to governance processes per Board member in the upcoming
year—using the same huddle process as frontline employees.

In regards to Senior Leadership, as Shilton points out, "Most senior leaders have
been very successful over the course of their careers, and during that time they
have developed a standard set of tools and strategies they apply to problems.
Now, with a new lean management system, senior leaders have to lead
differently, which requires throwing out the old tool box and assembling a new
one. Not all leaders can make this transition and those who can't need to leave, if
the organization is going to be successful with their lean journey.
"If I had to do this all over again," says President Don Shilton, "I would start with
the senior leadership team and make sure they understood they need to lead
differently. . . then I would implement the daily management system." With that
very system in place, the leadership team has to lead differently and have the
active support of the Board. Shilton continues, "Now, the hospital is positioned
better than ever before to have the right conversations at the right level with the
right frequency to implement focused improvements."

(D. Shilton, personal communication, April 2015)

First Improvement from Board of Directors at St Mary's General Hospital

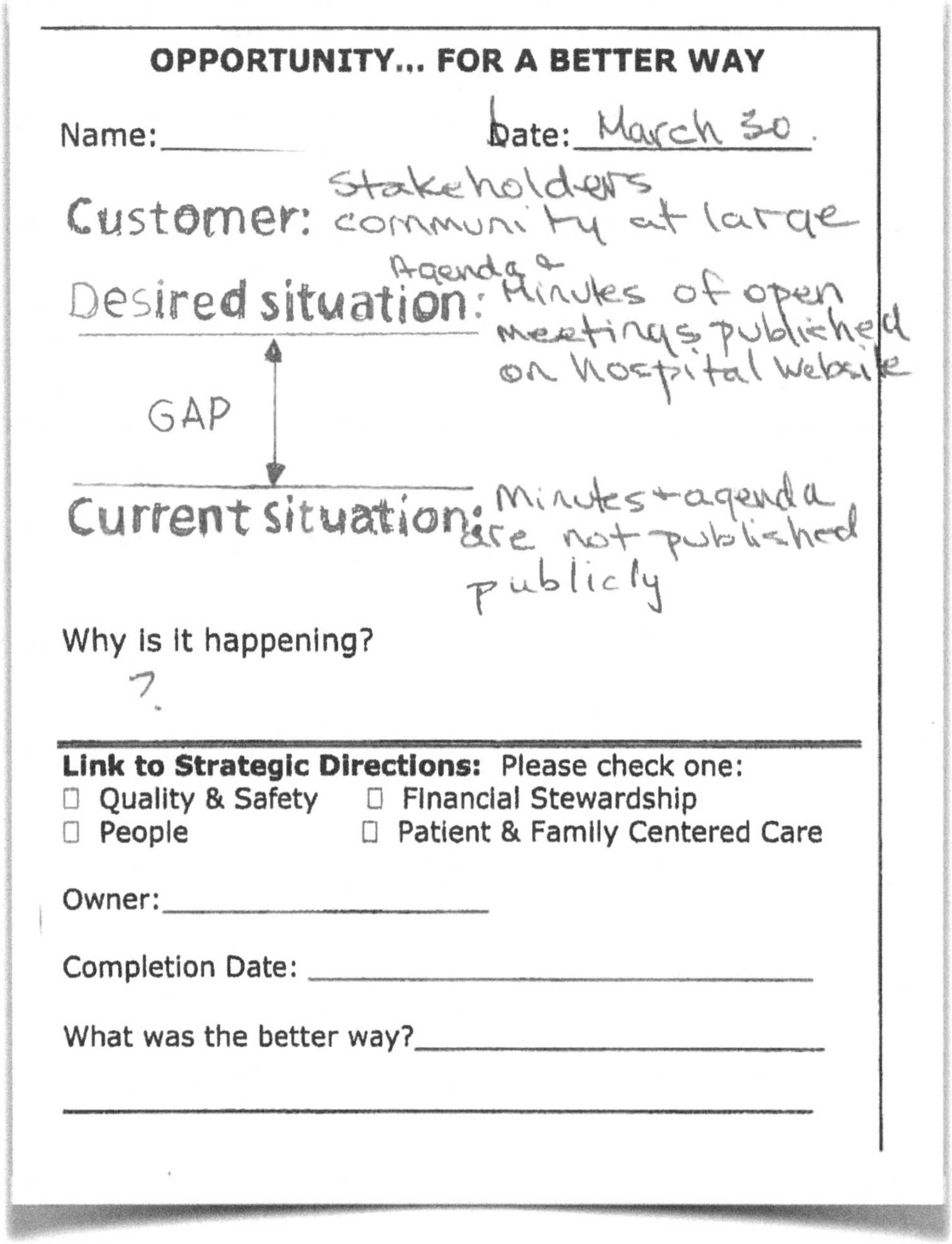

OPPORTUNITY... FOR A BETTER WAY

Name: _____

Date: March 30.

Customer: ~~Stakeholders~~ community at large

Desired situation: ~~Agenda &~~ Minutes of open meetings published on hospital website

GAP

Current situation: Minutes + agenda are not published publicly

Why is it happening?

?.

Link to Strategic Directions: Please check one:
- ☐ Quality & Safety   ☐ Financial Stewardship
- ☐ People   ☐ Patient & Family Centered Care

Owner: _____

Completion Date: _____

What was the better way? _____

_____

Figure 6.7. The first improvement from the Board of Directors at St Marys General Hospital. The improvement system at St Marys, introduced in the Chapter 6 case study, not only engages frontline team members but also the Board of Directors. The form, called an "Opportunity Ticket," states that the opportunity for improvement is for the board to post meeting agendas and minutes on the hospital's website to increase transparency.

Annual Improvement System Champion at Indiana Regional Medical Center

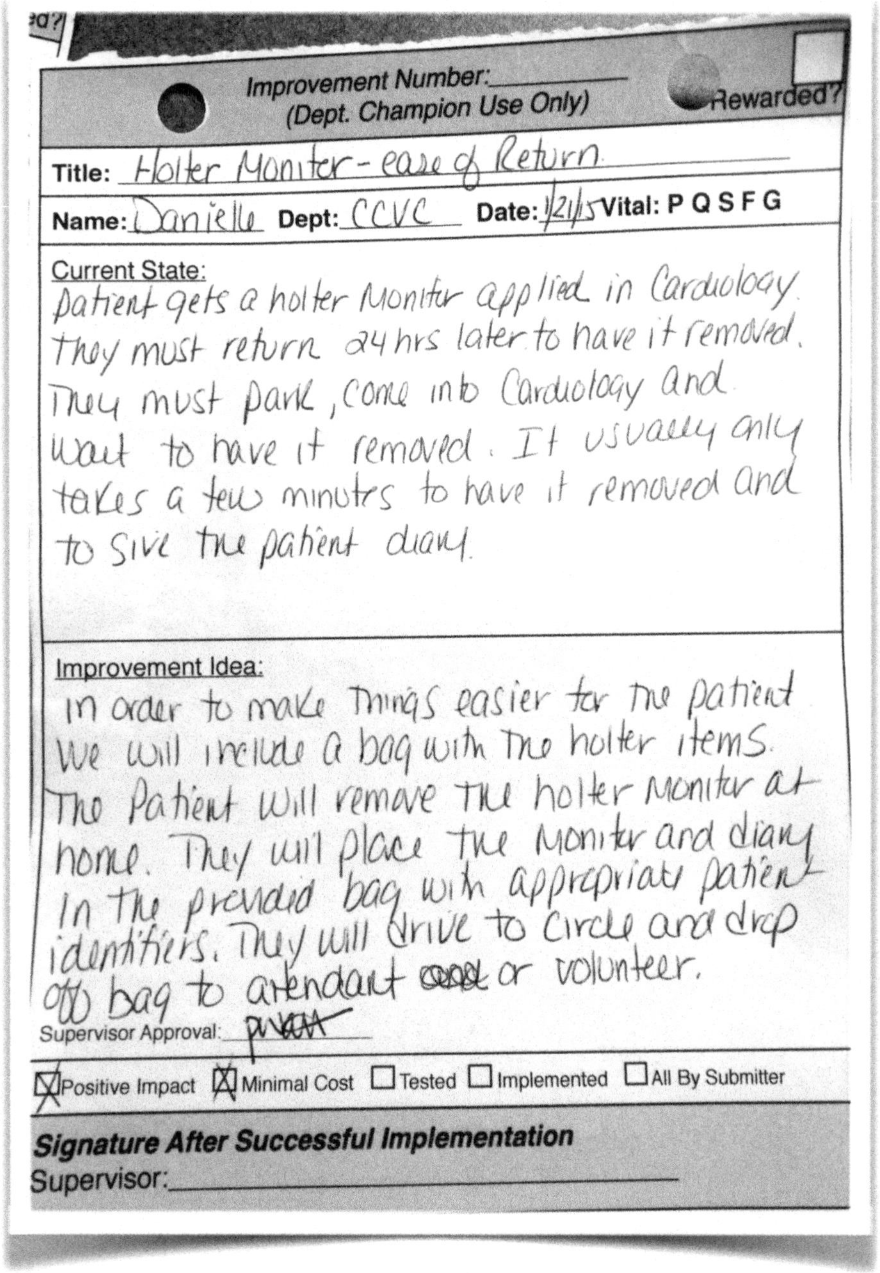
Improvement Number:
(Dept. Champion Use Only)
Rewarded?

Title: Holter Monitor - ease of Return

Name: Danielle Dept: CCVC Date: 1/21/15 Vital: P Q S F G

Current State:
Patient gets a holter Monitor applied in Cardiology. They must return 24 hrs later to have it removed. They must park, come into Cardiology and wait to have it removed. It usually only takes a few minutes to have it removed and to give the patient diary.

Improvement Idea:
In order to make things easier for the patient we will include a bag with the holter items. The Patient will remove the holter Monitor at home. They will place the Monitor and diary in the provided bag with appropriate patient identifiers. They will drive to circle and drop off bag to attendant or volunteer.

Supervisor Approval:

☒ Positive Impact ☒ Minimal Cost ☐ Tested ☐ Implemented ☐ All By Submitter

Signature After Successful Implementation
Supervisor:

Figure 6.8. Top Improvement of the Year from Indiana Regional Medical Center (IRMC). Danielle McCloskey, from IRMC in Indiana, Pennsylvania, generated and implemented an idea to increase patient safety and satisfaction by increasing the ease of returning a heart monitor. Previously patients would have to register and come back to the unit to have the heart monitor removed. Now, they can remove it at home and have a loved one drop it off at the hospital, or drop it off themselves without parking.

Example Safety Improvement from Excela Health

JUST DO IT IMPROVEMENT   Excela Health

Name: _____   Date: _7_/_1_/_14_

What is the problem? _Linen bags are not being_
emptied during the day and by the night
shift, they are too heavy to lift

Why is it happening? _No procedure in place to_
make sure bags are emptied during the day.

Potential solution: _Set up procedure to ensure bags_
are emptied during the day + during the
night

5 Pillars Impact (circle one)
Safety   Quality   Productivity   Human   Growth &
                                          Development   Margin

Owner: _____

	L	M	H
I			
I			
I			

Who will do   WHAT   by WHEN
use smaller linen bags & empty
when full according to new standard
Date Completed: _7_/_15_/_14_   work.

Figure 6.9. Excela Health's Solution System form, known as a "Just Do It." In this improvement, a standard was created which improved safety. Before the improvement, there was not a standard to empty linen bags on a daily basis.

Hallmark Healthcare Innovation System Board

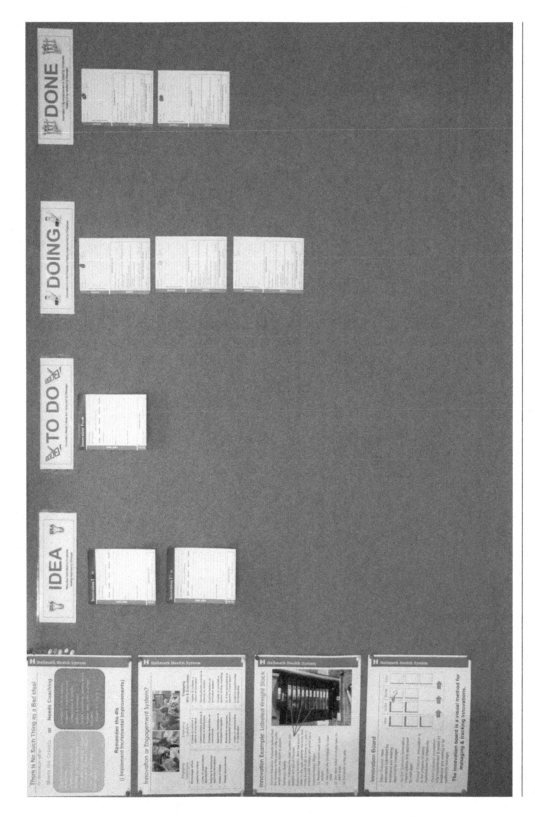

Figure 6.10. An example Innovation System board from Hallmark Health System in Medford, MA including training on the Innovation System (left) and Innovations in process.

Chapter 7
Safety System

This chapter will introduce your team to:

- *A system for increasing team member and patient safety.*

- *Safety system artifacts within a daily management system.*

- *Aligning safety with the daily management system.*

- *A case study about achieving world-class safety results.*

- *Example safety system artifacts.*

A System for Increasing Team Member and Patient Safety

"Safety is avoiding both short- and long-term harmful effects to people resulting from unsafe acts and preventable adverse events." (Joint Commission, 2012, p. vii). Healthcare workers' risk of safety incidents and accidents continues to rise because of the increasing age of the workforce, obesity of the patient population, and caregiver fatigue. As a result, the average cost of workers' compensation claims is $15,860. (OSHA, 2013, p. 2). "In terms of lost-time rates, it is more hazardous to work in a hospital than in construction or manufacturing." (OSHA, 2013, p. 1). All in all, "U.S. hospital workers are less healthy, consume more medical services, and accrue higher healthcare costs than the U.S. workforce at large." (Thomson Reuters, 2011). Figure 7.1 shows the top five causes of injury among hospital workers.

Poor workplace organization often results in poor safety for both employees and patients. For example, searching for safety devices, and supplies in general, both takes time away from patient care and leads to unsafe conditions. Disorganization leads to hazards such as tripping, slipping, and falling, for both employees and patients. With workers in the healthcare industry experiencing the highest rates for nonfatal illnesses and injuries (BLS, 2014) and preventable adverse events in healthcare being the leading cause of death in the United States (CQHCA, 2000, p. 26), having well defined roles and responsibilities around safety and workplace organization is a critical step in Lean culture change.

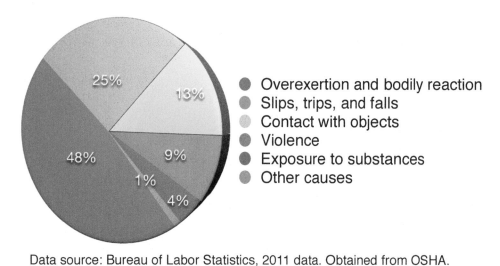

Data source: Bureau of Labor Statistics, 2011 data. Obtained from OSHA.

Figure 7.1. Top five causes of injury among hospital workers.

Safety System Artifacts within a Daily Management System

The **Safety System** is a systematic approach to improving employee, patient, visitor, and volunteer safety. This system consists of green crosses, safety audits, daily checks to increase Plan-Do-Check-Act cycles, and clearly-identified roles and responsibilities around these components. Problem solving and deployment of detailed plans (introduced in Chapter 5, Annual Planning) will support the ongoing development of customized safety leading indicators and actions. The purpose of the safety system in this phase is to begin building a safety mindset in healthcare staff by establishing clear visual management, Plan-Do-Check-Act cycles, and roles and responsibilities around safety. The components described throughout this chapter are not meant to be all-encompassing, but rather a baseline to start, continue, or build upon a culture of safety in healthcare organizations. Safety system artifacts include:

Green Cross. The green cross is a visual management tool to visualize safety in an area, department, and/or organization. It is based on a calendar and is typically a graph displayed on the balanced scoreboard.

Workplace Organization. Workplace organization goes hand in hand with both employee and patient safety. Having the right equipment at the right time is essential in keeping a safe environment.

Safety Audits and Checks. Safety audits are structured safety checks that include patient rooms, general areas, storerooms, and grounds. Audits are layered, and include specific roles of who will perform the audit and when.

End of Shift Restoration Checklist. The end of shift restoration checklist supports both a visual workplace and the safety system. It serves as a standard to-do list by an employee prior to shift change or the end of the day.

Leading Indicators for Safety. Visual displays include audit results, observation summaries, or near misses in an area. These process indicators help to track preventative and proactive safety initiatives.

Safety System Policy. The safety system policy includes how the artifacts of the safety system are deployed, monitored, and improved. It contains high-level safety expectations, references to standard process, roles, responsibilities, timeframe expectations for audits, and tiered problem solving.

OSHA states, "A safety and health management system can help your hospital build a 'culture of safety,' reduce injuries, and save money." (2013, p. 21)

The Green Crosses for Employee and Patient Safety

The green cross is a visual management tool used as a calendar to see safety problems, near misses, and safe days. In a daily management system, the employee safety cross is visualized under the People vital, and the patient safety cross is visualized under the Quality. The cross has each day color coded on a real-time basis to visualize safety. Figure 7.2 below is an example safety cross with color codes for both employee and patient safety status.

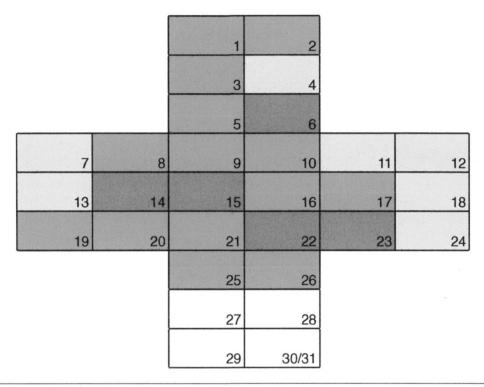

Figure 7.2. Safety cross shows the days of the month, color coded, at the huddle based on the days' safety results.

Table 7.1. Employee Safety Color Codes

Employee Safety Color Codes	
Red	OSHA Recordable/Reportable
Yellowl	ncident or Near Miss
Green	No Employee Safety Issues

Table 7.2. Patient Safety Color Codes

Patient Safety Color Codes	
Red	Serious Event
Yellowl	ncident or Near Miss
Green	No Patient Safety Issues

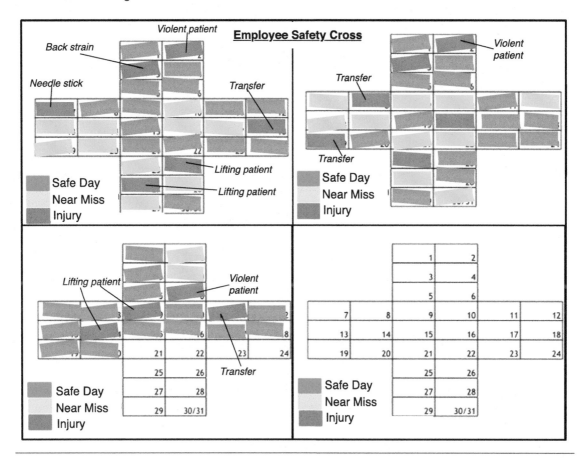

Figure 7.3. Safety crosses for employee safety used as a support row indicator on the balanced scoreboard. A general comment about the problem (e.g., needle stick) is written on the safety cross as a quick reference, but does not take the place of a problem-solving sheet.

The safety cross used as a support row indicator is seen in Figure 7.3. The safety champion or designee typically updates the green cross immediately before the daily huddle. Problems (yellow and red days) can be noted using short-hand problem statements, such as "lifting patient" or "transfer," but do not take the place of problem-solving sheets. As indicated in the case study at the end of this chapter, the organization-wide safety cross creates awareness on a daily basis about safety problems throughout the entire organization. The safety cross, colors, and communication mechanism should be adapted to meet the desired Lean culture change—keeping visuals simple, standardized, and focused on safety.

Did you know? The safety cross logo was used during the first safety week in Japan in 1919. A red cross is also used to symbolize many emergency rooms and the Red Cross. Today a safety flag is a symbol of a safety-first work environment (R. Horiguchi, personal communication, June 2014).

Workplace Organization

Workplace organization is not a program, project, or event; it consists of artifacts within a daily management system which align with safety and cultural change. Table 7.3 shows three acronyms for workplace organization, including 5S and CANDO. Serving the traditional operational purpose of eliminating waste and improving operations, workplace organization's other purpose is culturally based, providing a way for team members to think of and implement ideas within their span of control with high impact, yet minimal cost.

Table 7.3. Workplace Organization Acronyms

Workplace Organization		
Toyota's 5S (Japanese)	**5S (Translated)**	**Henry Ford's CANDO**
Seiri	Sort	Clean-up
Seiton	Straighten	Arrange
Seiso	Shine	Neatness
Seiketso	Standardize	Discipline
Shitsuke	Sustain	Ongoing Improvement

Note. Some organizations use 5S, 5S+1, 6S, CANDO, or other names. Stay consistent and focus on using the improvement system to change culture and create workplace organization.

Improving Culture. With an improvement system in place, team members can generate, test, and implement workplace organization ideas. These types of improvements are relatively easy ways for team members to make impactful improvements within their span of control at minimal cost and with little supervisor approval necessary. This begins to build excitement and additional cultural artifacts (visual improvement), which become prominent signs that the culture is changing.

Improving Operations. 5S/CANDO serves as the basis for more advanced traditional Lean tools such as kanban, set-up reduction, standard work, etc. Many workplace organization improvements during the cultural change phase will also improve operations by reducing time spent looking for items. As problem-solving sheets are used to identify root causes, countermeasures from problem solving may be added to the safety audit to prevent other problems from happening.

"A place for everything, everything in its place."

—Benjamin Franklin

CANDO, which stands for Clean-up, Arrange, Neatness, Discipline, and Ongoing Improvement, explains workplace organization within a system better than other acronyms, due to its close alignment with the safety audits and improvement system. CANDO can be conducted as an event-style group improvement activity to make fast operational improvements, or over time can be integrated with the improvement system to create incremental Lean culture change.

Clean-up (C). Workplace organization generally starts with cleaning up and sorting what's needed in that area and not needed. A ***Red Tag Area*** is a location where items that are not frequently used, are no longer needed, or are in the wrong area are placed for a period of time before being removed or relocated. A red tag, a visual identifier of a no-longer-needed item, can also be used to label items that are not easily moved or that cannot be relocated to a red tag area. An example of a red tag area is seen in Figure 7.4.

Arrange (A). Generally, determining the frequency of use for all items will help with arranging items most efficiently. Place items at the ***Point of Use***, or the location where the item is most utilized. Similarly, if an item such as a bariatric lift device is used less than once per month, it may be stored in the hospital's permanent storage.

Neatness (N). Neatness includes creating visual standards to help an area remain neat and organized. Labeling, outlining, and creating visual standards are great ways to keep areas neat and safe so that retrieving necessary supplies is easier and the standard is clear. Figures 7.5 and 7.6 are examples of creating visual standards.

Discipline (D). Disciplining and sustaining the improvements are essential components of a visual workplace, and often missed if 5S or CANDO is run as an event and not integrated into the daily management system. Layered audits and daily visual checks/inspections create discipline, identify problems proactively, and help identify opportunities for improvement to be shared via the improvement system. The Safety Audit and Checks section introduces a weekly safety/organization audit and daily safety/organization checks. Safety audit examples are shown in Figures 7.10 and 7.11. Other example audit items are in Table 7.4.

Ongoing Improvement (O). Visual workplace items are artifacts of Lean cultural change and deployment of a new daily management system. As leaders are using coaching and check cycles to energize teams around the improvement system, organization standards are introduced. As senior leaders conduct the 3Gs to reward and recognize improvements, they should look for opportunities for further improvement and standardization. CANDO provides a background to continually encourage improvements. One example is shown in Figure 7.7.

Figure 7.4. Example red tag system applied to a supply/equipment closet on a nursing unit.

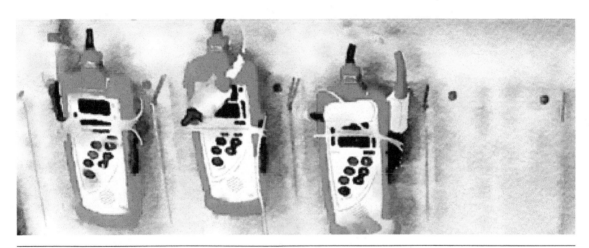

Figure 7.5. An improvement from a nurse's aid on a medical unit, standardizing the location of pulse oximeters. This workplace organization check can be added to the weekly audit.

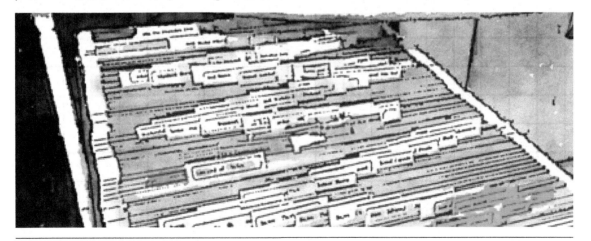

Figure 7.6. An improvement generated by a clinical secretary, who standardized the location of downtime forms in a quick, easy, and visual way.

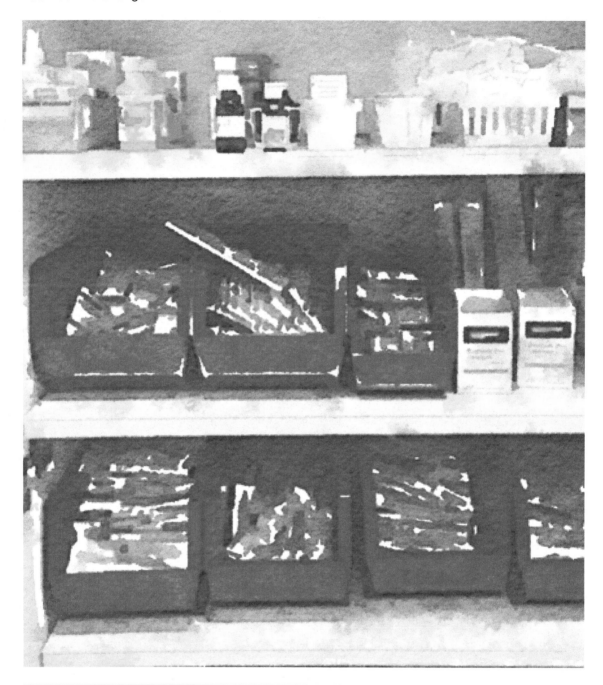

Figure 7.7. In an Urgent Care, one staff member noticed it was taking extra time and steps to lock and unlock three cabinets each evening and morning. She decided to combine the three cabinets into one. When the Senior Team member for her area came to see the improvement, he congratulated her, thanked her, awarded her, and asked, "What could you do to make this idea even better?" One of the many other ideas she had was to label each location so the items would have a higher chance of being in the same place each time. Other improvements that could be added to this improvement are labeling or visualizing the standard for the cabinet. These types of improvements and checks will serve as a prerequisite for a kanban system.

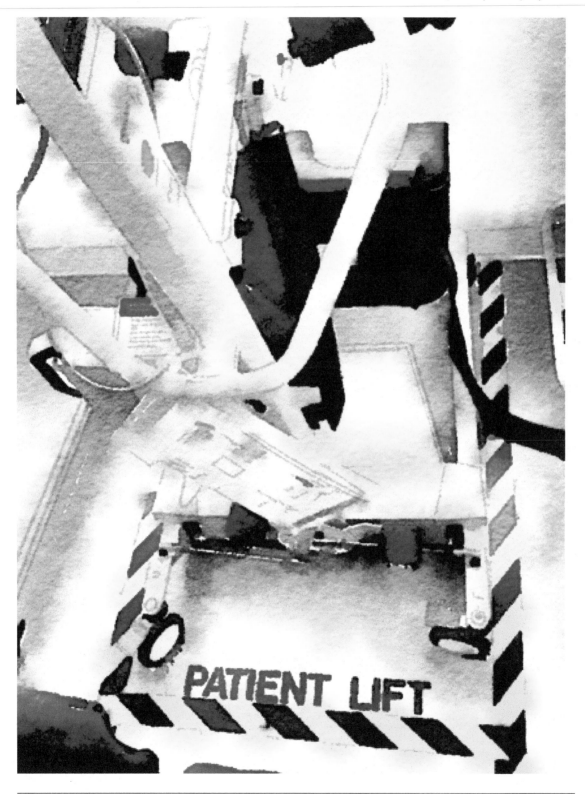

Figure 7.8. Standardized location of a patient lifting device helps staff solve problems proactively. Now, staff can know whether the lift is missing before it needs to be used.

141

Figure 7.9. This series of photos shows an Operating Room supply supermarket. This type of workplace organization was completed in a structured operational improvement event–based approach over time. The door is labeled, the floors have colored lines, and the shelving units are labeled to locate supplies faster.

Safety Audits and Checks

The **Safety Audit** is a standard check of the condition of patient rooms, shared areas, and common areas throughout the hospital and the rest of the organization. **End of Shift Restoration Checklists** are a standard to build mutual trust and respect between shifts. This may include restocking an operating room. There are generally two audits, one for patient rooms and one for general areas. Nonclinical units and units with no or only a small amount of patient rooms may only use one audit. As an organization, be sure to include all grounds, including the parking lot, entrances, and other areas. The audits yield a score so teams can visualize the unit's safety status and give the team leader direction on where to begin or continue problem solving. Later, the content of the audits will help guide safety walks and leaders' standard work.

Patient Room Safety Audit. This audit is typically a weekly audit (though done more frequently at the start of the system) to check the status of employee safety, patient safety, and overall environment of care. Typically, it is performed by a team leader aided by the area safety champion. The audit is a check tool to ensure that patients and patient rooms are in safe conditions.

General and Common Areas Safety Audit. The general area safety audit includes areas such as hallways, nurse's stations, storerooms, entrances, exits, public restrooms, and other locations outside of patient rooms. Examples for items to be checked during the general audit are listed below. Figure 7.10 shows an example of a safety audit. The safety audit form should be adapted to meet the needs of the organization and aligned with the management system. As the audit develops, more clear statements will be written clarifying each audit. Figure 7.11 is an example of the patient room safety audit and Table 7.4 shows example items in this audit. Note: audits should be updated and changed as different problems arise and other processes are hardwired. Adapt as needed!

End of Shift Restoration Checklist. Like the safety audit, this checklist is generally split into patient rooms and general areas. The end of shift restoration checklist is a list of to-dos which should be completed to ensure a successful hand-off from one shift to the next shift. A main purpose of this checklist is to increase transparency, mutual trust, and respect between shifts, making it clear what responsibilities need to be accomplished prior to the employees' end of shift. A patient room change of shift checklist will support hourly rounding and bedside reporting, giving the oncoming and off-going caregivers more time to focus on patients' healthcare needs. The checklist supports safety and visual workplace organization in clinical areas, administrative areas, and other areas. Table 7.4 is an example of items on an end of shift restoration checklist pertaining to patient rooms done on a medical unit.

Safety Audit

Completed By: _Suzy Q._   Date: _Oct 29._   Area: _8 med unit_

OK	NOT	Safety Item Checked	PSS?
X		Storage rooms have a standard visual and meet the standard.	
	X	Food/drink are not stored in refrigerators used for meds/drugs.	X
X		Personal protective equipment is available at appropriate locations.	
X		Soap and paper towels are available at each sink.	
X		Grab bars in bathrooms are in good condition.	
X		Crash carts are unobstructed.	
X		Grab bars to general bathrooms in hallway are unobstructed.	
	X	Linen carts are covered.	X
X		Area under sink is free from storage.	
X		Furniture in general areas is in good condition (not torn or broken).	
	X	IV poles on wheelchairs and stretcher are stored properly.	X
X		Narcotic keys are in possession of the on-duty RN/LPN.	
X		No narcotics are in common areas or out for easy access.	
X		Fire exits/routes are unobstructed.	
X		Exit lights are visible and lit.	
X		Fire extinguishers are placed in cabinet and are facing forward.	
X		Fire doors are positively latched.	
	X	Electrical cords are unplugged at wall, not the equipment.	X
X		Power strips are used for computer equipment only.	
X		Electrical equipment has current inspection.	

Total YES	16	* Divide Yes by Total to get %	
Total Items	20	**Place Audit Score (%) on BSB People Indicator	
Audit %	80%	***Start necessary problem solving sheets (PSS)	

Figure 7.10. Example weekly safety audit shows the status of standard audit items, as well as a compiled score. The score is tracked in the scoreboard and is a visual indicator of audit completion (see Figure 7.12 for an example). As problems are identified, appropriate problem-solving sheets or improvements should be generated.

Auditor(s):_____   **Date:**_____

Item to be checked (Y is positive, N is negative)	Room#	Room#	Room
Greet patient with a smile. Introduce yourself and the purpose of the visit.			
Have all the caregivers been introducing themselves?			
Have the staff been kind and courteous to you?			
Have you been happy with the care you are receiving?			
Has your pain been managed?			
Are your calls for help being answered promptly?			
Do you understand your plan of care? Next steps?			
Have the staff kept you informed about any delays?			
Call bell within reach?			
Room clean (no trash on the floor, floor not dirty)?			
No trip hazards in room, no loose cords, etc.?			
Patient looks presentable, clean and comfortable?			
Side rails up if appropriate?			
Bed Alarm if high risk for falls?			
White Board completed and accurate?			
Total Number of Y's for each room:			

Figure 7.11. Example medical unit's weekly safety audit integrating service excellence standards.

Table 7.4. Safety audit items for Urgent Care and Physician's office

Example safety audit from an Urgent Care Center
Storage rooms orderly, have standards, and meet standards.
All syringes are secured.
Personal protective equipment is available and in use.
Soap and paper towels are available at each sink.
Crash carts are unobstructed.
Furniture and floors are in good condition (not torn/broken).
Corridors are free from obstructions (carts, wheelchairs, etc.).
Prescription pads are secured.
Cabinets and counters have a standard and meet standard.
Oxygen cylinders are stored and secured properly.

> **_WARNING:_** The safety audit and results are not a punitive tools to score teams and identify people/teams "out of compliance." It should be used as a way to positively reinforce improvements and standards and a place to list countermeasures that will be checked on a frequent basis.

Safety System Leading Indicators

Leading indicators for safety are "proactive, preventative, and predictive measures that monitor and provide current information about effective performance, activities, and processes of an [Environmental Health and Safety] management system that can drive the identification and elimination or control of risks in the workplace that can cause incidents and injuries" (Campbell Institute, 2014, p. 44). Leading indicators may be used case by case, standardized across the organization, or used in a specific area with specific safety concerns. They may change as hardwiring of processes continues, more apparent problems arise, and visual management of the safety indicators is needed on the team's scoreboard. Leading indicators and support row metrics include:

- **Safety Audit Results.** Visualizing the safety audit results on the team's balanced scoreboard, as seen in Figure 7.12, an example of measuring safety as a leading indicator.

- **Safety Pat**. Visual management tools, like Safety Pat in Figure 7.13, can help show where safety problems are occurring, in this case measured by anatomy.

- **Process Indicators.** Leading process indicators, like those in Figure 7.14, can measure on a daily basis whether or not a process is being followed as the policy states.

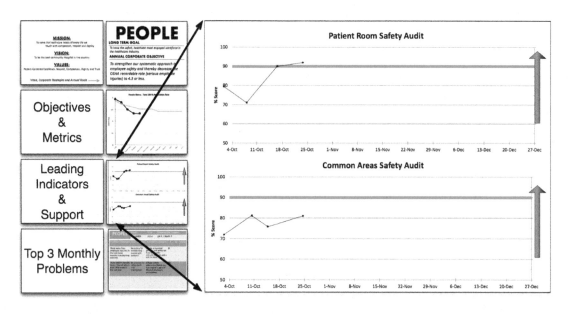

Figure 7.12. Safety audit leading indicators on a clinical unit. This example shows safety audit results from the weekly safety audit visualized on the balanced scoreboard.

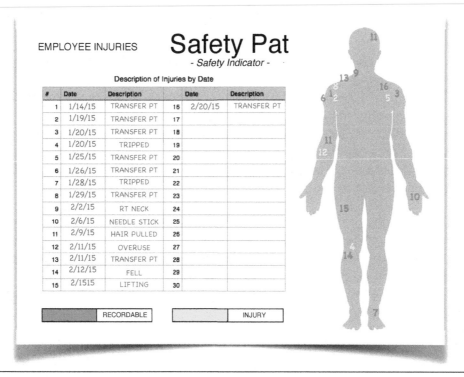

Figure 7.13. Safety pat, an indicator of employee safety.

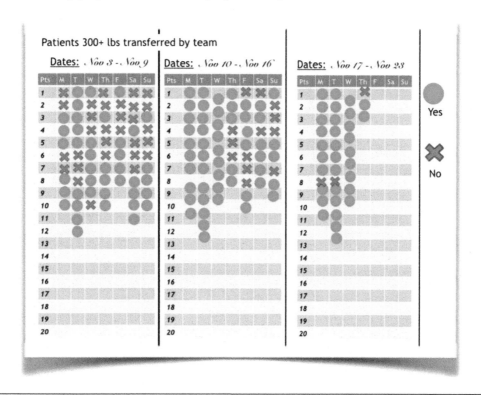

Figure 7.14. Example of leading indicators measuring adherence to the process/policy.

Aligning Safety with the Daily Management System

As leaders begin to develop standard work, and standard processes are being developed on following up with serious safety events (employee and patient), it is critical to begin to align responsibility and authority. At the beginning stages of building the system, follow-up and follow-though on problems to the root cause may be much more difficult than in mature problem-solving organizations where the skill has already been developed. The process below is an example process that should be standardized, engrained in the safety system policy, and monitored by the most appropriate departments (e.g., Quality).

Problem Solving. Standard roles, responsibilities, and timing around safety events using the problem-solving system and tiered daily huddles creates a reactive way to identify root causes and countermeasures. Agreeing to these standards creates alignment on minimum standards for problem solving. An example of how to align daily problem solving using committees, frontline teams, and the Senior Team is shown in Figure 7.15.

Problem Prevention. Layered safety audits and checks, from frontline staff to the CEO, are one way to proactively identify safety problems before they become realized problems. The standard frequency and content of safety audits becomes one of the elements of leaders' standard work.

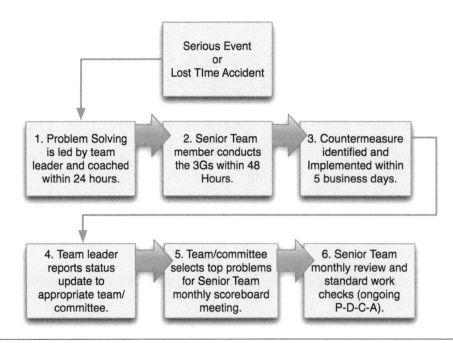

Figure 7.15. A process for integrating daily safety problems into the management system for the Senior Leadership team (VPs), existing committees, such as Medical Staff Quality Committee (MSQ) and Environment of Care Committee (EOC), and monthly checks.

1. **Team member/team leader conducts problem solving within 24 hours.** A problem-solving sheet and the problem-solving process should be started as soon as possible by the staff closest to the problem once the problem has been immediately contained. The root cause, countermeasures, and checking cycles should be identified within 24 hours and reported during the huddle.

2. **Senior Team conducts problem-solving review within 48 hours.** Within 48 hours, a member of the Senior Team should go and see where the problem occurred, i.e., conduct the 3Gs. The problem-solving sheet status will then be reported to the rest of the Senior Team during the next Senior Team daily huddle. During the 3G time, the Senior Team member(s) may need to start additional problem solving, coach the leaders and frontline staff member on their problem solving, and/or celebrate improvements that have been made as a result of problem solving.

3. **Test and implement countermeasure within 5 business days.** The countermeasure should be implemented as soon as possible after the root cause has been identified. The time limit of five business days is a standard that has been set in place for safety leaders to monitor how quickly the organization is implementing countermeasures to safety problems.

4. **Safety committee monthly checks.** The safety committees are responsible for checking the statuses of problem solving and proposing which countermeasures need to be adopted organization-wide. The leader of the area where the problem occurred must report to the meeting as one means to ensure follow-through on problem solving.

5. **Select top problems for Senior Team's monthly scoreboard meeting cycle.** After reviewing all outstanding lost time accidents and serious incidents, the respective committees, along with their respective Senior Leaders, select the top three problems to present to the Senior Team.

6. **Senior Team conducts the monthly balanced scoreboard meeting.** The monthly meeting, described in Chapter 4, is conducted by the Senior Team. During this meeting the Senior Team will review the top employee safety problems during the People vital overview and the top patient safety problems during the Quality vital overview. This meeting ensures a closed loop and communication among the Senior Team.

Baldrige Connections. Safety 6.2c(1): The safety system promotes and is one way to help provide a safe operating environment for employees, patients, visitors, volunteers, and non-employed care providers. The safety system addresses "accident prevention, inspection, root-cause analysis," and implementation of countermeasures at the department and organization-wide level. (NIST, 2015, p. 24)

How to Start a Safety System and Workplace Organization

Before starting a safety system in the pilot hall, ensure that the Senior Team has established a safety policy (or policies) and that there are time-frame expectations for safety problems.

1. **Integrate safety into the huddle.** Ensure that the huddle has both proactive and reactive safety prompts. Standardizing some prompts organization-wide may be helpful as well. Proactive prompts such as, "What improvements can we implement to keep our next patient from harm?" sustain huddles as transformational during this phase.

2. **Introduce the green crosses**. Introducing the crosses for employee and patient safety should be two of the first support indicators to be placed on the balanced scoreboard, especially in patient care areas. Begin to use these as soon as possible and update them during or just after the daily huddle to increase communication and awareness of safety problems.

3. **Encourage safety improvements**. Keeping it positive, encourage improvements using the improvement system around potential and actual safety problems. This can be done during end of shift checks, safety audits, and around the huddle.

4. **Coach problem solving of safety problems**. Continue to problem solve using the problem-solving process outlined in Chapter 3. On a daily basis, solve safety problems according to the timeframe standards in your policy (e.g., within 24 hours). Coach staff members on problem solving, giving support and guidance on an ongoing basis. Follow up on safety problems and near misses and follow through on countermeasures and actions. Remember, safety is the number one priority, so actions must follow suit.

5. **Establish unit-specific safety standards**. Using CANDO for an area within the unit or the entire unit, develop visual safety standards. Remember to clean up, arrange, establish neatness, create discipline through checks/ audits, and use the improvement system for ongoing improvement to the safety standards.

6. **Pilot the end of shift checklist**. Adapt the end of shift checklist to meet the needs of your unit. Get staff input and encourage changes to the checklist when needed. Pilot the flow of the checklist, key points for completion, and how team leaders will check/coach on a daily basis.

7. **Pilot the safety audits and checks**. Adapt the standard form to meet the needs of the area based on the organization's standard (e.g., number of beds, number of audits, etc). Adapt the criteria if necessary, or simply use

the standard audit until the audit becomes routine. Some units may be able to check on the actual status of the patient through visual safety checks and conversations, while other units may only be checking the condition of empty patient room. Visualize the results each week on the balanced scoreboard as leading indicators so the team knows the progress and current status.

8. **Follow the safety standards**. Review the policy or additions to the policy for employee and patient safety. Ensure that the unit will be able to comply with the standard timeframe goals for OSHA Recordables and Serious Events. Identify how and by whom problem solving will be completed on a daily basis.

9. **Develop leading indicators for safety**. Based on audit results, problems, and improvements, develop leading indicators to proactively identify safety issues and safe behaviors. Integrate those indicators with the daily management system's balanced scoreboard.

10. **Daily visual checks**. Team leaders should inspect each patient room and other areas immediately after or during shift change. This daily visual inspection is a check on the team member end of shift checklist and the overall status of safety.

11. **Integrate into the monthly balanced scoreboard meeting**. By integrating safety with the monthly meeting, a person (or persons) on the unit-based leadership team will be designated as the employee/patient safety champion. The weekly audit and daily problem solving informs top problem selection during the monthly balanced scoreboard meeting.

Safety System P-D-C-A Activities:

>   *Daily*: End of shift restoration checklists.
>
>   *Daily*: Visual safety inspections.
>
>   *Daily*: Identify safety problems and improvements.
>
>   *Weekly*: Safety audits for all areas.
>
>   *Monthly*: Update safety metrics and select top safety problems.

Note: A safety system serves both development and operational purposes. Later in the Transformation Curve, safety/organization checks will be used to sustain kanban (material management) systems. And the same P-D-C-A concepts will be used to check and coach process standards to stabilize and improve processes.

Roles and Responsibilities

Roles and responsibilities for safety are integrated into every layer of the organization. Below are example roles and responsibilities for a safety leader/champion, team member, team leader, and group/Senior Leader.

Safety Leader. Many healthcare organizations have safety leader(s) of some sort in departments like Safety/Security and/or Quality. In many cases, safety audits already exist but are done on a less than weekly basis, and not completed by managers or a unit safety champion. The safety leader should align, coach, and monitor the safety system, understanding that the objective is to increase both the number of safety checks the number of people responsible/support.

Team Member. Participate in the safety system by identifying safety problems proactively, implementing safety improvements via the improvement system, and following the guidelines set forth in the safety system policy. Complete the end of shift checklist to increase mutual trust and respect with patients, visitors, the leader, and a teammate for the oncoming shift. When a safety problem exists, whether or not it's an employee injury or preventable patient serious event, start the problem-solving process as soon as possible.

Team Leader. Be a role model for safety. Follow all of the safety guidelines on your unit and the guidelines set forth in the safety system. Complete daily safety checks, while inspecting 100 percent of patient areas. This means 100 percent of your patient rooms and 100 percent of the general areas. Complete the safety audit on a weekly basis, proactively identifying safety problems and reinforcing safety as the top priority. Encourage and suggest safety improvements to team members for their implementation. Be prompt with safety problem solving, following up with other leaders, and following up with staff on the status of safety problems.

Group Leader. Be a role model for safety. Conduct audits and safety rounds with team leaders on a regular basis to give a fresh perspective. Expect safety problems to be solved quickly by coaching, checking, and providing resources in a timely manner. Go, see, and coach according to the standard, and encourage proactive safety problem solving and safety improvements from staff.

"Train and sustain the primary lesson that any accident, incident, or shortcoming is essentially a 'message from the underlying system,' and that discovering and addressing virtually every supporting link in such a chain of causation (versus looking for someone to blame) is the only acceptable philosophy and methodology." (Naunce, 2012, p. 266) on "Just Culture."

—John Naunce

Summary: Lean Culture Change Using a Safety System

Once the Senior Team defines the basic safety system policy, the safety system artifacts are introduced to the pilot hall. A safety system summary includes:

☐ Healthcare organizations are by and large dangerous places to work, evidenced by a higher OSHA rate in healthcare.

☐ The safety system is a systematic approach to improving employee, patient, visitor, and volunteer safety. It is a sub-system of the daily management system.

☐ The green cross is an artifact to visualize safety in an area, department, and/ or organization. It can be used to show the status of employee and patient safety separately or combined.

☐ The green cross is integrated with the balanced scoreboard as a safety indicator/support metric.

☐ Workplace organization, CANDO, and 5S are ways to keep an area safe and organized. 5S stands for Sort, Straighten, Shine, Standardize, and Sustain. CANDO stands for Clean-up, Arrange, Neatness, Discipline, and Ongoing Improvement.

☐ Use red tags at the onset of CANDO and periodically during safety audits to visually indicate which items may be removed from the location in question.

☐ Safety audits and checks include a weekly safety audit for all areas of the organization, starting with the pilot hall. This may include general/common areas, patient rooms, supply/equipment rooms and other areas. This provides discipline in sustaining safety/organization improvements.

☐ The end of shift restoration checklist is a way to keep the workplace organized on a daily basis, using a standard hand-off as it relates to safety.

☐ Safety system leading indicators, visualized on the balanced scoreboard, are one way to track and communicate safety processes to team members.

☐ Safety pat is a visual management artifact to show types of bodily injury to aid in problem solving.

☐ Safety problems need specific timing for root cause analysis and countermeasure identification/implementation, which are spelled out in the safety system policy developed by the Senior Team and others.

Excela Health, Greensburg, Pennsylvania
Improving Employee Safety to World-Class

Excela Health first started Lean change in 2008 with a Laboratory pilot hall (model area for Lean) and focused improvement event. At that time, the number of OSHA recordables was nearly 233 at a rate of 6.8. Excela Health put "Safety" as the number one priority and used artifacts of a Lean management system to help keep the focus on safety and drive organizational change at all levels.

Each morning at Excela Health, the unit-based safety champion posts the organization-wide safety cross for employee and patient safety (Figure 7.16). Using the Solution System (Excela Health's Improvement System), self-implemented staff improvements have consisted of improving the safety, like Figure 6.9 in Chapter 6, Improvement System. In fact, Michael Pry, Director of Operational Excellence at Excela Health, boasts that 36% of the over 16,000 implemented solutions since 2008 have been focused on safety.

Laurie English, Sr. Vice President of Human Resources states, "Every other Tuesday our senior leadership group reviews our top three problems in safety and focuses our initiatives and priorities on projects that can improve and drive change." Additionally, when a top problem, like a blood body fluid exposure occurs, a meeting occurs with me, the department manager and VP to perform a root cause analysis with the team to determine opportunities for improvement." These daily actions, paired with strategic decisions such as sending our employee health coordinator to become certified in ergonomics, safety fairs, and cross-training Lean and Safety advocates are just some of the cultural change artifacts that have helped achieve a dramatic reduction in the number of employee injuries.

Some larger scale improvements improvements include establishing standard work around computer/cord set up, creating a flag system for visual management of high risk combative patients on the inpatient units, and standard work/training for safety devices. One major focus was and still is on winter slips, trips and falls by conducting a "What's on Your Feet" campaign and communication around wearing proper winter footwear. Excela Health's workers compensation has decreased from nearly $900,000 to around $130,000. Today, Excela Health boasts an OSHA rate of 1.8, which is one of the best OSHA rates in United States health care. Reflecting on their all-time low of 1.4, Excela Health's strategic corporate goal is to remain less than 2.0.

(Personal Interview, Laurie English, Sr. Vice President of Human Resources and Michael Pry, Director of Operational Excellence, Excela Health, 2015)

Excela Health's Organization-Wide Green Cross

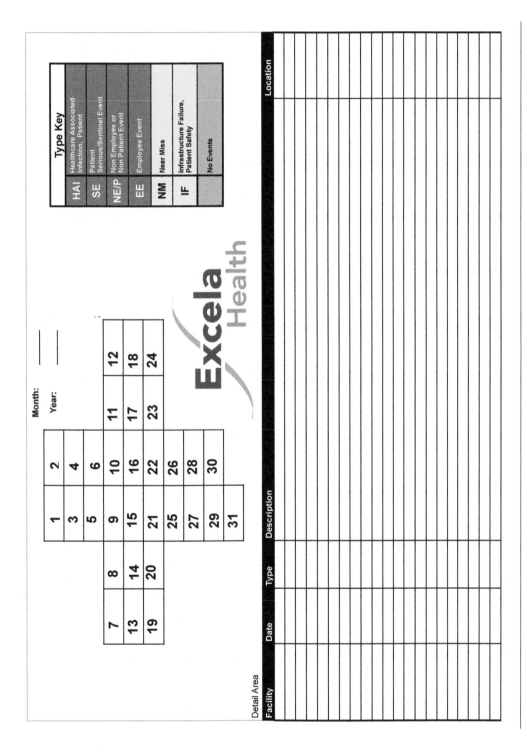

Figure. 7.16. Excela distributes the organization-wide safety cross for both employee and patient safety on a daily basis. Above is a blank organization wide safety cross.

Chapter 8
Sustaining and Next Steps

This chapter will introduce your team to:

- *The daily management system Introduction to Audit One.*

- *How to align and audit a daily management system.*

- *Performing and visualizing Audit One with Senior Leadership and the pilot hall.*

- *A leadership framework to support and implement.*

- *Foundations of Phase 1 Level B.*

The Daily Management System Audit One

The three dimensions to assessing a Lean management system include: 1) "clarify what you are working toward," i.e., standards for the team and organization; 2) "tell you where you stand relative to your standards and relative to your earlier status;" 3) "the results of an assessment will help you identify where you need to focus efforts to improve" (Mann, 2010, p. 212-213). The daily management system's Introduction to Audit One (DMS Audit One), coaching, and problem solving support these three dimensions to assessing, sustaining, and improving the management system.

Introduction to Audit One

Introduction to Audit One is an introduction to the first of the audits, consisting of organizational standards to assess the artifacts and interconnections of the daily management system (DMS). The Transformation Curve's Maturity Audit is between Phase 1 and Phase 2—this chapter is an introduction to that audit. The standards shown in this chapter focus on Senior Teams and the pilot hall, and should be adapted. The audit may be changed according to the organizational standard and team's standards. The artifacts assessed for frontline teams in the audit include the daily huddle, problem solving, balanced scoreboard, monthly meeting, leadership team, safety system, visual workplace, and improvement system. The Senior Team includes annual/master planning. As more daily management system components are introduced, the audit will expand.

The first dimension of the audit is to provide organizational standards for the daily management system. Secondly, it is a simple tool to assess the current status compared to those standards. Thirdly, audit results visualize the team's progress on and is integrated with the daily management system, as shown in Figure 8.1.

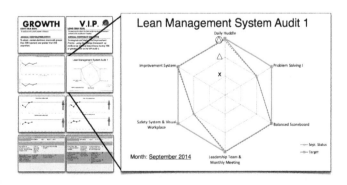

Figure 8.1. The audit visualized on the scoreboard using a radar chart to showcase the results.

Generating and Interpreting the Audit Results

The basic purpose of the audit is to have a process to sustain and improve the improvement process. Therefore, if a team does not have a DMS in place to a significant level, visualizing audit results serves little to no meaningful purpose. Though the audit will be used later to generate a score, a score should not be kept during the cultural change phase. At this stage of the daily management system, audit symbols are used rather than numbers. Similar to the problem-solving outlook learned in Chapter 3, the following symbols, seen in Figure 8.2, are used to communicate the current status

Figure 8.2. The audit symbols and general meaning.

Initially, a coach (e.g., external coach or CI team) determines the status of the team and helps visualize the results on the scoreboard. A seasoned coach has already been doing this continually to inform the coaching cycle, just not sharing it with the team until the time is right. Generally, the time is right when there are a few artifacts in the "controlled improvement" stage and a few components in the "needs improvement" stage. Visualizing audit results that are all triangles or X's only begins to demoralize a team leader and his/her team. Note, the "exceeds expectations" option is not available during this stage of the audit, because generally no team will exceed expectations beyond controlled improvement in the early stages of creating a daily management system.

Once a coach hands responsibility over to the leadership team for the audit, the team may start out generally accessing each artifact of the management system using visualizing the artifact names and status, as in Figure 8.3,. A standard time review of the Lean management system status is during the monthly balanced scoreboard review, along with check cycles that support that cycle. The Lean management system, visualized on the 6th column of the scoreboard, will have leading indicators and top monthly problems too. Once the auditing cycle is intertwined with the monthly meeting cycles, it may be time to introduce more specific standards for each component.

> **_WARNING:_** The audit is not a punitive tool used to rate a team, but rather a tool focused on positive improvement towards creating a Lean culture and management system. The audit is about learning to see and understanding the expectations of the new management system. If you score it you will fail.

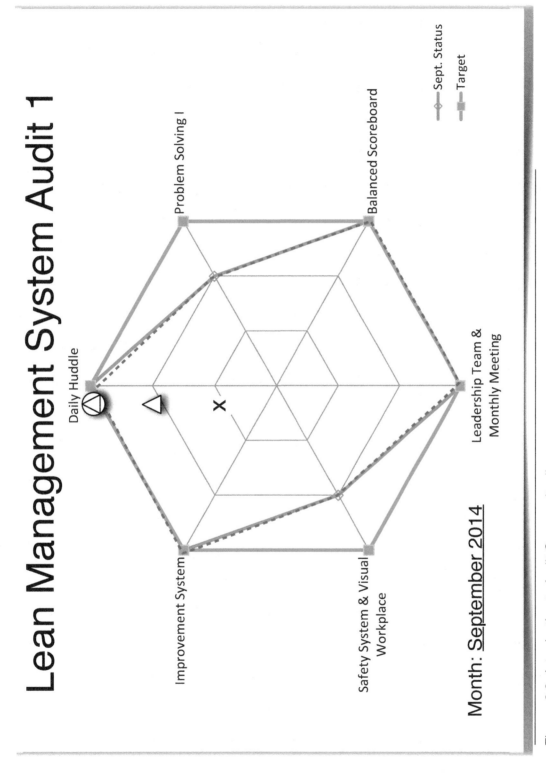

Figure. 8.3. Introduction to Audit One results diagram.

Auditing Senior Team and Pilot Halls

Keep it positive. The audit is a sustainment tool, not a tool to show Senior Leaders that a team is not performing. When a coach introduces the audit to either the Senior Team or the pilot hall(s), do not use the audit as a means to cast a shadow on a team or individuals. Ensure that teams are already doing well with the management system prior to introducing and adapting the audit. It is the responsibility of the coach, using a coaching cycle, to help the team use the daily management system to generate improvement. Use the audit to help integrate a formal P-D-C-A cycle around the daily management process, so the team can begin to self-identify and self-correct based on the standards presented in the audit. Audit standards are adapted to meet the adapted version of the management system as defined by organizational leaders. Integration with the monthly meeting is essential to sustain and build upon later artifacts.

Introduction to Audit 1 with the Senior Team. The audit for the Senior Team is seen in Figures 8.4 and 8.5. The audits are adapted to meet the needs of the organization's daily management system and expectations for the current phase of deployment. The artifacts, with ten expectations each, include:

1. Daily Huddle

2. Problem Solving One

3. Balanced Scoreboard, Leadership Team, and Monthly Meeting

4. Master Planning

5. Safety System and Workplace Organization

6. Improvement System

Introduction to Audit 1 with the Pilot Hall. This audit is very similar to the Senior Team audit, but does not contain annual planning (yet) and the wording of the audit is geared towards frontline teams. The audit for pilot hall(s) is seen in Figure 8.6 and 8.7. Artifacts of The audit for pilot hall(s) are in the following order:

1. Daily Huddle

2. Improvement System

3. Safety System and Workplace Organization

4. Balanced Scoreboard

5. Problem Solving One

6. Leadership Team and Monthly Meeting

1. HUDDLE

	Status	Average
The DAILY HUDDLE occurs at the same time and same place.		
There are HUDDLE PROMPTS that follow the vitals, including SAFETY prompts where applicable.		
There are completed HUDDLE RECORD SHEETS from recent days.		
There is evidence that staff are regularly facilitating the HUDDLES (check huddle record sheet for facilitator).		
Attendance is 75% or greater for all staff determined to be at the huddle and for team leaders on a daily basis.		
There are proactive prompts on the HUDDLE form.		
ACTIONS and FOLLOW-UP are being reported and checked at the HUDDLE (check the record sheet for evidence).		
PROBLEM-SOLVING SHEETS and IMPROVEMENTS are being reported out during the HUDDLE (GO AND SEE).		
The Team leader reports to another huddle with group leader (i.e., is the huddle aligned with the organization?).		
All staff attend HUDDLES frequently and have access to attend HUDDLES including all shifts and work-from-home staff.		

2. PROBLEM SOLVING ONE

	Status	Average
There is a PROBLEM-SOLVING BOARD, PROBLEM-SOLVING SHEETS, and PROBLEM-SOLVING STANDARDS in the department.		
RECOGNITION, TARGETS and CONTAINMENTS are listed on the PROBLEM SHEETS with detailed info on the top of the sheet.		
There's a large amount of PROBLEM SHEETS, evidence the TEAM LEADER is coaching his/her team on PROBLEM SOLVING.****		
PROBLEM SHEETS in bins B-D clearly identifying the PROBLEM STATEMENT (who, what, when, where, general why).		
PROBLEM SHEETS are used often and regularly, started by staff — and brought up at the HUDDLE (check for evidence).		
PROBLEM-SOLVING SHEETS have 5 whys done correctly to identify a ROOT CAUSE that we can change (use the "therefore" test).		
COUNTERMEASURES are being put in place to affect the ROOT CAUSE with a WHO and WHEN the action will be complete.		
CHECK CYCLES are visualized on the PROBLEM SHEETS and being checked and updated as needed.		
It is clear that PROBLEM-SOLVING SHEETS are moving in a timely manner through the PROBLEM-SOLVING BOARD.		
Confirmed PROBLEMS SHEETS when appropriate are being submitted via the IMPROVEMENT SYSTEM.		

3. BALANCED SCOREBOARD

	Status	Average
There is a 6-YEAR SCORECARD that aligns with the corporate SCORECARD that has been signed off by the Senior Leader.		
The team is using the standard SCOREBOARD layout (vitals, rows, and scorecards, watch numbers, and standards behind rows).		
Current year's SCORECARD TARGETS are visualized on the SCOREBOARD's METRIC row with graphs and show up to date status.		
The SCOREBOARD METRICS, LEADING INDICATORS, and TOP PROBLEMS are up to date (within a week).		
The SCOREBOARD contains LEADING INDICATORS that measure KEY PROCESSES to drive RESULTS including SAFETY.		
The TOP PROBLEMS on the SCOREBOARD generally represent the area's true TOP PROBLEMS.		
Generally, PROBLEM SHEETS for TOP PROBLEMS adhere to standards (see above) and have all have a clear PROBLEM STATEMENT.		
It is evident that the team is using the SCOREBOARD to manage and improve results, TOP PROBLEMS, and some processes.		
Many TOP PROBLEMS, METRICS, and INDICATORS are patient focused and VALUE STREAM focused.		
The area's SCOREBOARD is clearly a tool aligning daily management to monthly targets, annual goals, and the 6-year SCORECARD.		

Figure 8.4. Senior Team audit standards, page 1.

4. LEADERSHIP TEAM & Monthly Meeting

Item	Status	Average
The LEADERSHIP TEAM is established and visualized on the scoreboard (RESPONSIBLE/SUPPORT).		
The LEADERSHIP TEAM consists of key area leaders, SAFETY champion, and internal customer/supplier support when applicable.		
The LEADERSHIP TEAM has key stakeholder participation, including physician, quality, and finance representation (when applicable).		
The LEADERSHIP TEAM is scheduled for the MONTHLY MEETING for at least the next 3 months.		
The LEADERSHIP TEAM conducts the MONTHLY SCOREBOARD MEETING, reporting out on metrics, top problems, etc. as a team.		
Attendance at the MONTHLY PREPARATION MEETING by the LEADERSHIP TEAM has been at least 90% for 3+ months.		
Group leaders and/or Senior Leaders attend the MONTHLY MEETING report-out along with the LEADERSHIP TEAM.		
The MONTHLY MEETING follows the MONTHLY MEETING standards (KPS behind LEADING INDICATORS header).		
TOP PROBLEMS are checked at least WEEKLY to ensure movement on problems throughout the month.		
The top IMPROVEMENT winner is rewarded and recognized as a part of the MONTHLY MEETING.		

5. SAFETY SYSTEM & VISUAL WORKPLACE (6S)

Item	Status	Average
The area has an up-to-date GREEN CROSS for SAFETY.		
There are proactive and reactive SAFETY questions on the huddle prompt form.		
SAFETY and/or VISUAL WORKPLACE AUDITS are established, covering all locations, with scores visualized on SCOREBOARD.		
END OF SHIFT CHECKLIST established, in place, exposing problems, and checked frequently by TEAM LEADER.		
TEAM LEADER is conducting the SAFETY AUDIT and VISUAL WORKPLACE AUDIT at least weekly with daily visual inspections.		
PROBLEM SHEET for serious SAFETY events, ROOT CAUSE in 48 hours, COUNTERMEASURE within 5 days or better are being followed.		
VISUAL WORKPLACE standards exist, are posted, and followed in most areas (i.e., photos, diagrams, key points).		
A red tag area exists with standard process on how to frequently update/clear.		
High-use areas of material/information flow (nursing servers, nurses' station, etc.) have clear visual standards and audits.		
TEAM MEMBERS are frequently identifying and implementing IMPROVEMENTS to increase VISUAL MANAGEMENT and SAFETY.		

6. IMPROVEMENT SYSTEM

Item	Status	Average
The IMPROVEMENT SYSTEM is in place on the department (improvement board, blank forms, standards/training).		
TEAM MEMBERS are actively engaged in the IMPROVEMENT SYSTEM, as evidenced by IMPROVEMENTS in process of being implemented.		
Past implemented IMPROVEMENTS meet the acceptable criteria (use the improvement systems standard to check).		
IMPROVEMENTS are generally increasing SAFETY, VISUAL MANAGEMENT, standardization, and key point sheets.		
Generally IMPROVEMENTS are moving through the process rapidly (<2 weeks).		
Leaders are rewarding, and recognizing most implemented IMPROVEMENTS, including GOING and SEEING the IMPROVEMENT.		
The top IMPROVEMENT SYSTEM winner for the area is up-to-date and being recognized at the MONTHLY MEETING.		
Implemented IMPROVEMENTS are being shared and standardized throughout the department by the team leader.		
There are IMPROVEMENTS to already implemented IMPROVEMENTS.		
IMPROVEMENTS are being generated from completed PROBLEM-SOLVING SHEETS.		

Figure 8.5. Senior Team audit standards, page 2.

1. HUDDLE — Status / Average

Item	Status
The DAILY HUDDLE occurs at the same time and same place.	
There are HUDDLE PROMPTS that follow the vitals, including SAFETY prompts where applicable.	
There are completed HUDDLE RECORD SHEETS from recent days.	
There is evidence that staff are regularly facilitating the HUDDLES (check huddle record sheet for facilitator).	
Attendance is 75% or greater for all staff determined to be at the huddle and for team leaders on a daily basis.	
There are proactive prompts on the HUDDLE form.	
ACTIONS and FOLLOW-UP are being reported and checked at the HUDDLE (check the record sheet for evidence).	
PROBLEM-SOLVING SHEETS and IMPROVEMENTS are being reported out during the HUDDLE (GO AND SEE).	
Team members are reporting up from another huddle with their teams (i.e., is the huddle aligned with the organization?).	
All leaders attend HUDDLES frequently and have access to attend HUDDLES off campus.	

2. PROBLEM SOLVING ONE — Status / Average

Item	Status
There is a PROBLEM-SOLVING BOARD, PROBLEM-SOLVING SHEETS, and PROBLEM-SOLVING STANDARDS in the department.	
RECOGNITION, TARGETS and CONTAINMENTS are listed on the PROBLEM SHEETS with detailed info on the top of the sheet.	
There is a large amount of PROBLEM SHEETS — evidence the TEAM LEADER is coaching his/her team on PROBLEM SOLVING.****	
PROBLEM-SOLVING SHEETS in bins B-D clearly identifying the PROBLEM STATEMENT (who, what, when, where, general why).	
PROBLEM-SOLVING SHEETS are used often and regularly, started by staff, and brought up at the HUDDLE (check for evidence).	
PROBLEM-SOLVING SHEETS have 5 whys done correctly to identify a ROOT CAUSE that we can change (use the "therefore" test).	
COUNTERMEASURES are being put in place to affect the ROOT CAUSE with a WHO and WHEN the action will be complete.	
CHECK CYCLES are visualized on the PROBLEM-SOLVING SHEETS and being checked and updated as needed.	
It is clear that PROBLEM-SOLVING SHEETS are moving in a timely way through the PROBLEM-SOLVING BOARD.	
Confirmed PROBLEM SHEETS, when appropriate, are being submitted via the IMPROVEMENT SYSTEM.	

3. BALANCED SCORECARD, LEADERSHIP TEAM, & MONTHLY MEETING — Status / Average

Item	Status
There is a 6-YEAR SCORECARD approved by the BOARD OF DIRECTORS and COMMUNICATED to the organization.	
The team is using the standard SCOREBOARD layout, including annual targets, and with RESPONSIBLE and SUPPORT identified.	
The SCOREBOARD METRICS, LEADING INDICATORS, and TOP PROBLEMS are up-to-date KEY PROCESSES to drive RESULTS.	
The TOP PROBLEMS on the SCOREBOARD all have PROBLEM SHEETS and generally represent the area's true TOP PROBLEMS.	
The area's SCOREBOARD is clearly a tool aligning daily management to monthly targets, annual goals, and the 6-year SCORECARD.	
The SENIOR TEAM is established and visualized on the scoreboard (RESPONSIBLE/SUPPORT).	
The SENIOR TEAM conducts the MONTHLY SCOREBOARD MEETING, reporting out on metrics, top problems, etc. as a team.	
Attendance at the MONTHLY MEETING CYCLE has been at least 90% for 3+ months and planned for the next 3 months.	
Group leaders and/or Senior Leaders attend the MONTHLY MEETING report-out along with the LEADERSHIP TEAM.	
TOP PROBLEMS are checked at least WEEKLY to ensure movement on problems throughout the month.	

Figure 8.6. Pilot hall audit standards, page 1.

4. MASTER PLANNING — Status / Average

Item	Status
There is a MASTER PLAN for each ANNUAL OBJECTIVE on the 6-YEAR SCORECARD.	
MASTER PLANS include MASTER SCHEDULE ACTIVITIES and MASTER PLAN ACTIVITIES.	
Each MASTER PLAN ACTIVITY has a designated RESPONSIBLE and SUPPORT.	
Each MASTER PLAN ACTIVITY has a designated START DATE, END DATE, and CHECK POINTS visualized using the standard symbols.	
The MASTER PLANS have been signed off by the SENIOR TEAM and those RESPONSIBLE and SUPPORT for ACTIVITIES.	
Each MASTER PLAN has been COMMUNICATED with the organization.	
It is clear the SENIOR TEAM members are using the MASTER PLAN, as evidenced by the MASTER PLAN STATUS being up-to-date.	
The SENIOR TEAM is using the MASTER PLAN as a team to move the organization towards the vision.	
The SENIOR TEAM is using the MASTER PLAN to drive STRATEGY AND aligns organizational ACTIVITIES.	
The status of MASTER PLAN ACTIVITIES is reported to the BOARD OF DIRECTORS at least quarterly.	

5. SAFETY SYSTEM & VISUAL WORKPLACE (CANDO) — Status / Average

Item	Status
The organization has an up-to-date GREEN CROSS for SAFETY.	
There are proactive and reactive SAFETY questions on the huddle prompt sheet.	
There are SAFETY OBJECTIVES and TARGETS on the 6-YEAR SCORECARD.	
SAFETY and/or VISUAL WORKPLACE AUDITS are established, covering all locations (PILOT +), with scores visualized on a SCOREBOARD.	
PROBLEM SHEET for serious SAFETY events, ROOT CAUSE in 48 hours, COUNTERMEASURE within 5 days or better are being followed.	
SENIOR TEAM is conducting the SAFETY AUDIT and/or VISUAL WORKPLACE AUDIT at least monthly in PILOT and/or other areas.	
VISUAL WORKPLACE standards exist, are posted, and followed in most areas (i.e., photos, diagrams, key points).	
A red tag area exists with standard process on how to frequently update/clear.	
High-use areas of material/information flow (nursing servers, nurses' station, etc.) have clear visual standards and audits.	
TEAM MEMBERS are frequently identifying and implementing IMPROVEMENTS to increase VISUAL MANAGEMENT and SAFETY.	

6. IMPROVEMENT SYSTEM — Status / Average

Item	Status
There is an IMPROVEMENT SYSTEM policy and it has been communicated, including MONETARY REWARDS and POINTS.	
The IMPROVEMENT SYSTEM is in place in the department (PILOT +) (improvement board, blank forms, standards/training).	
Frontline staff are actively engaged in the IMPROVEMENT SYSTEM, as evidenced by IMPROVEMENTS in process of being implemented.	
Past implemented IMPROVEMENTS meet the acceptable criteria.	
IMPROVEMENTS are being implemented from problem sheets and previous improvements.	
IMPROVEMENTS are moving through the process rapidly, including REWARD and RECOGNITION by SENIOR TEAM (<2 weeks)	
SENIOR TEAM is encouraging further improvements by questioning when they GO AND SEE implemented IMPROVEMENTS.	
The IMPROVEMENT SYSTEM winner for the organization is recognized MONTHLY by the SENIOR TEAM.	
Implemented IMPROVEMENTS are being shared and standardized throughout the organization.	
The SENIOR TEAM uses and recognizes the IMPROVEMENT SYSTEM is positively affecting RESULTS.	

Figure 8.7. Pilot hall audit standards, page 2.

How to Align and Audit a Daily Management System

1. **Grasp the standards**. The audit standards are in place so that each team in the organization knows the standards. Once they have been adapted for your organization, know them well and use them with a coach to begin creating a daily management system. Generally, the standards are established in a particular order to help you build from one standard to the next and from one artifact to the next; however, a management system is not linear.

2. **Study the audit to advance the system**. By beginning to understand the audit, you will know where to make the next improvement within the daily management system. Improvements should be focused on both building the system and solving operational or people problems that exist with your team. As a leader, you can use the audit before visualizing the results.

3. **Use the audit to check the standards**. Generally, once you have most of the daily management system (the artifacts on the audit) in the process of being implemented, introduce the audit as a tool to get to the next level and to check existing standards. The audit is not a control tool, but rather a check tool to help sustain a maturing daily management system.

4. **Visualize results**. Using a radar chart, visualize results compared to the standard, with controlled improvement being the highest possible level of attainment at this point in implementation (circled triangle). As leaders, do not let this tempt you into scoring teams on the audit too early. When the radar chart is complete, with current, target, and previous month (if applicable), place it on the balanced scoreboard under the column dedicated to the daily management system.

5. **Integrate into the monthly meeting**. Like the other columns on the balanced scoreboard, check the metrics and leading indicators at the monthly meeting and at more frequent cycles as needed. Propose and select top problems in regards to deploying a daily management system using the audit as a guide. The audit will not encompass the different problems that you and your team are experiencing, so you may pick problems outside the scope of the audit as needed. Start problem-solving sheets and develop leading indicators as needed.

6. **Next steps**. As the daily management system matures, the audit will also mature. This includes more specific questions and detailed standards. Also, as other artifacts are introduced into the daily management system to different tiers of the organization, additional artifacts will be checked via the audit. Adapt the audit standards to meet the needs of the organization and the adapted daily management system.

A Leadership Framework to Support and Implement

Lean, in many cases, has been understood as a bottom-up and, at times, grass-roots effort, due to successful activities such as solving problems as close to the frontline as possible, implementing thousands of staff ideas, and empowering employees to design and deploy new processes. Both top-down and bottom-up leader styles must be developed and used to achieve world-class performance.

Lead from the Middle

Every leader within the organization must begin to lead from the middle and approach each situation determining what style of leadership is most appropriate for the situation—top down implementation leadership, or bottom-up supportive leadership, as seen in Figure 8.8. Implementation Leadership, or top down leadership, is associated with control. Supportive Leadership, or bottom-up leadership, is linked to frontline improvements. Neither style of leadership is better; every situation is different. A leader with a balanced approach can navigate the situation to best help individuals and the organization succeed, asking, "Do I need to be a supportive or directive leader?" The daily management system described in this book begins to give leaders a framework to lead from the middle, process the necessary information, and decide how they will help teams succeed, with either a top-down or bottom-up approach to leading.

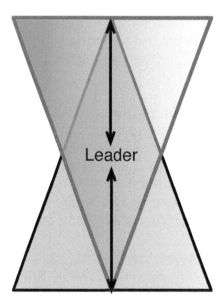

*Figure 8.8. **The Leadership Framework**. This framework demonstrates that leaders must approach each situation from the middle and decide which style of leadership is most appropriate. A robust daily management system provides leadership the artifacts to use the framework and navigate problems in order to develop people.*

166

Learning Implementation and Supportive Leadership

Start with Senior Leadership. For the most effective and efficient Lean transformation, Lean culture change must start with Senior Leadership. Senior Leadership not only has a disproportionate share of attention when it comes to new behaviors, but they must also use the daily management system to deploy strategy, develop leaders, and solve problems in order to improve organizational performance. This begins to create a new corporate culture. The Senior Team must learn the skills and stay ahead of the rest of the organization, make mistakes, learn, and lead differently. Lean culture change is a top-down, bottom-up effort led by leaders. Without a team to drive top-down implementation the organization will become unbalanced, losing confidence in the transformation.

Develop a Pilot Hall. Developing a pilot hall serves the operational purpose of introducing, testing, and learning new Lean tools, which is essential. More importantly, though, the pilot hall creates a counterculture aligned with the corporate culture. The pilot hall is a place to teach Senior Leaders how to support frontline team members (supportive leadership), establish and follow-through on plans to support the pilot hall (implementation leadership), and P-D-C-A the daily management system. Yes, a pilot hall is a place to develop standard work and change processes—but these changes are coming from team members through improvements and countermeasures to problems.

Introducing Phase 1 Level B, a Focus on Teamwork and the Pilot Hall

The primary focus on Phase 1 Level A in the Transformation Curve is on building individual capability, using the foundations at the Senior Team and pilot hall levels, and case by case throughout the organization.

Phase 1 Level B, the second phase of culture change in the Transformation Curve, includes a focus on teamwork with an emphasis on the Senior Leadership team and the pilot hall. The Teamwork Model, shown in Figure 8.9, visualizes a team leader's alignment and overlap with his/her group leader, team member, internal supplier, and internal customer. The same model is applied with the organization in the middle or a team in the middle.

As the daily management system begins to shift the culture of the organization, leaders will use the Leadership Framework and the Teamwork Model to navigate problems and build leaders. These models serve as the centerpiece of the next layer of foundations, known as the ***Management Cycle***, seen in Figure 8.10, as the daily management system is expanded throughout the organization with people development and operational improvement extending deep into the pilot hall, while changing the individual culture of Senior Team leaders.

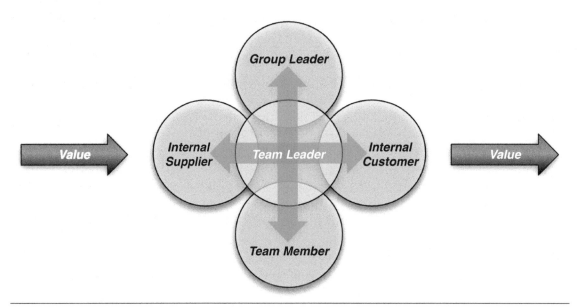

Figure 8.9. The **Teamwork Model** demonstrates how a leader or team aligns and overlaps with other individuals/teams. When implementing and coaching improvement, solving problems, establishing master plans, etc., be proactive with planning how decisions will impact the team(s) above, below, and side-to-side.

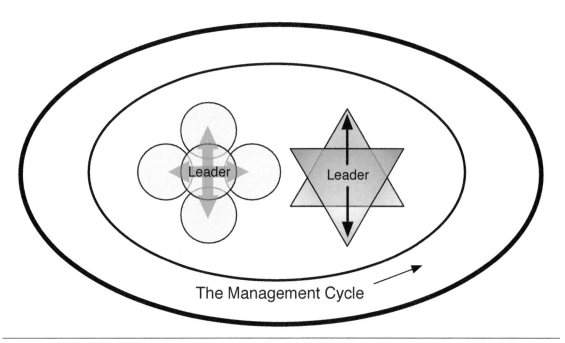

Figure 8.10. Introduction to the **Management Cycle**, a foundation of Phase 1 Level B of the Transformation Curve. The Management Cycle will help leaders align improvement activities of the daily management system introduced in the Transformation Curve's Phase 1 Level B.

Afterword
by Dr. Richard Kunkle

My journey toward Lean has taken twists and turns, as have most of ours. I served in the military as a Flight Surgeon and quickly learned the military system of command and control. It works quite well in some situations and is essential to military field operations and in certain healthcare circumstances. I learned the system well and relied upon it as I returned to civilian practice as an Emergency Department Director: I was good at designing protocols, initiating training and deploying solutions. But what I didn't see was much initiative on the part of a very talented staff to see and solve problems, proactively identify potential weaknesses or introduce new ideas or practices. I was lacking the bottom up support of creative ideas to achieve our goals. As Leuschel describes in the final chapter, both leadership styles, implementation and support, are necessary to become world-class. The leader must lead from the middle.

Through a number of roles from Emergency Department Director to Chief Quality Officer, my "Command and Control," leadership style which worked as a Flight Surgeon was failing. I did not have "my team" with me, lacking their innovative ideas, most of which were better than mine. I lacked creative input to change the work and support the improvements that necessary for operational improvement and cultural change. Once my very wise CEO asked me: "Rick, turn around. What do you see? I looked at him with the blank stare of utter confusion since what was behind me was his office wall. 'Where is your team?' was his response.

From there I began to search for a new system and read about the Toyota Production System (TPS). I was intrigued by the outcomes of the system, but could not understand how to create the environment in which it would work. I followed suggestions and after some considerable effort of exploring the system I came to the personal conclusion that while most of the tools of the system (5-S, visual management, kaizen, etc.) seemed to hold great promise, I had not seen nor had I any idea of how to introduce TPS into a system of multiple accountability and discordant motivations such as exists in healthcare.

So I began to try to tools. I had a modicum of success particularly when I applied the system within isolated areas. I had much less success applying them cross functionally. Even though I didn't recognize why this was happening, I was clearly seeing the culture, particularly the culture of mutual trust and respect at play.

Shortly after that, several events occurred in my life that lead to my departure from the active practice of medicine. As is wont to happen, at about the same time I engaged with Saint Vincent College, The Kennametal Center for Operational Excellence and my two Senseis, Mr. Rodger Lewis and Mr. David Adams. I have spent the last 10 years learning from them and answering many of the questions of how TPS is best introduced to organizations, in particular healthcare. Lewis' experience during the Toyota Georgetown ramp-up and the Transformation Curve provided a dramatically different approach to "Lean" than the tools-based approach I had previous learned and attempted. This approach was rooted in culture, mutual trust and respect, and provided a pathway for long-term organizational transformation— not just implementing isolated Lean tools.

Using the work that my Senseis have developed and that we at SVC and KCOE have evolved and that I have learned through hours of coaching experience, I have coached multiple manufacturing enterprises and healthcare systems both inside and outside the U.S. to successful applications of TPS to their organizations, using the Transformation Curve as my guide starting with leadership and a pilot hall—rooted in mutual trust and respect.

The Lean literature at first slowly and then more robustly began to take note of extremely high failure rates in Lean/TPS initiatives in U.S. industry. Our experience and proposition was that tools, introduced in isolation, enforced from above without a cultural underpinning of mutual trust and respect throughout the organization would never lead to a self sustaining, change embracing, learning organization. Conversely, a bottom-up approach without a top down implementation (i.e. leadership changing their personal and professional styles of leadership focused using the management system to communicate and execute strategy) might work, but would take far to long if not in tandem.

Once the organization is focusing on developing this core cultural value of mutual trust and respect, the more tools based activities are introduced at the lowest levels and the highest levels. Why the dichotomous introductions? So that leadership can gain a first hand understanding of the difficulties these changes bring to the front lines. So leadership can understand and coach. So leadership can practice the "3Gs": "Go and See, Get the Facts and Grasp the Situation" and the "3Ps": "People, Passion, Patience" at the front lines and Senior Leader level, while understanding the challenges the changes present to staff to practice the.

The implementation plan, the Transformation Curve, is a carefully designed, but infinitely adaptable pathway for introduction of both the cultural and technical tools of TPS/Lean/OE. Without it, it is much more likely you will achieve some isolated improvements; in the best cases, change will take a very long time. With the Transformation Curve your likelihood of success in achieving a high performing organization and world-class results is significantly enhanced.

— Dr. Richard Kunkle
Learner in Operational Excellence

Postscript
by Dominic Paccapaniccia

I have worked as the Chief Operating Officer at Indiana Regional Medical Center (IRMC) for 10 years. My background also includes both public accounting and human resources experience. As of the summer of 2013, IRMC leaders had not taken the traditional approach to Lean, but rather took the approach of starting with leadership learning, using, and leading a new leadership and management system. I had the opportunity to be a key instigator of the Senior Team starting daily huddles, one-by-one problem solving, visualizing results via a balanced scoreboard, and checking those results via daily, weekly, monthly, and quarterly checks. I then lead my operational direct reports through the same process, and am currently coaching these same direct reports to lead the same processes with frontline teams to engage frontline staff.

When presented with a daily Lean management system I jumped into the deep end because it made sense. It was clear that we needed to change the way we lead and manage and interact with each other regarding solving problems. It's been a challenge though, leading through this new system because I am learning, leading, and teaching in very short cycles.

Like many other healthcare organizations, for years we were successful. Now, though, healthcare is changing very rapidly and it's much more difficult to be successful. Being successful isn't as easy—yet leading and managing the same ways we've always have becomes a method of choice, because many times habit is easier than learning and leading a new way. We as leaders have a choice—do we continue the traditional way we lead and have always done things, or learn and try a new way of leadership and management?

Why would we continue to use/apply the traditional approaches to leading and managing people and work that we learned say 30 years ago? What else do we have from 30 years ago that works well in a completely different world and environment? Why would we do the same thing over and over and expecting a different result? That may be likened to an insanity approach.

When we first started the process, I didn't understand all the pieces of the system (I still don't), but it made sense. It seemed to be a viable alternative rather than to just doing more and more, or just doing things faster and faster (the previous way of thinking). This alternative approach focuses on teamwork; checks (Plan, Do, Check, Act cycles); and problem solving at most appropriate organizational level using root cause analysis instead of firefighting and crisis management. Now when I'm engaged in problem solving I am more inclined to gather people to produce a process map and focus on the process rather than focusing or faulting the people or an individual person.

This approach to deployment of the new management system not only showed me and our Senior Team's commitment to the process, but it reinforced my own knowledge base. Two years later, I know much more about the challenges that our staff face, exponentially more than before. My leadership theory emphasizes personal responsibility – each and every employee – each and every day – each and every customer encounter.

Am I an expert in daily huddles, problem solving, balanced scoreboards, monthly meetings, etc.? No. Am I learning? Yes. Is it making a difference? Yes. My approach is now very different – I used to be goal and results orientated only. That approach works early on and when there is low hanging fruit but it also has limitations. I have learned that to consistently improve and achieve results – ultimately – I'm responsible and I need to go deeper into the plan and process to engage staff to achieve results.

Strategically we have aligned our Board of Directors; Senior Team, middle management, and staff thorough our deployment of goals and ongoing checking and acting on problems and actions to achieve those goals. Now deployment is more robust and effective, which helps us engage more than superficial visions and goals, etc.

Our next steps include further deployment of the leadership system and more effective and frequent problem solving. Within our organization there's a multitude of leadership and management styles. This Lean management system works regardless of personality and leadership and management styles – in fact it enables us to transform our leadership and management styles.

It is clear that Leuschel has a long-term plan learned from Lewis, his Sensei, how to change organizations using key learnings from the Toyota Production System, i.e. the Transformation Curve. We are incrementally learning and applying that plan to change culture and strive for world-class results. The next steps for me are to continue to learn, lead, teach, and coach. What started as an intuitive decision has evolved into an intelligent choice to take us through the white waters ahead.

Alignment of strategies, initiatives, goals, objectives, tactics, etc. are imperative for a successful organization – often assumed, rarely achieved. This Lean leadership and management approach takes a while to assimilate into your work style (rather than additional work) – it took me a year. Master planning – coupled with PDCA cycles – are a requirement to ensure process improvement and ultimately goal achievement. Execution is the most important part of planning and this approach requires transparency and deployment. This approach engages employees in problem solving at the most appropriate organizational level. Root cause analysis drives to the cause of the problem so that they may be fixed rather than deal over and over again with the symptoms.

— Dominic Paccapaniccia
Chief Operating Officer at Indiana Regional Medical Center

A Theory of the Evolution and Professionalization of Lean in Healthcare

Lean is currently defined as "creating more value for customers with fewer resources" (LEI, 2015) and was previously defined as "eliminating waste." The term "Lean" describes the **Toyota Production System (TPS)**—a by-product of Toyota's culture. Lean/TPS has been adapted into many different organizations and industries, generally starting with automobile, disseminating into manufacturing, and then into healthcare and other industries. Now, healthcare organizations are adopting Lean faster than ever before, modeling their journeys on previous successes, adaptations, and professionalized best practices. Understanding the approach organizations have taken, as well as common conclusions and mistakes, is critical to grasping a better pathway towards transforming organizations and incremental culture change.

This chapter touches on several major points in North American Lean/TPS history, including Toyota's cultural revolutionary transformation New United Motor Manufacturing Inc. in 1983; incremental cultural change from Toyota's first fully owned North American plant in Georgetown, Kentucky, in 1986; the publication of *The Machine That Changed the World* (1990); establishment of the Toyota Supplier Support Center in 1992; an introduction of Lean in healthcare in 2002; and the breakthrough of a Lean management system in 2008, one of the best examples of Lean being utilized in healthcare in the country. Figure A.1 shows these and other critical moments in Lean transformation in North American healthcare. Understanding the process of **Professionalization** gives insight into common conclusions and evidence that the North American implementation of Lean needs to have a large-scale **Plan-Do-Study-Adjust (P-D-S-A)** cycle to grasp other methods of Lean transformation and adjust the common practices.

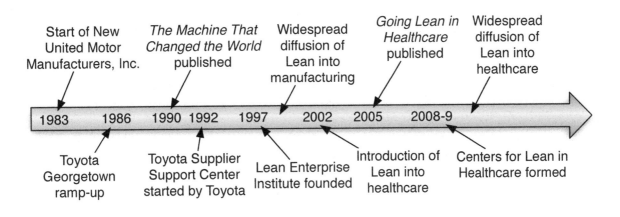

Figure A.1. An abbreviated history of Lean in healthcare.

Mechanisms for Change

Grasping why and how organizations learn from each other is essential in understanding how organizations have learned and adapted the TPS, aka "Lean." DiMaggio and Powell (1983) identify three mechanisms by which institutional isomorphic change occurs: *coercive*, *mimetic*, and *normative isomorphism*. "***Coercive Isomorphism*** results from both formal and informal pressures exerted on an organization by other organizations upon which they are dependent" (DiMaggio & Powell, 1983, p. 150). ***Mimetic Isomorphism*** results when an organization faces a problem with unclear solutions and a search yields a solution with little expense (p. 151). ***Normative Isomorphism*** stems primarily from ***Professionalization***, which includes "the resting of formal education and of legitimation in a cognitive base produced by university specialists; and the growth and elaboration of professional networks that span organizations and across which new models diffuse rapidly" (p. 152). Using these mechanisms as a lens to observe the Lean movement in North America provides evidence that the Lean healthcare industry must "Plan-Do-Study-Adjust" the approach as it moves forward.

New United Motor Manufacturing Inc., 1983.

The New United Motor Manufacturing, Inc. (NUMMI) was a 1983 joint venture between Toyota and General Motors. For Toyota, the main purposes of the alliance were rapid US market entry and learning to work with an American workforce (Inkpen, 2005, p. 117). The old culture, and workforce, at NUMMI was an "extraordinarily 'bad' one" that at the time "produced some of the worst quality in the GM system" (Shook, 2010, pp. 2–3). But within one year of partnering with Toyota, NUMMI had completely transformed its workforce by embodying the Toyota Culture, resulting in the best quality (Shook, 2010).

"One problem [of General Motors] was that managers assigned to NUMMI in the early years of the joint venture were given little preparation or training for their assignment from GM. Some managers were sent to NUMMI and told, 'Learn as much as you can,'" only to return to GM after two or more years not knowing where to begin. They learned the tools but did not grasp how to integrate them into an existing organization as an entire system (Inkpen, 2005, p. 120). Toyota achieved its human and operational objectives with NUMMI, learning how to work with an American workforce and capturing American market share. By and large the NUMMI transformation happened so quickly (within one year) that fully comprehending the Toyota approach to changing an organization using a systematic plan was extremely difficult for NUMMI employees.

Toyota Georgetown, 1986.

After Toyota achieved its objective of learning how to work with an American workforce at NUMMI, the next venture was its first fully owned and operated plant in Georgetown, Kentucky, where "developing human infrastructure was TMC's [Toyota Motor Company's] foremost priority—evidenced by a number of Toyota's actions" (Mishina & Takeda, 1995, p. 3). First, Toyota's construction started the same year it began hiring, which allowed TMC just as much time to develop "people infrastructure" as to develop "operational infrastructure." Second, the Camry's production line, which was already being mass produced, was replicated in Georgetown. Third, Toyota "set a deliberately slow ramp up schedule" (p. 3).

These decisions allowed for Toyota Motor Manufacturing (TMM) president at the time, Fuji Cho, and others to begin teaching/coaching a road map, transforming leaders to transform the organization—starting with the "people infrastructure." In addition, "every TMM manager was paired with a coordinator from TMC, who remained in Kentucky for a few years. These coordinators were charged to develop their counterparts only by persuasion—not to do things themselves. This intensely personal approach brought an 'eye-opening' moment to most TMM people. As TMC's plan unfolded in front of them, they could witness actions in the context around them, appreciate unexpectedly positive results, and have their coaches make sense of what lay behind these results" (Mishina & Takeda, 1995, p. 3).

Lean Defined in *The Machine That Changed the World*, 1990.

The Machine That Changed the World (Womack, Jones, & Roos, 1990) is a book based on an extensive study led by the Massachusetts Institute of Technology (MIT) that compared and contrasted mass versus Lean production, thinking, philosophies, and management. From this thorough five-year, five-million-dollar, fourteen-country study came the first book to reveal the Toyota Production System, called "Lean." The studies correctly predicted the triumph of Lean philosophies and production over mass production and the application of Lean into a variety of industries outside the automobile industry, including healthcare.

This groundbreaking, must-read book explains an extensive, mature Lean management and production system better than most, if not all, such books. It thoroughly describes the behaviors, philosophies, production, and management of the Toyota Production System in extensive detail and has been a driving force in reinvigorating organizations through a Lean transformation. After its publication and the successes that followed with Lean in manufacturing, improvement professionals became fixated on Toyota, trying to understand how to become a Lean organization.

Toyota Supplier Support Center, 1992.

In 1992, Toyota founded the Toyota Supplier Support Center (TSSC), now known as the Toyota Production System Support Center, in North America, to provide suppliers of Toyota and other North American companies training in the Toyota Production System. The operation of TSSC was based on Toyota's internal Operations Management Consulting Division (OMCD), based in Japan. The purpose of the OMCD was to give Toyota's employees the opportunity to solve complex problems through teaching, training, and coaching as they were "charged with leading improvement and training activities" (Spear & Bowen, 1999, p. 103). "The purpose of OMCD is to maintain a group of internal consultants with high levels of expertise in operations to assist in solving operational problems both at Toyota and at Toyota's suppliers" (Dyer & Nobeoka, 2000, p. 354). These improvement activities by OMCD and later TSSC were carried out in this order:

- Establish a theme for improvement.
- Implementation of Kaizen Improvement Activities.
- Repeated trial-and-error-style implementation until results were achieved.
- Presentation of results summary.
- Final evaluation of critical comments by Toyota's OMCD department. (Kato & Smalley, 2010, p. 12)

Essentially, if Toyota experiences a problem with a supplier, it must help the supplier to solve that problem. Complex problems are solved via Kaizen events, which were and are led by internal Toyota consultants/leaders (i.e., TSSC/ OMCD). As leaders within supply organizations learned the Kaizen event methodology for solving problems, they too began to apply it in order to solve their own internal problems. This coercive, yet positive, form of Kaizen event implementation of and introduction to Lean "results from both formal and informal pressures exerted on organizations by other organizations upon which they are dependent" (DiMaggio & Powell, 1983, p. 179).

Both the pressure and support from Toyota in helping suppliers to solve operational problems may have resulted in developing Toyota's leaders, solving operational problems, and suppliers learning the Kaizen event methodology to solving problems. Though the event is a necessary approach at times and the best approach for Toyota to help solve problems and develop leaders, it was always done within Toyota's culture and Toyota's daily management system.

One of the first general managers of TSSC, Hajime Ohba, recognized the discrepancy between traditional North American organizations and Toyota when stating: "It takes a very long time and tremendous commitment to implement the Toyota Production System. In many cases it takes a total cultural and organizational change. Many U.S. firms have management systems that contradict where you need to go" (Dyer & Nobeoka, 2000, p. 354). Therefore, if non-Lean organizations neglect the culture and management system, they will not become world-class using TPS. However, not knowing the best way to start, yet being familiar with Kaizen events, many organizations set out on an event-based journey to become "Lean," if not necessarily world-class.

The Spread of an Event-Based, Tools-Based Approach to TPS, 1980s–2000s.

Coercive and mimetic processes of a tools- and event-based approach yielded positive results, which has led to an abundance of successful professionals who learned, refined, and elaborated on the tools-based and Kaizen event–based pathway. The knowledge of what a Lean organization looks like was becoming readily available—and the main execution of becoming a Lean organization was Kaizen, aka "rapid improvement," events. Professionalization of and tools surrounding the Kaizen event rapidly diffused throughout North America as manufacturing organizations attempted to "become Lean."

Many organizations hired individuals or consultants with a narrow range of training and credentials, defined by professional networks and industry standards, like "belts," "Lean project specialists," etc. The Kaizen event professional of project facilitation and leadership development, similar to OMCD within its own organization or within a Lean organization, comprised a vast majority of Lean practitioners and professionals in the early years of Lean diffusion and still does today in most, if not all, industries.

Senior leaders within aspiring Lean organizations look to these professionals as both internal employees and external consultants to initiate Lean transformation. As Liker and Convis (2011) explain, "Traditionally the role of a lean consultant is to run a project and deliver an action plan. . . . They claim to have expertise in lean methods and guarantee that they can eliminate waste. . . . Blitzes and acting fast for results is the antithesis of good Lean practice, which is based on finding the root causes and the best solutions and sharing lessons for continuous improvement" (pp. 250–251). Yet, due to the professionalization of an event-based and/or tools-based approach to Lean, when healthcare found a solution in Lean, it generally started with Kaizen events.

Introducing Lean into Healthcare Organizations, 2002.

After the widespread diffusion of Lean into primarily the manufacturing sector, using the professionalized event-based, tools-based approach, early adopters of Lean in healthcare were turning to manufacturing for solutions to organizational and process problems. ThedaCare, Virginia Mason, Seattle Children's, and other healthcare organizations that were early adopters of Lean found the solution of "Lean" in 2002 (and the years leading up to 2002) from manufacturing. Generally, they began a journey very similar to that of Toyota's suppliers and most of the automobile and manufacturing industries—through Kaizen events.

Going Lean in Healthcare, an initial publication about Lean healthcare transformation, cites results of 175 RPIWs including positive changes in inventory, productivity, floor space, lead time, and set up time using Kaizen events called *Rapid Process Improvement Workshops/Weeks (RPIWs)* (IHI, 2005, p. 4). **RPIWs** are a seven-week cycle around a one-week focused improvement project (i.e., Kaizen event) that follow "intensive week-long sessions in which teams analyze processes and propose, test, and implement improvements" (IHI, 2005, p. 3). The event includes Lean training, developing a current state, a future state (based on the ideal), implementing the steps to get toward the future state, testing and standardizing the new process, and reporting out on the results (Toussaint, 2010), i.e., the OMCD/TSSC approach to Lean.

It was clear that the Kaizen events were exciting, led to results, were nicely packaged, and could be repeated to make operational improvement by a group of internal or external Lean specialists. Thus, the professional network continued to grow rapidly, and Kaizen events have been adapted to many industries using the same general format: *establish a theme for improvement, identify wastes in the current state, identify the Lean future state, implement the activities to achieve the future state*. Repeating this approach by and large became defined as the standard for becoming "Lean."

Learning from Great Lean Healthcare Organizations

ThedaCare is, without a doubt, one of the best examples of Lean healthcare. The Lean healthcare industry, however, must study mistakes that ThedaCare made in its journey of transformation and the causes of those mistakes, in order to grasp a better way to begin and continue transformation. ThedaCare's primary mode of improvement was events for many years until a turning point in 2008. One person in particular helped ThedaCare leaders recognize that their daily management system must change (or exist) when it was asked how the staff was supposed to change when leaders kept managing the same way (Toussaint, 2010). At the time, ThedaCare began to more deeply understand the problem: "Every manager at ThedaCare manages his or her own way. There is no one system" (Barnas, 2014, p. 11).

After twelve years on ThedaCare's Lean journey, the former senior vice president reflects, "Our goal was a new leadership system in which frontline supervisors, area managers, and upper-level executives all know today's goals, yesterday's performance, and how to work through problems" (Barnas, 2014, p. 11). Improvement became a way that managers accomplished work—"thus, a new management system emerged and it was clear that this was the secret sauce that so many had been seeking" (p. xii).

In 2015, former CEO of ThedaCare, Dr. John Toussaint, notes: "At one time, we were saving an average of $45,000 for every rapid-improvement event we did, week in and week out. Even then, however, we were setting ourselves up for failure. Our leaders should have been learning strategy deployment, visual management, and how to support the model cell" (Toussaint, 2015, para. 17). Many healthcare organizations not only experienced this mistake but also experienced it without successful results of rapid-improvement events. Other healthcare organizations and leaders need to not merely mimic what ThedaCare is now but rather grasp how an organization can be changed more effectively.

Plan-Do-Study-Act

Organizational isomorphism has led to a large number of successes throughout healthcare using an event-based journey for initiating organizational transformation and Lean improvement. Extensive Lean professionals' resources and understanding of how to make positive change using Kaizen events and the lack of resources for a systematic approach to becoming world-class have all perpetuated an event-based pathway to Lean. Though an event-based approach to Lean transformation has resulted in improvements, many of which are documented, shared, and expanded upon, this approach to reengineering processes has resulted in many failures in organizations that have gone undocumented and unpublished. Many of these failures most likely neglected culture and people development—the heart of Lean.

The concept is that many Lean organizations learned from individuals who mastered Kaizen events, and not necessarily leaders who have mastered organizational transformation using TPS. Very few people have experienced high levels of Toyota leadership compared to the number of individuals who have experienced Kaizen events. Furthermore, not many people have left leadership positions within Toyota to transform organizations using a systematic repeatable process, as demonstrated in Figure A.3. Therefore, it is time to P-D-S-A (Plan-Do-Study-Adjust) the approach to Lean over the last 25 years to grasp why organizations may have chosen an event-based, tools-based pathway. It is also time to grasp a time-tested approach to organizational transformation, which is summarized in the Transformation Curve.

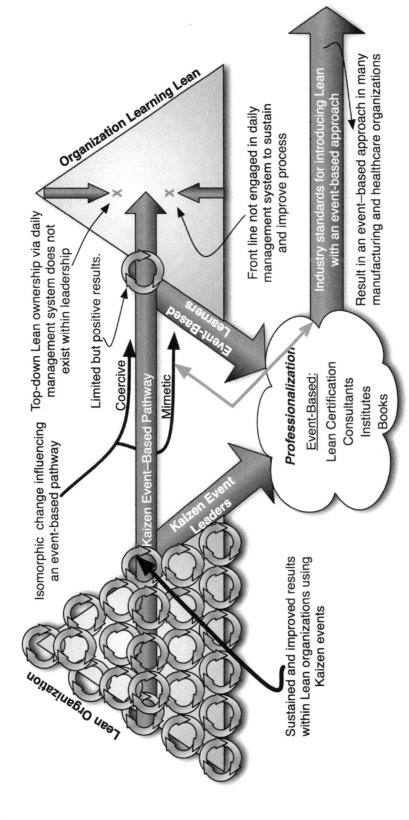

Figure A.2. The hypothesized development and popularization of an event-based pathway to introducing Lean. A mature Lean organization (left), like Toyota, has a robust management system and Lean culture. The Kaizen event and focused improvement yielded positive results and perpetuated the professionalization of an event-based approach to transformation, only later for thought leaders to realize that executive leadership, a new culture, and a daily management system are necessary in order to sustain any event-based improvements. *Note.* Theory of isomorphic change mechanisms via DiMaggio & Powell (1983).

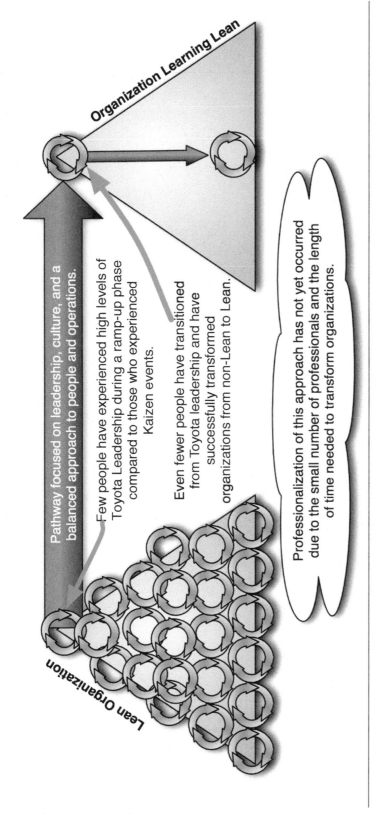

Figure A.3. The pathway of introducing Lean transformation to an organization, starting with leadership, focused on culture, and implementing a daily management system. This approach, adapted from Toyota Georgetown, and elaborated upon by Rodger Lewis, is currently less popular, due to a higher number of professionals experiencing Toyota's culture and methodologies via Kaizen events.

APPENDIX B
LEAN CULTURE CHANGE THEORY

Organizational Culture and How It's Expressed

Organizational Culture is defined by Edgar Schein (1985) as "the pattern of basic assumptions that a given group has invented, discovered, or developed in learning to cope with its problems of external adaptation and internal integration, and that have worked well enough to be considered valid, and, therefore, to be taught to new members as the correct way to perceive, think, and feel in relation to these problems" (p. 6).

Schein states that values produce artifacts, an expressions of culture. ***Values*** are "the social principles, goals, and standards that cultural members believe have intrinsic worth . . . and are revealed by their priorities" (Hatch & Cunliffe, 2013, p. 169). ***Artifacts*** are "manifestations or expressions of the same cultural core that produces and maintains the values and norms" and consists of objects, verbal expressions, and activities (p. 170). Examples of cultural artifacts as they relate to "Lean" organizations are in Table B.1.

Table 8.1. Example cultural artifacts in a Lean culture.

Artifacts	Examples in a Lean Culture
Objects	Andon lights and other signals Kanban cards and boards Balanced scoreboards and scorecards A3s, one page-reports, and problem-solving sheets Visual boards showcasing improvements
Verbal Expressions	Jargon around problem solving Storytelling of individual and team improvements Articulating processes about aligning goals/metrics "Let's start a problem-solving sheet" or "Just-Do-It" "Time for P-D-C-A"
Activities	Daily and monthly meeting cycles Cross-functional group problem solving (events) Leaders standard work in the Gemba Rituals of reward/recognition Hoshin kanri and the alignment of goals and plans

Source: Based on Hatch (2013); Dandridge, Mitroff, & Joyce (1980); Schultz (1995); Jones (1996).

Many times, artifacts (e.g., activities) are not the desired activity for Lean transformation, but this does not mean that individual and organizational values are complete off base. Their attitudes, however, may need to be changed to align the desired behavior with an existing value. Figure B.1 shows a physician's attitudes and activities based on the same values. Figure B.2 shows cultural expression by definition, comparing Toyota's long-term artifacts to most hospitals' short-term artifacts, which may be rooted also in similar values.

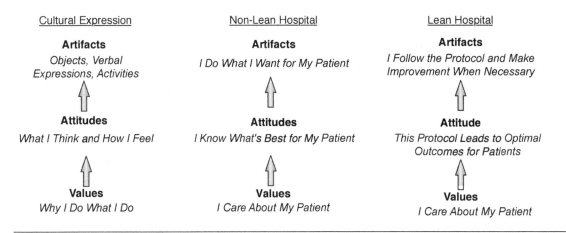

Figure B.1. Physicians at Lean and non-Lean hospitals may have similar value systems; however. the attitude towards standards may be expressed as different artifacts.
Adapted from Schein (1985), Shook (2010), Gagliardi (1986).

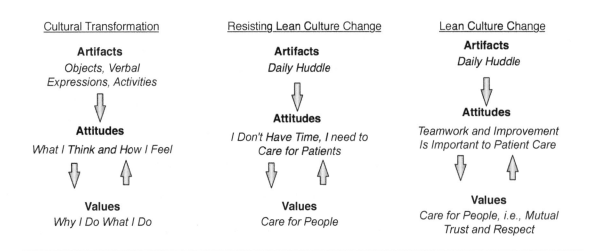

Figure B.2. Toyota's expression (middle) shows that the value of mutual trust and respect manifests in attitudes that "people are my number one resource," which is expressed in the cultural artifact of a no-layoff policy. The example on the right shows that laying off may be rooted in value systems associated with respect for community.
Adapted from Schein (1985), Shook (2010), Gagliardi (1986).

Types of Lean Culture Change

Different types of cultural change, the resources necessary, and the results gives understanding of why and how TPS was introduced and adapted so that leaders may decide which type of culture change is most appropriate for the organization.

Revolutionary Culture Change at NUMMI, 1983.

Revolutionary Culture Change describes the death of an old culture and the birth of a new culture (Gagliardi, 1986). Cultural change as a revolution describes the transformation that the New United Motor Manufacturing Inc. (NUMMI), the 1983 joint venture with Toyota and General Motors, experienced. The old culture and workforce at NUMMI was an "extraordinarily 'bad' one" that "produced some of the worst quality in the GM system" at the time (Shook, 2010, pp. 2–3). Within one year, NUMMI had the best quality within General Motors and a completely transformed workforce, which embodied the Toyota Culture (Shook, 2010).

Revolutionary culture change is the most effective approach to organizational transformation if the knowledge of TPS, standards for improvement, and standards for how to do the work exist in extensive detail with an extensive network of coaches. Most organizations, however, do not have the capacity or capability for revolutionary change, because of the high cost, need for large-scale defection of old and an influx of new personnel, disinvesting emotionally and financially, destruction of old symbols, new investments financially and emotionally, and the creation of new cultural artifacts (Gagliardi, 1986, p. 130).

Toyota at Georgetown, Kentucky, and Changing Leaders' Individual Culture

Most organizations do not have the capability, capacity, resources, or need for revolutionary change and must transform incrementally. During the Georgetown ramp-up, newly hired managers from Toyota "could witness actions in the context around them, appreciate unexpectedly positive results, and have their coaches make sense of what lay behind these results" (HBR, 1995, p. 3). Senior leadership, as coaches, must create and promote successes with Lean culture change artifacts in order to change attitudes and expand or reprioritize existing value systems, as demonstrated in Figure B.3. Figure B.4 shows how culture is transformed by using the foundations and artifacts to change attitudes, reorganize values, and express the new artifacts, essentially changing culture.

How to Initiate Lean Culture Change

If an organization needs Lean culture change, it should be initiated using the Transformation Curve using a daily management system. The following steps must be taken:

Have a Systematic Plan. Using "Lean" philosophies and tools is not about becoming "Lean" but creating a culture of mutual trust and respect, striving for perfection, and becoming world-class. Using the Transformation Curve as a guideline, a systematic approach to transforming culture towards "Lean" begins with senior leadership, is incremental, and is operationalized via a daily management system, reorganizing and reinforcing values on a daily basis.

Change Culture Incrementally. Most organizations do not have the capability, capacity, resources, or need for revolutionary change and must transform incrementally. The three conditions necessary for incremental culture change: (1) the change is not introducing a new value system different from the current value system; (2) the organization experiences success with the cultural change artifacts; and (3) leadership must promote the new culture and attribute successes back to the cultural change activities (Gigliardi, 1986, p. 131).

Start with Leadership. "Regardless of the perspective adopted, all organization culture researchers acknowledge that top managers are powerful members of an organization's culture. And, because power grants them a disproportionate share of attention, their behavior becomes a role model for others, their words are carefully attended, and their directives obeyed" (Hatch & Cunliffe, 2013, p. 185). Lean culture change, whether incremental or revolutionary, sporadic or systematic, must be not only supported by senior leadership but passionately and patiently led by senior leadership, with a focus on people development.

Use a Daily Management System. The objects, verbal expressions, and activities instilled using a daily management system first at the executive level, then at a frontline level, introduce new artifacts and thus norms. Using the foundations of continuous improvement (P-D-C-A, visual management, and roles/responsibilities) with the new artifacts (objects, verbal expressions, and activities/behaviors) begins to change attitudes and mind-sets around problems, which reprioritizes existing value systems or introduces new resonating values. The artifacts of daily management help teams focus on positive change through problem solving and continually reinforce the artifacts.

Learn in the Pilot Hall. Use a pilot hall to create a subculture that aligns with the corporate culture. The pilot hall is a place to learn and apply the foundations through a daily management system.

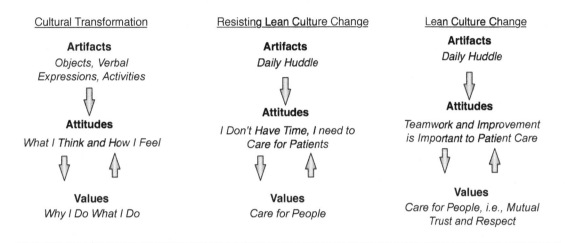

Figure B.3. Cultural transformation from current culture towards a Lean culture using incremental culture change. The artifact of a daily huddle, for example, may be met with resistance—not because the individual's or team's values are incompatible with Lean but because their attitudes and mind-sets towards problems in general may need to change in order to resonate with or reprioritize existing values. *Adapted from Schein (1985), Shook (2010), Gagliardi (1986).*

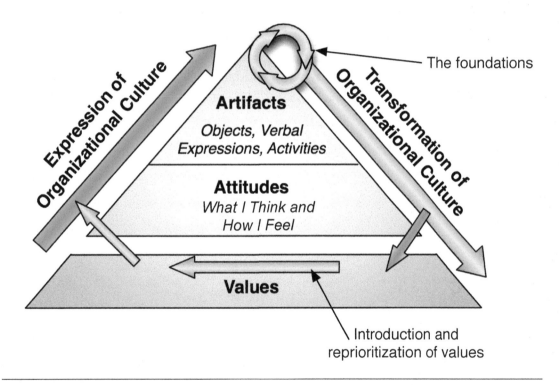

Figure B.4. The Incremental Cultural Change Pyramid* This visually depicts how culture is expressed and transformed. The foundations (P-D-C-A, visual management, and roles and responsibilities) of a daily management system reinforce cultural change artifacts, which begins to transform culture, reorganizes existing values, and in turn expresses new cultural artifacts and reinforces the existing cultural artifacts of a daily management system.

Cultural change pyramid adapted from Schein (1985), Shook (2010), and Gagliardi (1986).

For more templates, updates, and up-to-date information
visit www.alignkaizen.com

Glossary

3Gs: Go See, Get the Facts, Grasp the Situation—utilized when creating mutual trust and respect within an organization when balanced with the 3Ps.

3Ps: People, Passion, and Patience—utilized by creating mutual trust and respect within an organization when balanced with the 3Gs.

4Ps: Purpose, Process, People, and Problem Solving—used to help people understand the artifacts of a mature daily management system.

5S: Sort, Straighten, Shine, Standardize, and Sustain—a form of workplace organization that eliminates waste and improves operations.

5S+1: 5S plus safety.

5 Whys: A method of asking "why" to get from the point of occurrence to the root cause. The concept is that asking why 5 times will increase the chances of finding a root cause.

6-Year Scorecard: An artifact to organize the top organizational priorities, objectives, and targets, aiming toward achieving world-class organizational operations in 6 years or less.

A3: A one-page report that communicates a proposal, problem, status, project, or other information. It is typically reserved for larger-scale problem solving and/or team projects and is an essential part of organizational Lean transformation. The name A3 is after the size paper, A3.

Action Plan Modification: Adjusting master plans or detailed plans when the environments change and different ways to achieve the objective are planned.

Activity-R: The responsible person for an activity. The activity-R will come to any master plan check point prepared to report on status, coordinate, and elevate problems as needed.

Activity-S: Supports the responsible person for each activity and reports out the status to master plan R.

Annual Check Cycle: Includes setting objectives, creating master plans, establishing targets and metrics, setting the improvement theme, and creating the daily management system implementation plan.

Annual Objective: A clear link between the long-term goal and the metric. A goal statement including the target.

Annual Planning: A process for setting an improvement theme, recasting the 6-year scorecard, and establishing plans to achieve objectives and improve the organization's performance.

Annual Planning Cycle: A yearly organization-wide improvement cycle.

Annual Targets: A target set each year once a team clearly understands the 6-year world-class target, the current baseline, and the gaps.

Arrange (A): Organizing items by determining the frequency of use.

Artifacts: Include objects, verbal expressions, and activities (Schein, 1985). The tools and components of a daily management system introduced to change culture. Also the objects verbal expressions, and activities that are produced as a result of culture change.

Audit Process: Provides a framework to determine what is and is not working within a plan and adjust accordingly.

Balanced Scoreboard: A framework used to visualize specific objectives and metrics, key processes, indicators, and top monthly problems specific to the leadership team that is maintaining the scoreboard.

Balanced Scorecard: Shorthand for 6-year balanced scorecard. Also see BSC.

BSC: Abbreviation for 6-year balanced scorecard.

Baseline: Reflects a metric where the organization is currently at, or a more appropriate average over some period of time.

Best Practices: Organizational units or operations that are high-performing (internal) and world-class processes or practices (external).

CANDO: A form of Workplace Organization popularized by Henry Ford that includes: Clean-up, Arrange, Neatness, Discipline, and Ongoing Improvement.

CEO: Chief Executive Officer.

Check Cycle: A graphical representation of the total effect of the countermeasure compared to the plan.

CI Team: Continuous Improvement team—a group of internal coaches who learn, train, and coach the daily management system.

Clean-up (C): Workplace organization that begins with cleaning up and sorting what's needed in that area and not needed.

Coercive Isomorphism: When one organization places pressures (formal/informal) on another organization, which causes the two organizations to be come more similar. The example in the book is Toyota requiring its suppliers to solve problems facilitated by the Toyota Supplier Support Center using kaizen events. This coercive mechanism for change lead Toyota's suppliers to use kaizen events as a main mode of change. The term coercive isomorphism comes from DiMaggio & Powell (1983).

Communication Plan: Consists of the intention, strategy, and steps of Lean Culture Change and the general plan of the Transformation Curve.

Community: Businesses, families, government, patients, organizations, etc.

Complaint Management: Problem solving applied to patient complaints in order to avoid similar complaints in the future.

Containment Measure: The steps taken to fix a problem and/or ensure it does not get any larger. This is also known as a quick fix or a work around.

Continuous Improvement: Making small incremental changes moving towards world-class. In Japanese the term "kaizen" means continuous improvement.

Continuous Improvement (CI) Team: The core team responsible for coaching and supporting Lean culture change.

Countermeasure: An action or long-term solution that directly impacts or removes the root cause of a problem.

Countermeasure Owner: This is the person responsible for implementing the countermeasure.

Cultural Change: Shifting the culture from firefighting to root cause problem solving, while giving ownership to team members to develop countermeasures.

Culture Change Pyramid: Adapted from Shook (2010) and Schein (1985), this visualizes the interplay between artifacts, attitudes, and values in incremental culture change. By introducing new artifacts and using the foundations for continuous improvement to reinforce those artifacts, attitudes change which re-prioritize an existing value system to reinforce existing culture artifacts and new artifacts.

Customers: Patients, families, payers, providers, etc. This includes all direct and indirect, internal and external customers.

Daily Check Cycle: Includes the daily huddle, daily problem solving, daily going to see improvements, and daily checks of leading indicators.

Daily Huddle: A short, stand-up meeting that engages a team to make and sustain positive improvement through face-to-face communication.

Daily Management System: DMS—a system that incorporates many key Lean processes and components into a daily routine or practice.

Detailed Plans: These plans have the same structure as master plans. Detailed plans may be generated for selected master plan activities.

Discipline (D): Layered audits and daily visual checks/inspections create discipline, identify problems proactively, and help identify opportunities for improvement to be shared via the improvement system.

DMS: Daily Management System—a system that incorporates many key Lean processes and components into a daily routine or practice.

Employees: Staff, physicians, volunteers, leaders, etc.

End of Shift Restoration Checklist: A list of to-dos that should be completed to ensure a successful hand-off from one shift to the next shift.

Firefighting: First order problem solving—temporarily fixing, containing, or working around problems, with the chances being that the problem will resurface. First Order Problem Solving: Firefighting, temporarily fixing, containing, or working around problems, with the chances being that the problem will resurface.

Focus on Action: The annual planning process focuses on creating plans based on activities to achieve the objectives.

Gemba: A Japanese term referring to the actual place where a problem occurred and was first recognized.

Gembutsu: A Japanese term referring to the actual thing, not hearsay or speculation.

Genchi Gembutsu: A Japanese term meaning to go and observe.

Genijitsu: A Japanese term referring to the actual facts surrounding a problem and causes.

GL: Group Leader. This individual is the leader of team leaders.

Go, Get, Grasp: The 3Gs, utilized to help create mutual trust and respect within an organization. Go and see, Get the facts, and Grasp the situation.

Going Lean in Healthcare: A publication about Lean healthcare transformation, published by the Institute for Healthcare Improvement in 2005.

Green Cross: A visual management artifact to visualize safety in an area, department, and/or organization.

Group Leader: The "team leader" of multiple team leaders.

Huddle Prompt Sheet: An agenda with a simple, standard set of questions that the leader utilizes on a daily basis to conduct a daily meeting.

Huddle Record Sheet: A handwritten account of the daily huddle, used to capture statistics, undocumented problems, and undocumented improvement ideas.

Improvement Pathway: Helps to standardize positive recognition and embed it into the culture. These steps serve as a baseline process to guide leaders to reward, recognize, coach, and encourage improvement on a daily basis.

Improvement System: The creative ideas system for self-implemented improvements, with the purpose of engaging team members, team leaders and Senior Leadership.

Improvement System Board: A visual management artifact used to manage daily improvements that are owned and implemented by team members.

Improvement System Champion: Responsible for coaching the system to managers, proposing changes to the policy, and monitoring the overall performance, participation, rewards, and recognition of the improvement system.

Incremental Culture Change: Changing culture over time versus as a revolution. Three conditions must exist for incremental culture change: (1) the change is not introducing a new value system; (2) the organization experiences success with the cultural change artifacts; and (3) leadership must promote the new culture and attribute successes back to the cultural change activities (Gigliardi, 1986, p. 31).

Innovation System: Another name for the Improvement System.

Institutional Isomorphic Change: Includes three mechanisms: coercive, mimetic and normative isomorphism. These mechanisms presented by DiMaggio & Powell (1983) describe how organizations become more similar and how practices become professionalized and institutionalized.

Kaizen: Continuous improvement.

Kaizen Events: Continuous Improvement Events or Rapid Process Improvement Workshops. Generally a multi-day improvement event to visualize the current state, future state, and actions to achieve the future state.

Kanban: A Lean artifact generally for supply chain management that will be applied to patient, material, information, and other flow.

Knowledge Management: Employees collect and transfer workforce knowledge when utilizing the processes of a daily management system.

Leadership Framework: A model for leaders to lead from the middle, entering each situation asking what style of leadership is necessary: implementation (directive/command and control) or supportive (engaging improvement).

Leadership Team: A core group of people responsible for coaching and/ or solving top problems, maintaining the balanced scoreboard, preparing for and conducting the monthly balanced scoreboard meeting, overseeing the top implemented idea winners, leading annual planning sessions, and other responsibilities.

Leading Indicators: A visualization of key process drivers.

Lean: Currently defined as creating more value for customers with fewer resources while eliminating waste. (LEI, 2015). Defined in Lean Culture Change as mutual trust and respect.

Lean Consultant: Generally, the role of a Lean consultant is to run a project and deliver an action plan. (Liker & Convis, 2011, p. 250)

Lean Culture: Putting into practice Lean roles and responsibilities, which become behaviors and habits.

Lean Culture Change: Shifting the atmosphere to "problems are blessings" and opportunities for improvement, prepping the organization for full-scale implementation.

Learning and Development System: Supports organizational performance improvement, organizational change and innovation.

Long-Term Goal: A statement that is unchanging for the next several years. This statement should be broad enough to include everyone in the organization so that they can align with the statement in their day-to-day work

Management Cycle: A foundation of the Transformation Curve, with the centerpieces being the Teamwork Model and the Leadership Framework.

Maturity Audit: An advanced audit to measure the entire management system, typically introduced after Phase One of the Transformation Curve. Introduction to Audit 1, introduced in Chapter 8, is a very simplified version of the maturity audit for specific teams.

Master Plan: A tool used to visualize the master schedule, annual master plan activities, and timelines; contains master schedule activities, master plan activities, responsible and support persons, planned checkpoints, start dates, end dates, and other details necessary to achieve the objective of the plan.

Master Plan Activities: Specific steps or actions that are planned and needed in order to achieve an objective.

Master Schedule Activities: Previously planned activities or events that keep team members from completing master plan activities are included in master schedule activities, as is their timing.

Measurement Agility: Ensures that the performance measurement system can respond to rapid or unexpected organizational change.

Metrics: A quantifiable measure that is used to track and assess the status of a specific business process.

Mimetic Isomorphism: When an organization searches for a solution, and finds a solutions that will meet its relatively quickly, which is not necessarily the best or most effective long-term solution. (DiMaggio & Powell 1983)

Mission: A short statement that reflects an organization's core purpose.

Monthly Check Cycle: Includes checking performance to the annual targets, checking the status of annual plans, and generating top problems based on daily problem-solving cycles.

Monthly Balanced Scoreboard Meeting Cycle: A standard check on the previous month. It should morph into a proactive look at the next month. It takes the pulse of the unit/organization and serves as a time to check the status metrics, indicators, top problems, improvements, and overall performance of the unit or units the team leads.

Monthly Scoreboard Preparation Meeting: The first of two meetings, for the unit-based leadership team to understand the current situation via top metrics indicators, all the problem sheets, and any other sources of information. During this meeting the leadership team decides which problems they need to elevate as a top problem.

Monthly Winners: The form, the improvement, and the person's picture are all generally displayed on a visual board in a common area to showcase the improvement winner.

Neatness (N): Includes creating visual standards to help an area remain neat and organized.

Negotiation: A process that takes place formally and informally until the master plans and budgets are agreed upon and approved.

New United Motor Manufacturing, Inc. (NUMMI): A revolutionary Lean culture change (1983), involving the joint venture with Toyota and General Motors. (Inkpen, 2005, p. 117; Shook, 2010, p. 2-3)

Normative Isomorphism: A mechanism for change, where organizations become more similar based on professional networks and filtering of personnel from the same set of skills. (DiMaggio & Powell 1983)

NUMMI: New United Motor Manufacturing, Inc.

OMCD: Operations Management Consulting Division.

One Page Report: Also know as an A3. It is used to communicate a proposal, problem, status, project, or for another purpose.

Ongoing Improvement (O): Visual workplace items are artifacts of Lean cultural change and deployment of a new daily management system. Organization standards are introduced as leaders are using coaching and check cycles to energize teams around the improvement system.

Operations Management Consulting Division (OMCD): The purpose of the OMCD was to give Toyota's employees the opportunity to solve complex problems through teaching, training and coaching. (Spear & Bowen, 1991, p. 103)

Organizational Culture: "The pattern of basic assumptions that a given group has invented, discovered, or developed in learning to cope with its problems of external adaptation and internal integration, and that have worked well enough to be considered valid, and, therefore, to be taught to new members as the correct way to perceive, think, and feel in relation to these problems." (Schein, 1985, p. 6)

Organizational Leaning: Developing people to solve problems.

OSHA: Occupational Safety and Health Administration. A federal agency responsible for enforcing safety and health legislation.

OSHA Rate: "An incidence rate of injuries and illnesses is computed from the following formula: (Number of injuries and illnesses X 200,000) / Employee hours worked = Incidence rate." (OSHA.gov)

PDCA: Plan, Do, Check, Act—a foundation of continuous improvement and the Transformation Curve. Cultural activities mainly including standardized improvement cycles.

People: Third of the 4Ps. Describes the intention of the daily management system to engage every member of the organization in problem solving and improvement of their job and the product or service for the customers. Introduced in the Foreword by Mike Hoseus.

People, Passion, Patience: The 3Ps, utilized by creating mutual trust and respect within an organization.

Performance Analysis and Review: Problem solving helps team member to respond rapidly to changing organizational needs and challenges.

PICK Chart: (Possible, Implement, Challenge, and Kibosh)—a simple way to sort ideas and list as actions.

Pilot Hall: A frontline team to develop the new artifacts and culture. Also known as a model area or model cell.

Plan, Do, Check, Act (PDCA): Plan, Do, Check, Act—a foundation of continuous improvement and the Transformation Curve.

Point of Occurrence (PoO): The step, time, location, etc., where a problem originated.

Point of Recognition: The initial awareness of the problem that requires little or no investigation.

Point of Use: The location where an item is most utilized.

Points System: Each improvement is awarded a certain amount of points, based on the priorities on the balanced scorecard.

Problem Prevention (Safety): Layered safety audits and checks that proactively identify safety problems before they become realized problems.

Problem Solving: Fourth of the 4Ps. The point of the daily management system, which involves identifying and solving the right problems. Introduced in the Foreword by Mike Hoseus.

Problem-Solving Board: A standard board used to manage problem-solving sheets and lead towards problem solving.

Problem Solving One: A standard method to learn problem solving, solve problems one by one, and build problem-solving capability and capacity. It is focused on building individual problem solving.

Problem Solving One Process: Demonstrates how a problem is recognized and root cause is identified. It is the initial awareness of a problem.

Problem-Solving Sheet: A standard tool used to facilitate and communicate the status of problems within the Problem Solving One process individually, departmentally, and organizationally.

Problem-Solving Sheet Owner: This is the person who is seeing the problem-solving process through.

Problem Statement: A clear factual account of the problem that is generated from facts found at the point of occurrence and may include the 5 Whys.

Process: Second of the 4Ps, dealing with standardizing processes. Introduced in the Foreword by Mike Hoseus.

Process Indicators: Can measure on a daily basis whether or not a process is being followed as the policy states.

Professionalization: The collective struggle of members of an occupation to define the conditions and methods of work (DiMaggio & Powell, 1983, p. 151).

Project Plans: A visual management artifact to plan for, check, and adjust a project. Project plans look like a master plan, but are not necessarily linked directly to a 6-year scorecard.

Purpose: First of the 4Ps; this is about an organization having a clear plan communicated to the organization and a clear plan to get there. Introduced in the Foreword by Mike Hoseus.

Rapid Process Improvement Workshops (RPIWs): Rapid Process Improvement Workshops/Weeks, also known as kaizen events. The event includes Lean training, developing a current state, a future state (based on the ideal), implementing the steps to get toward the future state, testing and standardizing the new process, and reporting out on the results.

Recognition Per Improvement: Each improvement is recognized by a team leader or higher leader in the organization, depending on the stage of daily management system maturity.

Red Tag Area: A location where items that are not frequently used, are no longer needed, or are in the wrong area are placed for a period of time before being removed or relocated.

Responsible and Support (R/S): The R and S represent the leaders who will be primarily responsible for leading, coordinating, facilitating, and checking the progress of the efforts to achieve the annual objective.

Revolutionary Culture Change: Describes the death of an old culture and the birth of a new culture (Gagliardi, 1986).

Reward and Recognition: Should occur for each improvement until it is integrated into daily standard work for the leader.

Reward Per Improvement: A reward given whenever an improvement is implemented, regardless of its impact or cost savings.

Roles and Responsibilities: Defining individuals and teams along with expectations of the daily management system.

Root Cause: Underlying reason a problem occurred.

Root Cause Analysis: Understanding facts by asking questions to best determine the underlying reason why a problem occurred.

Root Cause Problem Solving: Finding and changing the root cause or underlying reason as to why a problem occurred. The 5 Whys are the most common form of root cause analysis.

RPIW: Rapid Process Improvement Workshops/Weeks.

Safety: Avoiding both short- and long-term harmful affects to people resulting from unsafe acts and preventable adverse events.

Safety Audit: A structured safety check that includes patient rooms, general areas, storerooms, and grounds.

Safety Audit Results: An informal result from the weekly safety audit visualized on the balanced scoreboard. The purpose of the results are to demonstrate that the audit is being completed, and generally if the team is sustaining/improving.

Safety Pat: A visual management tool that can help show where safety problems are occurring using anatomy.

Safety System: A systematic approach to improving employee, patient, provider, visitor, and volunteer safety.

Safety System Leading Indicators: Proactive measures that monitor and improve safety.

Safety System Policy: Includes how the artifacts of the safety system are deployed, monitored, and improved.

Scoreboard Review: The second of two meetings that follows the Monthly Scoreboard Preparation Meeting, which typically involves a senior leader. Leadership presents the current metrics, indicators, and top problems. The purpose of this meeting is to elevate top problems and for the group leader to understand all of the department's problems as an aid to selecting top problems.

Senior Team: The most executive team in the organization.

SMART Objectives: Objectives that are Specific, Measurable, Agreed-upon, Realistic, and Timed.

Solution System: Another common name for the improvement system or suggestion system that focuses on proactive problem solving.

Standardize Cycles: Standardize the time for preparing for and conducting the monthly meeting.

Steering Committee: A core group of leaders that sets and monitors the direction of the new daily management system.

Support Metrics: Any numbers, graphs, or other visual data that assist in giving more detail to a top metric or give further information in regards to a top problem.

SWOT Analysis: Strength, Weakness, Opportunity and Threats—grasping top problems and best practices.

Target: A metric from the balanced scoreboard or the ideal situation.

Team Leader: Team leaders are responsible for overall performance of the unit/ team as well as daily management system artifacts including improvement, balanced scorecard, problem solving, etc. The team leader leads team members and is lead by group leaders.

Teamwork Model: A visual representation showing the interconnections between a team or individual and the team above, below, and side to side.

The Machine that Changed the World: A publication that identified Toyota's Production System as Lean, and described in great detail what a Lean organization looks, feels, and acts like. (Womack, Jones, Roos, 1990)

Tier One Huddles: A start-up or change-of-shift huddle.

Tier Two Huddles: Generally, a value-stream-level meeting involving managers, which is usually done to discuss flow problems between units, discharge problems, bed placement problems, patient flow problems, and concerns that need to be elevated from frontline huddles.

Tier Three Huddles: Administration meets with team members as needed to ensure process adherence, coach elevated problems, and select problems to pass on to other Senior Team members.

Tier Four Huddles: The Senior Team's daily huddle where they can ensure that the others have followed up on the actions from the previous day, and to communicate any actions that must take place for the current day and upcoming days.

Tiered Huddles: Helps get the right information to the right person to ensure quick and appropriate follow-up.

TL: Team Leader.

Toyota Culture: A book written by Mike Hoseus and Jeffrey Liker.

Toyota Production System (TPS): Aims to intentionally expose problems and engage all members in solving them.

Toyota Supplier Support Center (TSSC): Known as the Toyota Production System Support Center in North America. Established in 1992.

TPS: Toyota Production System—aims to intentionally expose problems and engage all members in solving them.

Transactional: A meeting where problems and information are shared, but no action is taken or communicated.

Transformation Curve: A multi-phase, multi-year, adaptable pathway to organizational transformation rooted in the pathway learned in the Introduction.

Transformational: A meeting where countermeasures and improvements are presented formally and agreed upon, and where the total impact of past improvements is communicated to keep discussion positive.

The Ideal: A clearly communicated vision of where the company is going.

Unit-Based Improvement Coordinator: Person responsible for the unit coordination, submission, and tracking of the improvement system.

Values: "The social principles, goals, and standards that cultural members believe have intrinsic worth...and are revealed by their priorities." (Hatch & Cunliffe, 2013, p. 169)

Visual Management: Cultural objects that support the clear alignment of activities and roles/responsibilities with processes.

Visual Objects: Objects such as the safety cross, detailed plans, and metrics, that are integrated within a visual management plan.

Visual Recognition: Visual boards that are used to recognize monthly improvement winners, the quality of improvements, and recognize timelines.

Vitals: The organization's priorities, such as People, Quality, Service, Finance, Growth and VIP. Specific to Indiana Regional Medical Center.

Waste Walks: The purpose is to eliminate waste or to observe problems where the work is being done.

Watch Numbers: Serve as a simple tracking mechanism to aid in top problem selection and ongoing process monitoring.

Weekly Check Cycle: Includes checking the status/progress of monthly top problems, weekly checks on safety and workplace organization, and other weekly checks.

Workplace Organization: Consists of artifacts with a daily management system that align with safety and cultural change.

World-Class Metric: Indicates where the organization needs to go in order to be a world-class organization.

Bibliography

Barnas, K. (2014). *Beyond heroes: A lean management system for healthcare.* Appleton, WI: ThedaCare Center for Healthcare Value.

Bluedorn, A., Kalliath, T., Strube, M., & Martin, G. (1999). Polychronicity and the inventory of polychronic values (IPV). *Journal Of Managerial Psych*, 14(3/4), 205-231. doi:10.1108/02683949910263747

Burke, L., & Hutchins, H. (2008). A study of best practices in training transfer and proposed model of transfer. *Human Resource Development Quarterly*, 19(2), 107-128. doi:10.1002/hrdq.1230

Cameron, K. S., & Quinn, R. E. (2011). Diagnosing and changing organizational culture: Based on the competing values framework. San Francisco: John Wiley & Sons.

Campbell Institute. (2014). Transforming EHS performance measurement through leading indicators.

Committee on Quality of Health Care in America,Institute of Medicine. (2000). To err is human: Building a safer health system. (L.T. Kohn, J.M. Corrigan, & M.S. Donaldson, Eds.). Washington: National Academies Press.

Culig, M., Kunkle, R., Frndak, D., Grunden, N., Maher, T., & Magovern, G. (2011). Improving Patient Care in Cardiac Surgery Using Toyota Production System Based Methodology. *The Annals Of Thoracic Surgery*, 91(2), 394-399. doi:10.1016/j.athoracsur.2010.09.032

Dandridge, T. C., Mitroff, I., & Joyce, W. F. (1980). Organizational Symbolism: A Topic To Expand Organizational Analysis. *Academy of Management Review*, 5, 77-82.

DiMaggio, P. J., & Powell, W. W. (1983). The iron cage revisited-institutional isomorphism and collective rationality in organizational fields. *The American Sociological Association*, 48, 147-160.

Doran, G. T. (1981). "There's a S.M.A.R.T. Way to Write Management's Goals and Objectives", *Management Review*, Vol. 70, Issue 11, pp. 35-36.

Dyer, J., & Nobeoka, K. (2000). Creating and managing a high performance knowledge-sharing network: the Toyota case. *Strategic Management Journal*, 21, 345–367.

Drucker, P. (1954). The practice of management. New York: Harper & Row.

Gannon, J. R., Butler, J., & Gilbert, L. J. (1981). Deaf heritage: A narrative history of deaf America. Cincinnati: National Association of the Deaf.

Gagliardi, P. (1986). The creation and change of organizational cultures: A conceptual framework. *Organization studies*, 7(2), 117-134.

Goffee, R., & Jones, G. (1996). What holds the modern company together?. *Harvard Business Review*, 74(6), 133.

Graban, M. (2008). Lean hospitals: Improving quality, patient safety, and employee satisfaction. Boca Raton: CRC Press.

Guindon-Nasir,J. (2010). *Transferring service excellence best practices from the hospitality industry to the healthcare industry* (Doctoral dissertation). Retrieved from Proquest. (AAI3421861)

Hatch, J. M., & Cunliffe, A. L. (2013). Organization theory: Modern, symbolic and postmodern perspectives. Oxford: Oxford University Press.

Hernández, B. M. V., & Handal, R. Y. (2014). Implementación de un programa de excelencia operacional como una herramienta para la mejora continua en el Centro Médico ABC. *An Med* (Mex), 59(3), 179-184.

Institute for Healthcare and Improvement (IHI). (2015). Going Lean in Health Care. Retrieved 31 July 2015, from https://www.entnet.org/sites/default/files/GoingLeanin-HealthCareWhitePaper-3.pdf

Inkpen, A. (2005). Learning through alliances: General Motors and NUMMI. *California Management Review*, 47(4), 114-136.

Jones, M. (1996). Studying organizational symbolism: What, how, why? Thousand Oaks: Sage Publications.

Kato, I., & Smalley, A. (2010). Toyota Kaizen methods: Six steps to improvement. Boca Raton: CRC Press.

LEI (2015). What is Lean?. Retrieved 4 June 2015, from Lean Enterprise Institute (LEI) http://www.lean.org/WhatsLean/

Liker, J., & Convis, G. (2011). The Toyota way to lean leadership: Achieving and sustaining excellence through leadership development. New York: McGraw-Hill.

Liker, J., & Hoseus, M. (2008). Toyota culture. New York: McGraw-Hill.

Liker, J., & Meier, D. (2005). The Toyota way fieldbook. New York: McGraw-Hill.

Mann, D. (2010). Creating a lean culture. New York: Productivity Press.

Miller, J. (2003). The suggestion system is no suggestion (3rd ed.). Mukilteo: Gemba Research LLC.

Mishina, K. & Takeda, K. (1995). Toyota motor manufacturing, U.S.A, Inc. Harvard Business Review.

Nance, J. J., & Bartholomew, K. (2012). Charting the course: Launching patient-centric healthcare. Bozeman: Second River Healthcare Press.

NIST. (2015). 2015-2016 Health Care Criteria for Performance Excellence. Retrieved July 2015, from The National Institute of Standards and Technology (NIST), http://www.nist.gov/baldrige/publications/purchase_criteria.cfm

OSHA. (2013). Facts about Hospital Worker Safety. USA Department of Labor: Occupational Safety and Health Admiration. Retrieved July 2015, https://www.osha.gov/dsg/hospitals/documents/1.2_Factbook_508.pdf.

Rother, M. (2009). Toyota Kata: Managing people for improvement, adaptiveness and superior results. New York: McGraw-Hill.

Schultz, M. (1995). On studying organizational cultures: Diagnosis and understanding (Vol. 58). Walter de Gruyter.

Schein, E. H.(1985). Organizational culture and leadership (2nd ed.). San Francisco: Jossey-Bass

Shook, J. (2010). How to change a culture: Lessons from NUMMI. MIT *Sloan Management Review*, 51(2), 42-51.

Sherman, V. (1993). Creating the new American hospital. San Francisco: Jossey-Bass.

Spear, S., & Bowen, H. K. (1999). Decoding the DNA of the Toyota production system. *Harvard Business Review*, 77, 96-108.

Spear, S. J. (2005). Fixing health care from the inside, today. *Harvard Business Review*, (83), 78-91.

Studer, Q. (2003). Hardwiring excellence. Gulf Breeze: Fire Starter Pub.

Toussaint, J. (2013). A management, leadership, and board road map to transforming care for patients. *Front Health Serv Manage*, 29(3), 3-15.

Toussaint, J. (2009). Writing the new playbook for US health care: Lessons from Wisconsin. *Health Affairs*, 28(5), 1343-1350.

Toussaint, J., & Gerard, R. (2010). *On the mend: Revolutionizing healthcare to save lives and transform the industry.* Cambridge, MA: Lean Enterprise Institute, Inc.

Toussaint, J. (2015). *Management on the mend: The healthcare executive guide to system transformation.* Appleton, WI: ThedaCare Center for Healthcare Value.

Thomson Reuters. (2011). Sicker and costlier: Healthcare utilization of U.S. hospital employees. Retrieved from http://img.en25.com/Web/ThomsonReuters/H_PAY_EMP_1108_10237_HHE_ Report_WEB.PDF

Womack, J. P., Jones, D. T., & Roos, D. (1990). The machine that changed the world. New York: Simon and Schuster.

Acknowledgments

First and foremost, thank you to my wife and best friend, Mary, for your loving support, patience, guidance, and our two beautiful children— Edie and Henry.

Rodger Lewis, thank you for giving me the opportunity to publish the learnings that only scratch the surface of the *Transformation Curve* and your time at Toyota Georgetown, General Motors, and beyond. My personal and professional culture has changed. Shifting organizations, leaders, and communities to embody mutual trust and respect is now a life-long mission using your teaching and "the curve" as a way to operationalize the cultural underpinnings of TPS.

David Adams, hands down one of the best leaders, coaches, and mentors for other leaders and organizations aspiring to become world-class. Your thought leadership and skill as a coach are evidenced by the immense culture change at Signature Healthcare and a multitude of other organizations—including most of the case studies throughout this book. I am forever grateful for your guidance and coaching as your leadership provided shaping of this book over many years. When deeply learning the Transformation Curve at Saint Vincent College, our vision was to shift the North American approach to "Lean," especially in healthcare away from events and tools towards culture and daily management. As you focus the vision by executive coaching and organizational transformation through Adams Strategy Group, Inc., with world-class coaches like Dan Niemiec, this book aid leaders of tomorrow in the same vision.

Mike Hoseus, for a robust foreword and a passion to expand Toyota's Culture throughout the world via your writing and coaching as the Executive Director of Center for Quality People and Organizations. You are an inspiration personally and professionally. After hearing a keynote presentation from you nearly a decade ago, it was clear that many individuals in the room began to shift their thinking away from tools and events towards creating a Lean culture by developing people. The current understanding of Lean and the Toyota Production System is shifting in this same direction in a large part due to your writings, coaching, and speaking.

Dr. Richard Kunkle, "Doc," for your mentoring, coaching, and friendship over the last decade. In the classroom, as the former Graduate Director of the Management: Operational Excellence Program at Saint Vincent College, you have inspired a multitude of professional students to focus on culture. As a coach and mentor, especially at hospitals, your insight is transforming leaders and physicians to believe in Lean and use the Transformation Curve as a guide is evidenced by the case studies from Forbes Hospital and ABC Medical Center, plus a multitude of unnamed organizations.

Dominic Paccapaniccia, thank you for your candid zeal for improvement, leadership, and willingness to learn a new system. Your transparency on the difficulty, but necessity to learn, lead, and learn a new way to develop people and achieve results in a new model of thinking and behavior for other leaders. The Postscript you provided on your experience with this phase of the Transformation Curve will aid leaders in learning and leading in a more effective way.

My completion of this project would not have been accomplished without key case studies which were coordinated with Dr. Jill Guindon-Nasir, Blanca Velazquez Hernandez, Dr. Mike Culig, Dr. James Kinneer, Larry Sedlemeyer, Don Shilton, David Marshall, Michael Pry, and Laurie English. Additional artifacts shared throughout the book compliments of Jessa Cardelli, Lori Hennessey, Dr. Bruce Bush, Deana Szentmiklosi, Danielle McCloskey, and Heather Glance. A special thanks to David Marshall for ongoing collaboration.

Mark Graban, thank you for helping me navigate the Lean landscape and providing insight on writing, publication, and marketing in the realm of Lean healthcare. Your early publications on Lean and current work are aiding in healthcare organizations becoming world-class.

Indiana Regional Medical Center, especially the Senior Leadership Team, those who participated in this book, and early adopters throughout the organization.

Saint Vincent College, my alma mater, and the Kennametal Center for Operational Excellence (KCOE) at Saint Vincent—the values that the Transformation Curve instill in leaders and organizations resonate with the Benedictine Values. As one of the very first graduates of the Masters in Management: Operational Excellence program, I believe it is one of the best Lean/management/improvement Masters in the country, which incorporates the human element of improvement. As the founder of Saint Vincent, Archabbot Boniface Wimmer, O.S.B. states, "Forward, always forward, everywhere forward!"

The Pittsburgh Regional Health Initiative (PRHI) for creating a collaborative atmosphere in the southwestern Pennsylvania region around Lean transformation. Your work has cultivated many organizations, especially those in health care, to strive for excellence.

To my editors throughout the process, Emily Mahan, Sandra Ripley Distelhorst, Mary Rose Dawson, Zeke Woods, Cheryl Fenske—thank you for your assistance, advice, and changes at many different stages in this book.

Leah Nicholson, Yvonne Roehler, and the team at the Jenkins Group, thank you for helping this book cross the finish line, I look forward to working with you on future projects.

Index

Page numbers in italics are figures or tables.

About the Author

STEVEN R. LEUSCHEL, a Lean Culture Change Coach, has aided in the adaptation and implementation of the Transformation Curve at a number of manufacturing, healthcare, and service industries, teaching and coaching a Lean daily management system at both executive and frontline levels. With a Masters in Management: Operational Excellence and a Masters Certificate in Health Services Leadership from Saint Vincent College, Leuschel is pursuing his Ph.D. in Administration and Leadership Studies at the Indiana University of Pennsylvania.

About the Sensei

RODGER B. LEWIS, is the originator of the Transformation Curve and long-time adapter of the Toyota Production System (TPS). Lewis was hired as one of the initial leaders at Toyota's first fully owned and operated plant in North America in 1986. After his learnings in Georgetown, Kentucky, Lewis has lead organizations to develop cultures of mutual trust and respect by adapting TPS. His leadership has helped transform General Motors, Bombardier, and a number of other organizations around the world.